T0268913

The Posthuman

The Posthuman

Rosi Braidotti

polity

Copyright © Rosi Braidotti 2013

The right of Rosi Braidotti to be identified as Author of this Work has been asserted in accordance with the UK Copyright, Designs and Patents Act 1988.

First published in 2013 by Polity Press

Polity Press
65 Bridge Street
Cambridge CB2 1UR, UK

Polity Press
350 Main Street
Malden, MA 02148, USA

All rights reserved. Except for the quotation of short passages for the purpose of criticism and review, no part of this publication may be reproduced, stored in a retrieval system, or transmitted, in any form or by any means, electronic, mechanical, photocopying, recording or otherwise, without the prior permission of the publisher.

ISBN-13: 978-0-7456-4157-7
ISBN-13: 978-0-7456-4158-4 (pb)

A catalogue record for this book is available from the British Library.

Typeset in 10.5 on 12 pt Sabon
by Toppan Best-set Premedia Limited
Printed and bound in Great Britain by MPG Books Group Limited, Bodmin, Cornwall

The publisher has used its best endeavours to ensure that the URLs for external websites referred to in this book are correct and active at the time of going to press. However, the publisher has no responsibility for the websites and can make no guarantee that a site will remain live or that the content is or will remain appropriate.

Every effort has been made to trace all copyright holders, but if any have been inadvertently overlooked the publisher will be pleased to include any necessary credits in any subsequent reprint or edition.

For further information on Polity, visit our website: www.politybooks.com

Contents

Acknowledgements

I want to thank my publisher John Thompson for suggesting the idea of this book to begin with. I am proud of being a long-standing Polity author. My sincere thanks also to Jennifer Jahn for her advice and support. I benefited greatly from conversations with my colleagues on the CHCI Board (Consortium of Humanities Centres and Institutes) and within ECHIC (European Consortium of Humanities Institutes and Centres). Henrietta Moore and Claire Colebrook, Peter Galison and Paul Gilroy proved to be formidable readers and I thank them for their critical comments. My research assistant Goda Klumbyte helped me greatly especially with bibliographical work. All my gratitude to Nori Spauwen and to Bolette Blaagaard for their insightful critical comments. My thanks also to Stephanie Paalvast for critical and editorial assistance. To Anneke, who endured, commented and supported me throughout the process, all my love, as ever.

Introduction

Not all of us can say, with any degree of certainty, that we have always been human, or that we are only that. Some of us are not even considered fully human now, let alone at previous moments of Western social, political and scientific history. Not if by 'human' we mean that creature familiar to us from the Enlightenment and its legacy: 'The Cartesian subject of the cogito, the Kantian "community of reasonable beings", or, in more sociological terms, the subject as citizen, rights-holder, property-owner, and so on' (Wolfe, 2010a). And yet the term enjoys widespread consensus and it maintains the re-assuring familiarity of common sense. We assert our attachment to the species as if it were a matter of fact, a given. So much so that we construct a fundamental notion of Rights around the Human. But is it so?

While conservative, religious social forces today often labour to re-inscribe the human within a paradigm of natural law, the concept of the human has exploded under the double pressure of contemporary scientific advances and global economic concerns. After the postmodern, the post-colonial, the post-industrial, the post-communist and even the much contested post-feminist conditions, we seem to have entered the post-human predicament. Far from being the nth variation in a sequence of prefixes that may appear both endless and somehow arbitrary, the posthuman condition introduces a qualitative shift in our thinking about what exactly is the basic unit of common reference for our species, our polity and our relationship to the other inhabitants of this planet. This issue raises serious questions as to the very structures of our shared identity – as humans – amidst the complexity of contemporary science, politics and international relations. Discourses and representations of the non-human, the inhuman, the anti-human, the inhumane and the posthuman proliferate and overlap in our globalized, technologically mediated societies.

The debates in mainstream culture range from hard-nosed business discussions of robotics, prosthetic technologies, neuroscience and bio-genetic capital to fuzzier new age visions of trans-humanism and techno-transcendence. Human enhancement is at the core of these debates. In academic culture, on the other hand, the posthuman is alternatively celebrated as the next frontier in critical and cultural theory or shunned as the latest in a series of annoying 'post' fads. The posthuman provokes elation but also anxiety (Habermas, 2003) about the possibility of a serious de-centring of 'Man', the former measure of all things. There is widespread concern about the loss of relevance and mastery suffered by the dominant vision of the human subject and by the field of scholarship centred on it, namely the Humanities.

In my view, the common denominator for the posthuman condition is an assumption about the vital, self-organizing and yet non-naturalistic structure of living matter itself. This nature–culture continuum is the shared starting point for my take on posthuman theory. Whether this post-naturalistic assumption subsequently results in playful experimentations with the boundaries of perfectibility of the body, in moral panic about the disruption of centuries-old beliefs about human 'nature' or in exploitative and profit-minded pursuit of genetic and neural capital, remains however to be seen. In this book I will try to examine these approaches and engage critically with them, while arguing my case for posthuman subjectivity.

What does this nature–culture continuum amount to? It marks a scientific paradigm that takes its distance from the social constructivist approach, which has enjoyed widespread consensus. This approach posits a categorical distinction between the given (nature) and the constructed (culture). The distinction allows for a sharper focus in social analysis and it provides robust foundations to study and critique the social mechanisms that support the construction of key identities, institutions and practices. In progressive politics, social constructivist methods sustain the efforts to de-naturalize social differences and thus show their man-made and historically contingent structure. Just think of the world-changing effect of Simone de Beauvoir's statement that 'one is not born, one becomes a woman'. This insight into the socially bound and therefore historically variable nature of social inequalities paves the road to their resolution by human intervention through social policy and activism.

My point is that this approach, which rests on the binary opposition between the given and the constructed, is currently being replaced by a non-dualistic understanding of nature–culture interaction. In my view the latter is associated to and supported by a monistic philosophy, which rejects dualism, especially the opposition nature–culture and stresses instead the self-organizing (or auto-poietic) force of living matter. The boundaries between the categories of the natural and the cultural have been displaced and to a large extent blurred by the effects of scientific and technological advances. This book starts from the assumption that social theory needs to take stock of the transformation of concepts, methods and political practices brought about by this change of paradigm. Conversely, the question of what kind of political analysis and which progressive politics is supported by the approach based on the nature–culture continuum is central to the agenda of the posthuman predicament.

The main questions I want to address in this book are: firstly what is the posthuman? More specifically, what are the intellectual and historical itineraries that may lead us to the posthuman? Secondly: where does the posthuman condition leave humanity? More specifically, what new forms of subjectivity are supported by the posthuman? Thirdly: how does the posthuman engender its own forms of inhumanity? More specifically, how might we resist the inhuman(e) aspects of our era? And last, how does the posthuman affect the practice of the Humanities today? More specifically, what is the function of theory in posthuman times?

This book rides the wave of simultaneous fascination for the posthuman condition as a crucial aspect of our historicity, but also of concern for its aberrations, its abuses of power and the sustainability of some of its basic premises. Part of the fascination is due to my sense of what the task of critical theorists should be in the world today, namely, to provide adequate representations of our situated historical location. This in itself humble cartographic aim, that is connected to the ideal of producing socially relevant knowledge, flips over into a more ambitious and abstract question, namely the status and value of theory itself.

Several cultural critics have commented on the ambivalent nature of the 'post-theoretical malaise' that has struck the contemporary Human and Social Sciences. For instance, Tom Cohen, Claire Colebrook and J. Hillis Miller (2012) emphasize the positive aspect of this 'post-theory' phase, namely the fact that it actually registers the new opportunities as well as the threats that emerge from contemporary science. The negative aspects, however, are just as striking, notably the lack of suitable critical schemes to scrutinize the present.

I think that the anti-theory shift is linked to the vicissitudes of the ideological context. After the official end of the Cold War, the political movements of the second half of the twentieth century have been discarded and their theoretical efforts dismissed as failed historical experiments. The 'new' ideology of the free market economy has steamrolled all oppositions, in spite of massive protest from many sectors of society, imposing anti-intellectualism as a salient feature of our times. This is especially hard on the Humanities because it penalizes subtlety of analysis by paying undue allegiance to 'common sense' – the tyranny of doxa – and to economic profit – the banality of self-interest. In this context, 'theory' has lost status and is often dismissed as a form of fantasy or narcissistic self-indulgence. Consequently, a shallow version of neo-empiricism – which is often nothing more than data-mining – has become the methodological norm in Humanities research.

The question of method deserves serious consideration: after the official end of ideologies and in view of the advances in neural, evolutionary and bio-genetic sciences, can we still hold the powers of theoretical interpretation in the same esteem they have enjoyed since the end of the Second World War? Is the posthuman predicament not also linked to a post-theory mood? For instance, Bruno Latour (2004) – not exactly a classical humanist in his epistemological work on how knowledge is produced by networks of human and non-human actors, things and objects – recently commented on the tradition of critical theory and its connection to European humanism. Critical thought rests on a social constructivist paradigm which intrinsically proclaims faith in theory as a tool to apprehend and represent reality, but is such faith still legitimate today? Latour raised serious self-questioning doubts about the function of theory today.

There is an undeniably gloomy connotation to the posthuman condition, especially in relation to genealogies of critical thought. It is as if, after the great explosion of theoretical creativity of the 1970s and 1980s, we had entered a zombified landscape of repetition without difference and lingering melancholia. A spectral dimension has seeped into our patterns of thinking, boosted, on the right of the political spectrum, by ideas about the end of ideological time (Fukuyama, 1989) and the inevitability of civilizational crusades (Huntington, 1996). On the political left, on the other hand, the rejection of theory has resulted in a wave of resentment and negative thought against the previous intellectual generations. In this context of theory-fatigue, neo-communist intellectuals (Badiou and Žižek, 2009) have argued for the need to return to concrete political action, even violent antagonism if necessary, rather than indulge in more theoretical speculations. They have contributed to push the philosophical theories of post-structuralism way out of fashion.

In response to this generally negative social climate, I want to approach posthuman theory as both a genealogical and a navigational tool. I find it useful as a term to explore ways of engaging affirmatively with the present, accounting for some of its features in a manner that is empirically grounded without being reductive and remains critical while avoiding negativity. I want to map out some of the ways in which the posthuman is circulating as a dominant term in our globally linked and technologically mediated societies. More specifically, posthuman theory is a generative tool to help us re-think the basic unit of reference for the human in the bio-genetic age known as 'anthropocene', the historical moment when the Human has become a geological force capable of affecting all life on this planet. By extension, it can also help us re-think the basic tenets of our interaction with both human and non-human agents on a planetary scale.

Let me give some examples of the contradictions offered by our posthuman historical condition.

Vignette 1
In November 2007 Pekka-Eric Auvinen, an eighteen-year-old Finnish boy, opened fire on his classmates in a high school near Helsinki, killing eight people before shooting himself. Prior to the carnage, the young killer posted a video on YouTube, in which he showed himself, wearing a t-shirt with the caption 'Humanity is overrated'.

That humanity be in a critical condition – some may even say approaching extinction – has been a *leitmotif* in European philosophy ever since Friedrich Nietzsche proclaimed the 'death of God' and of the idea of Man that was built upon it. This bombastic assertion was meant to drive home a more modest point. What Nietzsche asserted was the end of the self-evident status attributed to human nature as the common sense belief in the metaphysically stable and universal validity of the European humanistic subject. Nietzschean genealogy stresses the importance of interpretation over dogmatic implementation of natural laws and values. Ever since then, the main items on the philosophical agenda have been: firstly, how to develop critical thought, after the shock of recognition of a state of ontological uncertainty, and, secondly, how to reconstitute a sense of community held together by affinity and ethical accountability, without falling into the negative passions of doubt and suspicion.

As the Finnish episode points out, however, philosophical anti-humanism must not be confused with cynical and nihilistic misanthropy. Humanity may well be over-rated, but as the human population on earth reaches its eighth billion mark, any talk of extinction seems downright silly. And yet, the issue of both ecological and social sustainability is at the top of most governmental programmes across the world, in view of the environmental crisis and climate change. Thus, the question Bertrand Russell formulated in 1963, at the height of the Cold War and of nuclear confrontation, sounds more relevant than ever: has Man a future indeed? Does the choice between sustainability and extinction frame the horizon of our shared future, or are there other options? The issue of the limits of both humanism and of its anti-humanist critics is therefore central to the debate on the posthuman predicament and I will accordingly devote the first chapter to it.

Vignette 2

The Guardian *reported that people in war-torn lands like Afghanistan were reduced to eating grass in order to survive.[1] At the same point in history, cows in the United Kingdom and parts of the European Union were fed meat-based fodder. The agricultural bio-technological sector of the over-developed world had taken an unexpected cannibalistic turn by fattening cows, sheep and chickens on animal feed. This action was later diagnosed as the source for the lethal disease Bovine spongiform encephalopathy (BSE), vulgarly called 'mad cow disease', which caused the brain structure of the animals to corrode and turn to pulp. The madness here, however, is decidedly on the side of the humans and their bio-technological industries.*

Advanced capitalism and its bio-genetic technologies engender a perverse form of the posthuman. At its core there is a radical disruption of the human–animal interaction, but all living species are caught in the spinning machine of the global economy. The genetic code of living matter – 'Life itself' (Rose, 2007) – is the main capital. Globalization means the commercialization of planet Earth in all its forms, through a series of inter-related modes of appropriation. According to Haraway, these are the techno-military proliferation of micro-conflicts on a global scale; the hyper-capitalist accumulation of wealth; the turning of the ecosystem into a planetary apparatus of production, and the global infotainment apparatus of the new multimedia environment.

The phenomenon of Dolly the sheep is emblematic of the complications engendered by the bio-genetic structure of contemporary technologies and their stock-market backers. Animals provide living material for scientific experiments.

[1] *The Guardian Weekly*, 3–5 January 2002, p. 2.

They are manipulated, mistreated, tortured and genetically recombined in ways that are productive for our bio-technological agriculture, the cosmetics industry, drugs and pharmaceutical industries and other sectors of the economy. Animals are also sold as exotic commodities and constitute the third largest illegal trade in the world today, after drugs and arms, but ahead of women.

Mice, sheep, goats, cattle, pigs, rabbits, birds, poultry and cats are bred in industrial farming, locked up in battery-cage production units. As George Orwell prophetically put it, however, all animals may be equal, but some are definitely more equal than others. Thus, because they are an integral part of the bio-technological industrial complex, livestock in the European Union receives subsidy to the tune of US$803 per cow. This is considerably less than the US$1,057 that is granted to each American cow and US$2,555 given to each cow in Japan. These figures look all the more ominous when compared to the gross national income *per capita* in countries like Ethiopia (US$120), Bangladesh (US$360), Angola (US$660) or Honduras (US$920).[2]

The counterpart of this global commodification of living organisms is that animals have become partly humanized themselves. In the field of bio-ethics, for instance, the issue of the 'human' rights of animals has been raised as a way of countering these excesses. The defence of animals' rights is a hot political issue in most liberal democracies. This combination of investments and abuse is the paradoxical posthuman condition engendered by advanced capitalism itself, which triggers multiple forms of resistance. I will discuss the new post-anthropocentric views of animals at length in chapter 2.

Vignette 3
On 10 October 2011, Muammar Gaddafi, deposed leader of Libya, was captured in his hometown of Sirte, beaten and killed by members of the National Transitional Council of Libya (NTC). Before he was shot by the rebel forces, however, Colonel Gaddafi's convoy was bombed by French jets and by an American Predator Drone which was flown out of the

[2] *The Guardian Weekly*, 11–17 September 2003, p. 5.

American Air Force base in Sicily and controlled via satellite from a base outside Las Vegas.[3]

Although world media focused on the brutality of the actual shooting and on the indignity of the global visual exposure of Gaddafi's wounded and bleeding body, less attention was paid to what can only described as the posthuman aspect of contemporary warfare: the tele-thanatological machines created by our own advanced technology. The atrocity of Gaddafi's end – his own tyrannical despotism notwithstanding – was enough to make one feel slightly ashamed of being human. The denial of the role played by the advanced world's sophisticated death-technology of drones in his demise, however, added an extra layer of moral and political discomfort.

The posthuman predicament has more than its fair share of inhuman(e) moments. The brutality of the new wars, in a globalized world run by the governance of fear, refers not only to the government of the living, but also to multiple practices of dying, especially in countries in transition. Bio-power and necro-politics are two sides of the same coin, as Mbembe (2003) brilliantly argues. The post-Cold War world has seen not only a dramatic increase in warfare, but also a profound transformation of the practice of war as such in the direction of a more complex management of survival and of extinction. Contemporary death-technologies are posthuman because of the intense technological mediation within which they operate. Can the digital operator that flew the American Predator Drone from a computer room in Las Vegas be considered a 'pilot'? How does he differ from the Air Force boys who flew the Enola Gay plane over Hiroshima and Nagasaki? Contemporary wars have heightened our necro-political power to a new level of administration of 'the material destruction of human bodies and population' (Mbembe, 2003: 19). And *not* only human.

The new necro-technologies operate in a social climate dominated by a political economy of nostalgia and paranoia on the one hand, and euphoria or exaltation on the other.

[3] *The Daily Telegraph*, 21 October 2011.

This manic-depressive condition enacts a number of variations: from the fear of the imminent disaster, the catastrophe just waiting to happen, to hurricane Katrina or the next environmental accident. From a plane flying too low, to genetic mutations and immunity breakdowns: the accident is there, just about to unfold and virtually certain; it is just a question of time (Massumi, 1992). As a result of this state of insecurity, the socially enforced aim is not change, but conservation or survival. I shall return to these necro-political aspects in chapter 3.

Vignette 4
At a scientific meeting organized by the Dutch Royal Academy of Sciences about the future of the academic field of the Humanities a few years ago, a professor in Cognitive Sciences attacked the Humanities head-on. His attacks rested on what he perceived as the two major shortcomings of the Humanities: their intrinsic anthropocentrism and their methodological nationalism. The distinguished researcher found these two flaws to be fatal for the field, which was deemed unsuitable for contemporary science and hence not eligible for financial support by the relevant Ministry and the government.

The crisis of the human and its posthuman fallout has dire consequences for the academic field most closely associated with it – the Humanities. In the neo-liberal social climate of most advanced democracies today, Humanistic studies have been downgraded beyond the 'soft' sciences level, to something like a finishing school for the leisurely classes. Considered more of a personal hobby than a professional research field, I believe that the Humanities are in serious danger of disappearing from the twenty-first-century European university curriculum.

Another motivation behind my engagement with the topic of the posthuman therefore can be related to a profound sense of civic responsibility for the role of the academic today. A thinker from the Humanities, a figure who used to be known as an 'intellectual', may be at a loss to know what role to play in contemporary social public scenarios. One could say that my interest in the posthuman emerges from an all too human concern about the kind of knowledge and intellectual values we are producing as a society today. More specifically, I worry about the status of university research in what we are still calling, for lack of a better word, the human sciences or the Humanities. I will develop my ideas about the university today in chapter 4.

This sense of responsibility also expresses a habit of thought which is dear to my heart and mind, as I belong to a generation that had a dream. It was and still is the dream of actually constituting communities of learning: schools, universities, books and curricula, debating societies, theatre, radio, television and media programmes – and later, websites and computer environments – that look like the society they both reflect, serve and help to construct. It is the dream of producing socially relevant knowledge that is attuned to basic principles of social justice, the respect for human decency and diversity, the rejection of false universalisms; the affirmation of the positivity of difference; the principles of academic freedom, anti-racism, openness to others and conviviality. Although I am inclined towards anti-humanism, I have no difficulty in recognizing that these ideals are perfectly compatible with the best humanist values. This book is not about taking sides in academic disputes, but rather aims to make sense of the complexities we find ourselves in. I will propose new ways of combining critique with creativity, putting the 'active' back into 'activism', thus moving towards a vision of posthuman humanity for the global era.

Posthuman knowledge – and the knowing subjects that sustain it – enacts a fundamental aspiration to principles of community bonding, while avoiding the twin pitfalls of conservative nostalgia and neo-liberal euphoria. This book is motivated by my belief in new generations of 'knowing subjects' who affirm a constructive type of pan-humanity by working hard to free us from the provincialism of the mind, the sectarianism of ideologies, the dishonesty of grandiose posturing and the grip of fear. This aspiration also shapes my vision of what a university should look like – a *universum* that serves the world of today, not only as the epistemological site of scientific production, but also as the epistemophilic yearning for the empowerment that comes with knowledge and sustains our subjectivity. I would define this yearning as a radical aspiration to freedom through the understanding of

the specific conditions and relations of power that are imminent to our historical locations. These conditions include the
power that each and every one of us exercises in the everyday
network of social relations, at both the micro- and macro-
political levels.

In some ways, my interest in the posthuman is directly
proportional to the sense of frustration I feel about the
human, all too human, resources and limitations that frame
our collective and personal levels of intensity and creativity.
This is why the issue of subjectivity is so central to this book:
we need to devise new social, ethical and discursive schemes
of subject formation to match the profound transformations
we are undergoing. That means that we need to learn to think
differently about ourselves. I take the posthuman predicament
as an opportunity to empower the pursuit of alternative schemes
of thought, knowledge and self-representation. The posthuman
condition urges us to think critically and creatively about who
and what we are actually in the process of becoming.

Chapter 1

Post-Humanism:
Life beyond the Self

At the start of it all there is He: the classical ideal of 'Man', formulated first by Protagoras as 'the measure of all things', later renewed in the Italian Renaissance as a universal model and represented in Leonardo da Vinci's Vitruvian Man (see figure 1.1). An ideal of bodily perfection which, in keeping with the classical dictum *mens sana in corpore sano*, doubles up as a set of mental, discursive and spiritual values. Together they uphold a specific view of what is 'human' about humanity. Moreover, they assert with unshakable certainty the almost boundless capacity of humans to pursue their individual and collective perfectibility. That iconic image is the emblem of Humanism as a doctrine that combines the biological, discursive and moral expansion of human capabilities into an idea of teleologically ordained, rational progress. Faith in the unique, self-regulating and intrinsically moral powers of human reason forms an integral part of this high-humanistic creed, which was essentially predicated on eighteenth- and nineteenth-century renditions of classical Antiquity and Italian Renaissance ideals.

This model sets standards not only for individuals, but also for their cultures. Humanism historically developed into a civilizational model, which shaped a certain idea of Europe as coinciding with the universalizing powers of self-reflexive reason. The mutation of the Humanistic ideal into

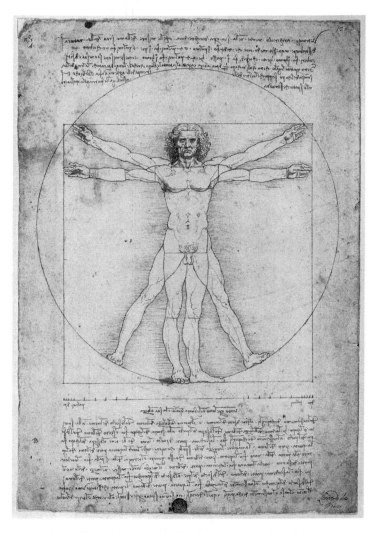

Figure 1.1   Vitruvian Man, 1492, Leonardo da Vinci
Source: Wikimedia Commons

a hegemonic cultural model was canonized by Hegel's philosophy of history. This self-aggrandizing vision assumes that Europe is not just a geo-political location, but rather a universal attribute of the human mind that can lend its quality to any suitable object. This is the view espoused by Edmund Husserl (1970) is his celebrated essay 'The crisis of European sciences', which is a passionate defence of the universal powers of reason against the intellectual and moral decline symbolized by the rising threat of European fascism in the 1930s. In Husserl's view, Europe announces itself as the site of origin of critical reason and self-reflexivity, both qualities resting on the Humanistic norm. Equal only to itself, Europe as universal consciousness transcends its specificity, or, rather, posits the power of transcendence as its distinctive character- istic and humanistic universalism as its particularity. This makes Eurocentrism into more than just a contingent matter of attitude: it is a structural element of our cultural practice, which is also embedded in both theory and institutional and pedagogical practices. As a civilizational ideal, Humanism fuelled 'the imperial destinies of nineteenth-century Germany, France and, supremely, Great Britain' (Davies, 1997: 23).

This Eurocentric paradigm implies the dialectics of self and other, and the binary logic of identity and otherness as respec- tively the motor for and the cultural logic of universal Human- ism. Central to this universalistic posture and its binary logic is the notion of 'difference' as pejoration. Subjectivity is equated with consciousness, universal rationality, and self- regulating ethical behaviour, whereas Otherness is defined as its negative and specular counterpart. In so far as difference spells inferiority, it acquires both essentialist and lethal con- notations for people who get branded as 'others'. These are the sexualized, racialized, and naturalized others, who are reduced to the less than human status of disposable bodies. We are all humans, but some of us are just more mortal than others. Because their history in Europe and elsewhere has been one of lethal exclusions and fatal disqualifications, these 'others' raise issues of power and exclusion. We need more ethical accountability in dealing with the legacy of Human- ism. Tony Davies puts it lucidly: 'All Humanisms, until now, have been imperial. They speak of the human in the accents and the interests of a class, a sex, a race, a genome. Their embrace suffocates those whom it does not ignore. [. . .] It is almost impossible to think of a crime that has not been com- mitted in the name of humanity' (Davies, 1997: 141). Indeed, but it is also the case unfortunately that many atrocities have been committed in the name of the hatred for humanity, as shown by the case of Pekka-Eric Auvinen in the first vignette in the introduction.

Humanism's restricted notion of what counts as the human is one of the keys to understand how we got to a post-human turn at all. The itinerary is far from simple or predictable. Edward Said, for instance, complicates the picture by introducing a post-colonial angle: 'Humanism as protective or even defensive nationalism is [. . .] a mixed blessing for its [. . .] ideological ferocity and triumphalism, although it is sometimes inevitable. In a colonial setting for example, a revival of the suppressed languages and cultures, the attempts at national assertion through cultural tradition and glorious ancestors [. . .] are explainable and understandable' (Said, 2004: 37). This qualification is crucial in pointing out the importance of where one is actually speaking from. Differences of location between centres and margins matter greatly, especially in relation to the legacy of something as complex and multi-faceted as Humanism. Complicitous with genocides and crimes on the one hand, supportive of enormous hopes and aspirations to freedom on the other, Humanism somehow defeats linear criticism. This protean quality is partly responsible for its longevity.

Anti-Humanism

Let me put my cards on the table at this early stage of the argument: I am none too fond of Humanism or of the idea of the human which it implicitly upholds. Anti-humanism is so much part of my intellectual and personal genealogy, as well as family background, that for me the crisis of Humanism is almost a banality. Why?

Politics and philosophy are the main reasons for the glee with which I have always greeted the notion of the historical decline of Humanism, with its Eurocentric core and imperial tendencies. Of course, the historical context has a lot to do with it. I came of age intellectually and politically in the turbulent years after the Second World War, when the Humanist ideal came to be questioned quite radically. Throughout the 1960s and 1970s an activist brand of anti-Humanism was developed by the new social movements and the youth cultures of the day: feminism, de-colonization and anti-racism, anti-nuclear and pacifist movements. Chronologically linked to the social and cultural politics of the generation known as the baby-boomers, these social movements produced radical political, social theories and new epistemologies. They challenged the platitudes of Cold War rhetoric, with its emphasis on Western democracy, liberal individualism and the freedom they allegedly ensured for all.

Nothing smacks more like a theoretical mid-life crisis than to acknowledge one's affiliation to the baby-boomers. The public image of this generation is not exactly edifying at this point in time. Nonetheless, truth be said, that generation was marked by the traumatic legacy of the many failed political experiments of the twentieth century. Fascism and the Holocaust on the one hand, Communism and the Gulag on the other, strike a blood-drenched balance on the comparative scale of horrors. There is a clear generational link between these historical phenomena and the rejection of Humanism in the 1960s and 1970s. Let me explain.

At the levels of their own ideological content, these two historical phenomena, Fascism and Communism, rejected openly or implicitly the basic tenets of European Humanism and betrayed them violently. They remain, however, quite different as movements in their structures and aims. Whereas fascism preached a ruthless departure from the very roots of Enlightenment-based respect for the autonomy of reason and the moral good, socialism pursued a communitarian notion of humanist solidarity. Socialist Humanism had been a feature of the European Left since the utopian socialist movements of the eighteenth century. Admittedly, Marxist-Leninism rejected these 'soft-headed' aspects of socialist humanism, notably the emphasis on the fulfilment of the human beings' potential for authenticity (as opposed to alienation). It offered as an alternative 'proletarian Humanism', also known as the 'revolutionary Humanism' of the USSR and its ruthless pursuit of universal, rational human 'freedom' through and under Communism.

Two factors contributed to the relative popularity of communist Humanism in the post-war era. The first is the disastrous effects of Fascism upon European social but also intellectual history. The period of Fascism and Nazism enacted a major disruption in the history of critical theory in Continental Europe in that it destroyed and banned from Europe the very schools of thought – notably Marxism, psychoanalysis, the Frankfurt School and the disruptive charge of Nietzschean genealogy (though the case of Nietzsche is admittedly quite complex) – which had been central to philosophy in the earlier part of the twentieth century. Moreover, the Cold War and the opposition of the two geo-political blocks, which followed the end of the Second World War kept Europe split asunder and dichotomized until 1989, and did not facilitate the re-implantation of those radical theories back into the Continent which had cast them away with such violence and self-destruction. It is significant, for instance, that most of the authors which Michel Foucault singled out as heralding the philosophical era of critical post-modernity (Marx, Freud, Darwin) are the same authors whom the Nazis condemned and burned at the stake in the 1930s.

The second reason for the popularity of Marxist Humanism is that Communism, under the aegis of the USSR, played a pivotal role in defeating Fascism and hence, to all ends and purposes came out of the Second World War as the winner. It follows therefore that the generation that came of age politically in 1968 inherited a positive view of Marxist praxis and ideology as a result of socialists' and communists' opposition to fascism and to the Soviet Union's war effort against Nazism. This clashes with the almost epidermic anti-communism of American culture and remains to date a point of great intellectual tension between Europe and the USA. It is sometimes difficult at the dawn of the third millennium to remember that Communist parties were the single largest emblem of anti-fascist resistance throughout Europe. They also played a significant role in national liberation movements throughout the world, notably in Africa and Asia. André Malraux's seminal text: *Man's Fate* (*La condition humaine*, 1934) bears testimony to both the moral stature and the tragic dimension of Communism, as does, in a different era and geo-political context, Nelson Mandela's (1994) life and work.

Speaking from his position within the United States of America, Edward Said adds another significant insight:

> Antihumanism took hold on the United States intellectual scene partly because of widespread revulsion with the Vietnam War. Part of that revulsion was the emergence of a resistance movement to racism, imperialism generally and the dry-as-dust aca-

demic Humanities that had for years represented an apolitical, unworldly and oblivious (sometimes even manipulative) attitude to the present, all the while adamantly extolling the virtues of the past. (2004: 13)   `

The 'new' Left in the USA throughout the 1960s and 1970s embodied a militant brand of radical anti-humanism, which was posited in opposition not only to the Liberal majority, but also to the Marxist Humanism of the traditional Left.

I am fully aware of the fact that the notion that Marxism, by now socially coded as an inhumane and violent ideology, may actually be a Humanism will shock the younger generations and all who are unschooled in Continental philosophy. Suffice it, however, to think of the emphasis that philosophers of the calibre of Sartre and de Beauvoir placed on Humanism as a secular tool of critical analysis, to see how the argument may have shaped up. Existentialism stressed Humanist conscience as the source of both moral responsibility and political freedom.

France occupies a very special position in the genealogy of anti-humanist critical theory. The prestige of French intellectuals was linked not only to the formidable educational structure of that country, but also to contextual considerations. Foremost among them is the high moral stature of France at the end of the Second World War, thanks to the anti-Nazi resistance of Charles de Gaulle. French intellectuals continued accordingly to enjoy a very high status, especially in comparison with the wasteland that was post-war Germany. Hence the huge international reputation of Sartre and de Beauvoir, but also Aron, Mauriac, Camus and Malraux. Tony Judt sums it up succinctly (2005: 210):

Despite France's shattering defeat in 1940, its humiliating subjugation under four years of German occupation, the moral ambiguity (and worse) of Marshall Petain's Vichy regime, and the country's embarrassing subordination to the US and Britain in the international diplomacy of the post-war years, French culture became once again the centre of international attention: French intellectuals acquired a special international significance as spokesmen for the age, and the tenor of French political arguments epitomised the ideological rent in the world at large. Once more – and for the last time – Paris was the capital of Europe.

Throughout the post-war years, Paris continued to function as a magnet that attracted and engendered all sorts of critical thinkers. For example, Alexandr Solzhenitsyn's *The Gulag Archipelago* was first published in France in the 1970s, after being smuggled out of the USSR in samizdat form. It was out of his Parisian retreat that the Ayatollah Khomeini led the Iranian revolution of 1979, which installed the world's first Islamist government. In some ways, the French context of those days was open to all sorts of radical political movements. As a matter of fact, so many critical schools of thought flourished on the Left and Right Bank in that period, that French philosophy became almost synonymous with theory itself, with mixed long-term consequences, as we shall see in chapter 4.

Up until the 1960s, philosophical reason had escaped relatively unscathed from the question of its responsibilities in perpetuating historical models of domination and exclusion. Both Sartre and de Beauvoir, influenced by Marxist theories of alienation and ideology, did connect the triumph of reason with the might of dominant powers, thus disclosing the complicity between philosophical ratio and real-life social practices of injustice. They continued, however, to defend a universalist idea of reason and to rely on a dialectical model for the resolution of these contradictions. This methodological approach, while being critical of hegemonic models of violent appropriation and consumption of the 'others', also defined the task of philosophy as a privileged and culturally hegemonic tool of political analysis. With Sartre and de Beauvoir, the image of the philosopher-king is built into the general picture, albeit in a critical mode. As a critic of ideology and the conscience of the oppressed, the philosopher is a thinking human being who continues to pursue grand theoretical systems and overarching truths. Sartre and de Beauvoir consider humanistic universalism as the distinctive trait of Western culture, i.e. its specific form of particularism. They use the conceptual tools provided by Humanism to precipitate a confrontation of philosophy with its own historical responsibilities and conceptual power-brokering.

This humanistic universalism, coupled with the social constructivist emphasis on the man-made and historically variable nature of social inequalities, lays the grounds for a robust political ontology. For instance, de Beauvoir's emancipatory

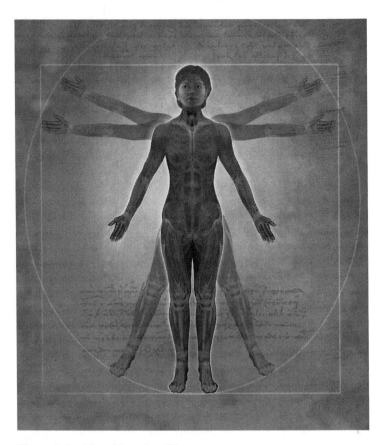

Figure 1.2   New Vitruvian Woman
Source: Friedrich Saurer/Science Photo Library

feminism builds on the Humanist principle that 'Woman is the measure of all things female' (see figure 1.2) and that to account for herself, the feminist philosopher needs to take into account the situation of all women. This creates on the theoretical level a productive synthesis of self and others. Politically, the Vitruvian female forged a bond of solidarity between one and the many, which in the hands of the second feminist wave in the 1960s was to grow into the principle of political sisterhood. This posits a common grounding among women, taking being-women-in-the-world as the starting point for all critical reflection and jointly articulated political praxis.

Humanist feminism introduced a new brand of materialism, of the embodied and embedded kind (Braidotti, 1991). The cornerstone of this theoretical innovation is a specific brand of situated epistemology (Haraway, 1988), which evolved from the practice of 'the politics of locations' (Rich, 1987) and infused standpoint feminist theory and the subsequent debates with postmodernist feminism throughout the 1990s (Harding, 1991). The theoretical premise of humanist feminism is a materialist notion of embodiment that spells the premises of new and more accurate analyses of power. These are based on the radical critique of masculinist universalism, but are still dependent on a form of activist and equality-minded Humanism.

Feminist theory and practice worked faster and more efficiently than most social movements of the 1970s. It developed original tools and methods of analysis that allowed for more incisive accounts of how power works. Feminists also explicitly targeted the masculinism and the sexist habits of the allegedly 'revolutionary' Left and denounced them as contradictory with their ideology, as well as intrinsically offensive.

Within the mainstream Left, however, a new generation of post-war thinkers had other priorities. They rebelled against the high moral status of post-war European Communist parties in Western Europe, as well as in the Soviet empire. This had resulted in an authoritarian hold over the interpretation of Marxist texts and their key philosophical concepts. The new forms of philosophical radicalism developed in France and throughout Europe in the late 1960s expressed a vocal critique of the dogmatic structure of Communist thought and practice. They included a critique of the political alliance between philosophers like Sartre and de Beauvoir and the Communist Left,[1] which lasted at least until the Hungarian insurrection of 1956. In response to the dogma and the violence of Communism, the generation of 1968 appealed directly to the subversive potential of the texts of Marx, so as to recover their anti-institutional roots. Their radicalism was expressed in terms of a critique of

[1] Although Sartre and de Beauvoir were not members of the French Communist Party.

the humanistic implications and the political conservatism of the institutions that embodied Marxist dogma.

Anti-humanism emerged as the rallying cry of this generation of radical thinkers who later were to became world-famous as the 'post-structuralist generation'. In fact, they were post-communists *avant la lettre*. They stepped out of the dialectical oppositional thinking and developed a third way to deal with changing understandings of human subjectivity. By the time Michel Foucault published his ground-breaking critique of Humanism in *The Order of Things* (1970), the question of what, if anything, was the idea of 'the human' was circulating in the radical discourses of the time and had set the anti-humanist agenda for an array of political groups. The 'death of Man', announced by Foucault formalizes an epistemological and moral crisis that goes beyond binary oppositions and cuts across the different poles of the political spectrum. What is targeted is the implicit Humanism of Marxism, more specifically the humanistic arrogance of continuing to place Man at the centre of world history. Even Marxism, under the cover of a master theory of historical materialism, continued to define the subject of European thought as unitary and hegemonic and to assign him (the gender is no coincidence) a royal place as the motor of human history. Anti-humanism consists in de-linking the human agent from this universalistic posture, calling him to task, so to speak, on the concrete actions he is enacting. Different and sharper power relations emerge, once this formerly dominant subject is freed from his delusions of grandeur and is no longer allegedly in charge of historical progress.

The radical thinkers of the post-1968 generation rejected Humanism both in its classical and its socialist versions. The Vitruvian ideal of Man as the standard of both perfection and perfectibility (as shown in figure 1.1) was literally pulled down from his pedestal and deconstructed. This humanistic ideal constituted, in fact, the core of a liberal individualistic view of the subject, which defined perfectibility in terms of autonomy and self-determination. These are precisely the qualifications the post-structuralists objected to.

It turned out that this Man, far from being the canon of perfect proportions, spelling out a universalistic ideal that by now had reached the status of a natural law, was in fact a historical construct and as such contingent as to values and locations. Individualism is not an intrinsic part of 'human nature', as liberal thinkers are prone to believe, but rather a historically and culturally specific discursive formation, one which, moreover, is becoming increasingly problematic. The deconstructive brand of social constructivism introduced by post-structuralist thinkers like Jacques Derrida (2001a) also contributed to a radical revision of the Humanist tenets. An entire philosophical generation called for insubordination from received Humanist ideas of 'human nature'.

Feminists like Luce Irigaray (1985a, 1985b) pointed out that the allegedly abstract ideal of Man as a symbol of classical Humanity is very much a male of the species: it is a he. Moreover, he is white, European, handsome and able-bodied; of his sexuality nothing much can be guessed, though plenty of speculation surrounds that of its painter, Leonardo da Vinci. What this ideal model may have in common with the statistical average of most members of the species and the civilization he is supposed to represent is a very good question indeed. Feminist critiques of patriarchal posturing through abstract masculinity (Hartsock, 1987) and triumphant whiteness (hooks, 1981; Ware, 1992) argued that this Humanist universalism is objectionable not only on epistemological, but also on ethical and political grounds.

Anti-colonial thinkers adopted a similar critical stance by questioning the primacy of whiteness in the Vitruvian ideal as the aesthetic canon of beauty (see figure 1.2). Regrounding such lofty claims onto the history of colonialism, anti-racist and post-colonial thinkers explicitly questioned the relevance of the Humanistic ideal, in view of the obvious contradictions imposed by its Eurocentric assumptions, but at the same time they did not entirely cast it aside. They held the Europeans accountable for the uses and abuses of this ideal by looking at colonial history and the violent domination of other cultures, but still upheld its basic premises. Frantz Fanon, for instance, wanted to rescue Humanism from its European perpetuators arguing that we have betrayed and misused the humanist ideal. As Sartre put it in his preface to Fanon's *The Wretched of the Earth* (1963: 7): 'the yellow and black voices still spoke of our Humanism, but only to reproach us with our inhumanity'. Post-colonial thought asserts that if Humanism has a future at all, it has to come from outside the Western world and by-pass the limitations of Eurocentrism. By extension, the claim to universality by scientific rationality is challenged on both epistemological and political grounds (Spivak, 1999; Said, 2004), all knowledge claims being expressions of Western culture and of its drive to mastery.

French post-structuralist philosophers pursued the same post-colonial aim through different routes and means.[2] They argued that in the aftermath of colonialism, Auschwitz, Hiroshima and the Gulag – to mention but a few of the horrors of modern history – we Europeans need to develop a critique of Europe's delusion of grandeur in positing ourselves as the moral guardian of the world and as the motor of human evolution. Thus, the philosophical generation of the 1970s, that proclaimed the 'death of Man' was anti-fascist, post-communist, post-colonial and post-humanist, in a variety of different combinations of the terms. They led to the rejection of the classical definition of European identity in terms of Humanism, rationality and the universal. The feminist philosophies of sexual difference,[3] through the spectrum of the critique of dominant masculinity, also stressed the ethnocentric nature of European claims to universalism. They advocated the need to open it up to the 'others within' (Kristeva, 1991) in such a way as to re-locate diversity and multiple belongings to a central position as a structural component of European subjectivity.

Anti-humanism is consequently an important source for posthuman thought. It is by no means the only one, nor is the connection between anti-humanism and the posthuman logically necessary or historically inevitable. And yet it turned out to be so for my own work, although this story is still unfinished and in some ways, as I will argue in the next section, my relation to Humanism remains unresolved.

---

[2] This line is pursued in philosophy by Deleuze's rejection of the transcendental vision of the subject (1994); Irigaray's de-centring of phallogocentrism (1985a, 1985b); Foucault's critique of Humanism (1977) and Derrida's deconstruction of Eurocentrism (1992).

[3] See, for instance, Irigaray (1993), Cixous (1997) and Braidotti (1991).

The Death of Man, the Deconstruction of Woman

As indicated in the genealogical itinerary I have just sketched, anti-humanism is one of the historical and theoretical paths that can lead to the posthuman. I owe my anti-humanism to my beloved post-1968 teachers, some of whom were amazing philosophers whose legacy I continue to respect and admire: Foucault, Irigaray and Deleuze especially. The human of Humanism is neither an ideal nor an objective statistical average or middle ground. It rather spells out a systematized standard of recognizability – of Sameness – by which all others can be assessed, regulated and allotted to a designated social location. The human is a normative convention, which does not make it inherently negative, just highly regulatory and hence instrumental to practices of exclusion and discrimination. The human norm stands for normality, normalcy and normativity. It functions by transposing a specific mode of being human into a generalized standard, which acquires transcendent values as *the* human: from male to masculine and onto human as the universalized format of humanity. This standard is posited as categorically and qualitatively distinct from the sexualized, racialized, naturalized others and also in opposition to the technological artefact. The human is a historical construct that became a social convention about 'human nature'.

My anti-humanism leads me to object to the unitary subject of Humanism, including its socialist variables, and to replace it with a more complex and relational subject framed by embodiment, sexuality, affectivity, empathy and desire as core qualities. Equally central to this approach is the insight I learned from Foucault on power as both a restrictive (*potestas*) and productive (*potentia*) force. This means that power formations not only function at the material level but are also expressed in systems of theoretical and cultural representation, political and normative narratives and social modes of identification. These are neither coherent, nor rational and their makeshift nature is instrumental to their hegemonic force. The awareness of the instability and the lack of coherence of the narratives that compose the social structures and relations, far from resulting in a suspension of political and moral action, become the starting point to elaborate new forms of resistance suited to the polycentric and dynamic structure of contemporary power (Patton, 2000). This engenders a pragmatic form of micro-politics that reflects the complex and nomadic nature of contemporary social systems and of the subjects that inhabit them. If power is complex, scattered and productive, so must be our resistance to it. Once this deconstructive move is activated, both the standard notion of Man and his second sex, Woman, are challenged in terms of their internal complexities.

This clearly affects the task and the methods status of theory. Discourse, as Michel Foucault argues in *Discipline and Punish* (1977), is about the political currency that is attributed to certain meanings, or systems of meaning, in such a way as to invest them with scientific legitimacy; there is nothing neutral or given about it. Thus, a critical, materialist link is established between scientific truth, discursive currency and power relations. This approach of discourse analysis primarily aims at dislodging the belief in the 'natural' foundations of socially coded and enforced 'differences' and of the systems of scientific validity, ethical values and representation which they support (Coward and Ellis, 1977).[4]

Feminist anti-Humanism, also known as postmodernist feminism, rejected the unitary identities indexed on that Eurocentric and normative humanist ideal of 'Man' (Braidotti, 2002). It went further, however, and argued that it is impossible to speak in one unified voice about women, natives and other marginal subjects. The emphasis falls instead on issues of diversity and differences among them and on the internal fractures of each category. In this respect, anti-humanism rejects the dialectical scheme of thought, where difference or otherness played a constitutive role, marking off the sexualized other (woman), the racialized other (the native) and the naturalized other (animals, the environment or earth). These others were constitutive in that they fulfilled a mirror

---

[4] This approach has also been adopted by intersectional analysis, which argues for the methodological parallelism of gender, race, class and sexual factors, without flattening out any differences between them but rather investing politically the question of their complex interaction (Crenshaw, 1995).

function that confirmed the Same in His superior position (Braidotti, 2006). This political economy of difference resulted in passing off entire categories of human beings as devalued and therefore disposable others: to be 'different from' came to mean to be 'less than'. The dominant norm of the subject was positioned at the pinnacle of a hierarchical scale that rewarded the ideal of zero-degree of difference.[5] This is the former 'Man' of classical Humanism.

The negative dialectical processes of sexualization, racialization and naturalization of those who are marginalized or excluded have another important implication: they result in the active production of half-truths, or forms of partial knowledge about these others. Dialectical and pejorative otherness induces structural ignorance about those who, by being others, are posited as the outside of major categorical divides in the attribution of Humanity. Paul Gilroy (2010) refers to this phenomenon as 'agnatology' or enforced and structural ignorance. This is one of the paradoxical effects of the alleged universalist reach of humanist knowledge. The 'bellicose dismissiveness' of other cultures and civilizations is what Edward Said criticizes as: 'self-puffery, not humanism and certainly not enlightened criticism' (2004: 27). The reduction to sub-human status of non-Western others is a constitutive source of ignorance, falsity and bad consciousness for the dominant subject who is responsible for their epistemic as well as social de-humanization.

These radical critiques of humanistic arrogance from feminist and post-colonial theory are not merely negative, because they propose new alternative ways to look at the 'human' from a more inclusive and diverse angle. They also offer significant and innovative insights into the image of thought that is implicitly conveyed by the humanistic vision of Man as the measure of all things, standard-bearer of the 'human'. Thus, they further the analysis of power by developing the

[5] Deleuze calls it 'the Majority subject' or the Molar centre of being (Deleuze and Guattari, 1987). Irigaray calls it 'the Same', or the hyper-inflated, falsely universal 'He' (Irigaray, 1985b, 1993), whereas Hill Collins calls to account the white and Eurocentric bias of this particular subject of humanistic knowledge (1991).

tools and the terminology by which we can come to terms with masculinism, racism, white superiority, the dogma of scientific reason and other socially supported systems of dominant values.

Having practically grown up with theories about the death of God (Nietzsche), the end of Man (Foucault) and the decline of ideologies (Fukuyama), it took me a while to realize that, actually, one touches humanism at one's own risk and peril. The anti-humanist position is certainly not free of contradictions. As Badmington wisely reminds us: 'Apocalyptic accounts of the end of "man" [. . .] ignore Humanism's capacity for regeneration and, quite literally, recapitulation' (2003: 11). The Vitruvian Man rises over and over again from his ashes, continues to uphold universal standards and to exercise a fatal attraction.

The thought did occur to me, as I was listening to Diamanda Galas' 'Plague Mass' (1991) for the victims of AIDS: it is one thing to loudly announce an anti-humanist stance, quite another to act accordingly, with a modicum of consistency. Anti-humanism is a position fraught with such contradictions that the more one tries to overcome them, the more slippery it gets. Not only do anti-humanists often end up espousing humanist ideals – freedom being my favourite one – but also, in some ways, the work of critical thought is supported by intrinsic humanist discursive values (Soper, 1986). Somehow, neither humanism nor anti-humanism is adequate to the task.

The best example of the intrinsic contradictions generated by the anti-humanist stance is emancipation and progressive politics in general, which I consider one of the most valuable aspects of the humanistic tradition and its most enduring legacy. Across the political spectrum, Humanism has supported on the liberal side individualism, autonomy, responsibility and self-determination (Todorov, 2002). On the more radical front, it has promoted solidarity, community-bonding, social justice and principles of equality. Profoundly secular in orientation, Humanism promotes respect for science and culture, against the authority of holy texts and religious dogma. It also contains an adventurous element, a curiosity-driven yearning for discovery and a project-oriented approach that is extremely valuable in its pragmatism. These principles are so deeply entrenched in our habits of thought that it is difficult to leave them behind altogether.

And why should we? Anti-humanism criticizes the implicit assumptions about the human subject that are upheld by the humanist image of Man, but this does not amount to a complete rejection.

For me it is impossible, both intellectually and ethically, to disengage the positive elements of Humanism from their problematic counterparts: individualism breeds egotism and self-centredness; self-determination can turn to arrogance and domination; and science is not free from its own dogmatic tendencies. The difficulties inherent in trying to overcome Humanism as an intellectual tradition, a normative frame and an institutionalized practice, lie at the core of the deconstructive approach to the posthuman. Derrida (2001a) opened this discussion by pointing out the violence implicit in the assignation of meaning. His followers pressed the case further: 'the assertion that Humanism can be decisively left behind ironically subscribes to a basic humanist assumption with regard to volition and agency, as if the "end" of Humanism might be subjected to human control, as if we bear the capacity to erase the traces of Humanism from either the present or an imagined future' (Peterson, 2011: 128). The emphasis falls therefore on the difficulty of erasing the trace of the epistemic violence by which a non-humanist position might be carved out of the institutions of Humanism. The acknowledgment of epistemic violence goes hand in hand with the recognition of the real-life violence which was and still is practised against non-human animals and the dehumanized social and political 'others' of the humanist norm. In this deconstructive tradition, Cary Wolfe (2010b) is especially interesting, as he attempts to strike a new position that combines sensitivity to epistemic and word-historical violence with a distinctly transhumanist faith (Bostrom, 2005) in the potential of the posthuman condition as conducive to human enhancement.

I have great respect for deconstruction, but also some impatience with the limitations of its linguistic frame of reference. I prefer to take a more materialist route to deal with the complexities of the posthuman as a key feature of our historicity. That road, too, is fraught with perils, as we shall see in the next section.

The Postsecular Turn

As a progressive political creed, Humanism bears a privileged relation to two other interlocked ideas: human emancipation in the pursuit of equality, and secularism through rational governance. These two premises emerge from the concept of Humanism just like the classical goddess Athena is raised from Zeus' head, fully clad and armed for battle. As John Gray (2002: xiii) argued: 'Humanism is the transformation of the Christian doctrine of salvation into a project of universal human emancipation. The idea of progress is a secular version of the Christian belief in providence. That is why among the ancient pagans it was unknown'. It is not surprising, therefore, that one of the side-effects of the decline of Humanism is the rise of the post-secular condition (Braidotti, 2008; Habermas, 2008).

If the death of Man proved to be a bit of a hasty statement, that of God turned out to be positively delusional. The first cracks in the edifice of self-assured secularity appeared at the end of the 1970s. As the revolutionary zeal cooled off and social movements started to dissipate, conform or mutate, former militant agnostics joined a wave of conversions to a variety of conventional monotheistic or imported Eastern religions. This turn of events raised serious doubts as to the future of secularity. The doubt crept into the collective and individual mind: how secular are 'we' – feminists, anti-racists, post-colonialists, environmentalists, etc. – really?

The doubt was even sharper for intellectual activists. Science is intrinsically secular, secularity being a key tenet of Humanism, alongside universalism, the unitary subject and the primacy of rationality. Science itself, however, in spite of its secular foundations, is far from immune from its own forms of dogmatism. Freud was one of the first critical thinkers to warn us against the fanatical atheism of the supporters of scientific reason. In *The Future of an Illusion* (1928), Freud compares different forms of rigid dogmatism, classifying rationalist scientism alongside religion as a source of superstitious belief, a position best illustrated today by the extremism with which Richard Dawkins defends his atheist faith (Dawkins, 1976). Moreover, the much-celebrated objectivity of science has also been shown to be quite flawed. The uses and abuses of scientific experimentation under Fascism and in the colonial era prove that science is not immunized against nationalist, racist and hegemonic discourses and practices. Any claim to scientific purity, objectivity and autonomy needs therefore to be firmly resisted. Where does that leave Humanism and its anti-humanist critics?

Secularity is one of the pillars of Western Humanism, thus an instinctive form of aversion to religion and to the church is historically an integral aspect of emancipatory politics. The socialist humanist tradition, which was so central to the European Left and the women's movements in Europe since the eighteenth century, is justified in claiming to be secular in the narrow sense of the term: to be agnostic if not atheist and to descend from the Enlightenment critique of religious dogma and clerical authority. Like other emancipatory philosophies and political practices, the feminist struggle for women's rights in Europe has historically built on secular foundations. The lasting influence exercised by existentialist feminism (de Beauvoir, 1973), and Marxist or socialist feminisms[6] on the second feminist wave, may also account for the perpetuation of this position. As the secular and rebellious daughters of the Enlightenment, European feminists were raised in rational argumentation and detached self-irony. The feminist belief-system is accordingly civic, not theistic and viscerally opposed to authoritarianism and orthodoxy. Feminist politics is also and at the same time a double-edged vision (Kelly, 1979) that combines rational arguments with political passions and creates alternative social blueprints and value systems.

However proud twentieth-century feminism may be of its secular roots, it is nonetheless the case that it has historically produced various alternative spiritual practices alongside and often in antagonism to the mainstream political secularist line. Major writers in the radical feminist tradition of the second American wave, notably Audre Lorde (1984), Alice

---

[6] Central figures in this tradition are: Firestone (1970), Rowbotham (1973), Mitchell (1974), Barrett (1980), Davis (1981), Coward (1983) and Delphy (1984).

Walker (1984) and Adrienne Rich (1987), acknowledged the importance of the spiritual dimension of women's struggle for equality and symbolic recognition. The work of Mary Daly (1973), Schussler Fiorenza (1983) and Luce Irigaray (1993), to name but a few, highlights a specific feminist tradition of non-male-centred spiritual and religious practices. Feminist theology in the Christian (Keller, 1998; Wadud, 1999), Muslim (Tayyab, 1998) and Judaic (Adler, 1998) traditions produced well-established communities of both critical resistance and affirmation of creative alternatives. The call for new rituals and ceremonies makes the fortune of the witches' movement, currently best exemplified by Starhawk (1999) and reclaimed among others by the epistemologist Stengers (1997). Neo-pagan elements have also emerged in technologically mediated cyber-culture, producing various brands of posthuman techno-asceticism (Halberstam and Livingston, 1995; Braidotti, 2002).

Black and post-colonial theories have never been loudly secular. In the very religious context of the USA, African-American women's literature is filled with references to Christianity, as bell hooks (1990) and Cornell West (1994) demonstrate. Furthermore, as we shall see later on in this chapter, post-colonial and critical race theories today have developed non-theistic brands of situated neo-humanism, often based on non-Western sources and traditions.

Contemporary popular culture has intensified the post-secular trend. Madonna, known in her Judaic (con)version as Esther, has a standing dialogue and stage act as/with Jesus Christ and has revived the tradition of female crucifixions. Evelyn Fox Keller (1983), in her seminal work on feminist epistemology, recognizes the importance of Buddhism in the making of contemporary microbiologist McClintock's Nobel-prize winning discoveries. Henrietta Moore's recent anthropological research on sexuality in Kenya (2007) argues that, considering the impact of grass-roots religious organizations, being white is less of a problem in the field today than being a failed Christian. Recently Donna Haraway came out as a failed secularist (Haraway, 2006); while Helen Cixous (2004) saw it fit to write a book entitled *Portrait of Jacques Derrida as a Young Jewish Saint*. Now, let me ask once again: how secular is all this?

The notion that flatly and hastily equates secularity and secularism with women's emancipation emerges therefore as problematic. As Joan Scott cogently argues (2007), this notion can be easily challenged by contradictory historical evidence. If we take, for instance, the French Revolution as the historical point of origin of European secularism, there is no evidence that a concern for the equal status of women was a priority for those who acted to separate church from state. High secularism is essentially a political doctrine of the separation of powers, which was even historically consolidated in Europe and is still prominent in political theory today (British Humanist Association, 2007). This tradition of secularism, however, introduces a polarization between religion and citizenship, which is socially enacted in a new partition between a private belief system and the public political sphere. This public–private distinction is thoroughly gendered. Historically, women in Europe have been assigned to both the private domain and to the realm of faith and religion, Humanism being 'white Man's burden'. This traditional attribution of religious faith to women stands in the way of granting them full political citizenship. European women were encouraged to engage in religious activity, rather than to participate in public affairs. This is not only a source of social marginalization, but also a dubious privilege, in view of the entrenched sexism of monotheistic religions and their shared conviction of the necessity to exclude women from the ministry and the administration of sacred functions. Secularity therefore reinforced the distinction between emotions or un-reason, including faith and rational judgement. In this polarized scheme, women were assigned to the pole of un-reason, passions and emotions, including religion, and these factors combined to keep them in the private sphere. Thus secularism actually re-enforces the oppression of women and their exclusion from the public sphere of rational citizenship and politics. The fact that idealized secularism in European political history does not guarantee that women were considered the political equals of men opens a series of critical questions, according to Joan Scott. What are European feminists to make of the fact that, both logically and historically, equality within the secular state does not guarantee the respect for difference, let alone diversity?

These sobering and important questions can be raised in the aftermath of decades of anti-humanist critical theory, which generated innovative feminist, post-colonial and environmental insights. Complexity becomes the key word, as it is clear that one single narrative does not suffice to account for secularity as an unfinished project and its relationship to Humanism and emancipatory politics. A post-secular approach, posited on firm anti-humanist grounds makes manifest the previously unacceptable notion that rational agency and political subjectivity, can actually be conveyed through and supported by religious piety and may even involve significant amounts of spirituality. Belief systems and their rituals are perhaps not incompatible with critical thought and practices of citizenship. Simone de Beauvoir would be distressed at the very suggestion of such a possibility.

Let me approach the limits of the feminist secular position from another angle. My monistic philosophy of becomings rests on the idea that matter, including the specific slice of matter that is human embodiment, is intelligent and self-organizing. This means that matter is not dialectically opposed to culture, nor to technological mediation, but continuous with them. This produces a different scheme of emancipation and a non-dialectical politics of human liberation. This position has another important corollary, namely that political agency need not be critical in the negative sense of oppositional and thus may not be aimed solely or primarily at the production of counter-subjectivities. Subjectivity is rather a process of auto-poiesis or self-styling, which involves complex and continuous negotiations with dominant norms and values and hence also multiple forms of accountability (Braidotti, 2006). This process-oriented political ontology can accommodate a post-secular turn, a position that is also defended within feminism by a variety of thinkers, such as Harding (2000) and Mahmood (2005). The double challenge of linking political subjectivity to religious agency and of disengaging both from oppositional consciousness, and from critique defined as negativity, is one of the main issues raised by the posthumanist condition.

Things around Humanism, however, are always more complex than one expects them to be. The return of religion in the public sphere and the strident tone reached by the global public debate on the 'clash of civilizations', not to speak of the permanent state of war on terror that ensued from this context, took many anti-humanists by surprise. To speak of a 'return' of religion is inappropriate, as it suggests a regressive movement. What we are experiencing at present is a more complicated situation. The crisis of secularism, defined as the essentialist belief in the axioms of secularity, is a phenomenon that takes place within the social and political horizon of late globalized post-modernity, not in pre-modern times. It is of the here and now. Moreover, it spreads across all religions, amidst both second and third generation descendants of Muslim immigrants; and amidst born-again fundamentalist Christians and by Hindi, Hebrew and others.

This is the paradoxical and violent global context where the posture of Western 'exceptionalism' has taken the form of self-aggrandizing praise of the Enlightenment Humanist legacy. This claim to an exceptional cultural status foregrounds the emancipation of women, gays and lesbians as the defining feature of the West, coupled with extensive geo-political armed interventions against the rest. Humanism has once again become enlisted in a civilizational crusade. Simultaneously over-estimated in its emancipatory historical role and manipulated for xenophobic purposes by populist politicians across Europe, Humanism may need to be rescued from these over-simplifications and violent abuses. I wonder, therefore, whether nowadays one can continue to uphold a simple anti-humanist position. Is a residual form of Humanism inevitable, intellectually, politically and methodologically, after all? If the new belligerent discourses about the alleged superiority of the West are expressed in terms of the legacy of secular Humanism, while the most vehement opposition to them takes the form of post-secular practices of politicized religion, where can an anti-humanist position rest? To be simply secular would be complicitous with neo-colonial Western supremacist positions, while rejecting the Enlightenment legacy would be inherently contradictory for any critical project. The vicious circle is stifling.

It is out of contradictions of this magnitude that the seemingly endless polemic between Humanism and anti-humanism reaches a dead-end. This position is not only unproductive; it also actively prevents an adequate reading of our immediate context. Leaving behind the tensions that surround Humanism and its self-contradictory refutation is now a priority. Another option becomes increasingly desirable and necessary: posthumanism as a move beyond these lethal binaries. Let us turn to it next.

The Posthuman Challenge

Posthumanism is the historical moment that marks the end of the opposition between Humanism and anti-humanism and traces a different discursive framework, looking more affirmatively towards new alternatives. The starting point for me is the anti-humanist death of Wo/Man which marks the decline of some of the fundamental premises of the Enlightenment, namely the progress of mankind through a self-regulatory and teleological ordained use of reason and of secular scientific rationality allegedly aimed at the perfectibility of 'Man'. The posthumanist perspective rests on the assumption of the historical decline of Humanism but goes further in exploring alternatives, without sinking into the rhetoric of the crisis of Man. It works instead towards elaborating alternative ways of conceptualizing the human subject. I will emphasize the priority of the issue of posthuman subjectivity throughout this book.

   The crisis of Humanism means that the structural others of the modern humanistic subject re-emerge with a vengeance in postmodernity (Braidotti, 2002). It is a historical fact that the great emancipatory movements of postmodernity are driven and fuelled by the resurgent 'others': the women's rights movement; the anti-racism and de-colonization movements; the anti-nuclear and pro-environment movements are the voices of the structural Others of modernity. They inevitably mark the crisis of the former humanist 'centre' or dominant subject-position and are not merely anti-humanist, but move beyond it to an altogether novel, posthuman project. These social and political movements are simultaneously the symptom of the crisis of the subject, and for conservatives even its 'cause', and also the expression of positive, pro-active alternatives. In the language of my nomadic theory (Braidotti, 2011a, 2011b), they express both the crisis of the majority and the patterns of becoming of the minorities. The challenge for critical theory consists in being able to tell the difference between these different flows of mutation.

In other words, the posthumanist position I am defending builds on the anti-humanist legacy, more specifically on the epistemological and political foundations of the post-structuralist generation, and moves further. The alternative views about the human and the new formations of subjectivity that have emerged from the radical epistemologies of Continental philosophy in the last thirty years do not merely oppose Humanism but create other visions of the self. Sexualized, racialized and naturalized differences, far from being the categorical boundary-keepers of the subject of Humanism, have evolved into fully fledged alternative models of the human subject. The extent to which they bring about the displacement of the human will become even clearer in the next chapter, which analyses the post-anthropocentric turn. For now, I want to emphasize this shift away from anti-Humanism towards an affirmative posthuman position and examine critically some of its components.

I see three major strands in contemporary posthuman thought: the first comes from moral philosophy and develops a reactive form of the posthuman; the second, from science and technology studies, enforces an analytic form of the posthuman; and the third, from my own tradition of anti-humanist philosophies of subjectivity, proposes a critical post-humanism. Let us look at each of these in turn.

The reactive approach to the posthuman is defended, both conceptually and politically, by contemporary liberal thinkers like Martha Nussbaum (1999, 2010). She develops a thorough contemporary defence of Humanism as the guarantee of democracy, freedom and the respect for human dignity, and rejects the very idea of a crisis of European Humanism, let alone the possibility of its historical decline. Nussbaum does acknowledge the challenges presented by contemporary, technology-driven global economies, but responds to them by re-asserting classical humanist ideals and progressive liberal politics. She defends the need for universal humanistic values as a remedy for the fragmentation and the relativistic drift of our times, which is the result of globalization itself. Humanistic cosmopolitan universalism is also presented as an antidote against nationalism and ethnocentrism, which plague the contemporary world, and to the prevailing American attitude of ignorance of the rest of the world.

Central to the reactive or negative post-humanism of Nussbaum is the idea that one of the effects of globalization is a sort of re-contextualization induced by the market economy. This produces a new sense of inter-connection which in turn calls for a neo-humanist ethics. For Nussbaum, abstract universalism is the only stance that is capable of providing solid foundations for moral values such as compassion and respect for others, which she firmly attaches to the tradition of American liberal individualism. I am very happy that Nussbaum stresses the importance of subjectivity, but less happy about the fact that she re-attaches it to a universalistic belief in individualism, fixed identities, steady locations and moral ties that bind.

In other words, Nussbaum rejects the insights of the radical anti-humanist philosophies of the last thirty years. Notably, she embraces universalism over and against the feminist and post-colonial insights about the importance of the politics of location and careful grounding in geo-political terms. By embracing dis-embedded universalism, Nussbaum ends up being paradoxically parochial in her vision of what counts as the human (Bhabha, 1996a). There is no room for experimenting with new models of the self; for Nussbaum the posthuman condition can be solved by restoring a humanist vision of the subject. As we shall see in the next section, whereas Nussbaum fills the ethical vacuum of the globalized world with classical Humanistic norms, critical post-humanists take the experimental path. They attempt to devise renewed claims to community and belonging by singular subjects who have taken critical distance from humanist individualism.

A second significant posthuman development comes from science and technology studies. This contemporary interdisciplinary field raises crucial ethical and conceptual questions about the status of the human, but is generally reluctant to undertake a full study of their implications for a theory of subjectivity. The influence of Bruno Latour's anti-epistemology and anti-subjectivity position accounts partly for this reluctance. Concretely, it results in parallel and noncommunicating lines of posthuman enquiry. A new segregation of knowledge is produced, along the dividing lines of the 'two cultures', the Humanities and the Sciences, which I will discuss in depth in chapter 4.

For now, let me stress that there is a posthuman agreement that contemporary science and biotechnologies affect the very fibre and structure of the living and have altered dramatically our understanding of what counts as the basic frame of reference for the human today. Technological intervention upon all living matter creates a negative unity and mutual dependence among humans and other species. The Human Genome Project, for instance, unifies all the human species on the basis of a thorough grasp of our genetic structure. This point of consensus, however, generates diverging paths of enquiry. The Humanities continue to ask the question of the epistemological and political implications of the posthuman predicament for our understanding of the human subject. They also raise deep anxieties both about the moral status of the human and express the political desire to resist commercially owned and profit-minded abuses of the new genetic know-how.

Contemporary science and technology studies, on the other hand, adopt a different agenda. They have developed an analytic form of posthuman theory. For instance, Franklin, Lury and Stacey, working within a socio-cultural frame of reference, refer to the technologically mediated world of today as 'panhumanity' (2000: 26). This indicates a global sense of inter-connection among all humans, but also between the human and the non-human environment, including the urban, social and political, which creates a web of intricate inter-dependences. This new pan-humanity is paradoxical in two ways: firstly, because a great deal of its inter-connections are negative and based on a shared sense of vulnerability and fear of imminent catastrophes and, secondly, because this new global proximity does not always breed tolerance and peaceful co-existence; on the contrary, forms of xenophobic rejection of otherness and increasing armed violence are key features of our times, as I will argue in chapter 3.

Another relevant example of the same analytic posthuman thought, within the disciplinary field of science studies, is the work of sociologist Nicholas Rose (2007). He has written eloquently about the new forms of 'bio-sociality' and bio-citizenship that are emerging from the shared recognition of the bio-political nature of contemporary subjectivity. Resting on a Foucauldian understanding of how bio-political management of Life defines advanced capitalist economies today, Rose has developed an effective, empirically grounded analysis of the dilemmas of the posthuman condition. This posthuman analytic frame advocates a Foucauldian brand of neo-Kantian normativity. I find this position quite helpful, also because it defends a vision of the subject as a relational process, with reference to the last phase of Foucault's work (Foucault 1978, 1985, 1986). As I will argue in detail in the next chapter, however, the return to a notion of Kantian moral responsibility re-instates the individual at the core of the debate. This is not compatible with the Foucauldian process ontology and creates both theoretical and practical contradictions that defeat the stated purpose of developing a posthuman approach.

Another significant case for analytic post-humanism is advocated by Peter-Paul Verbeek (2011). Starting from the recognition of the intimate and productive association between human subjects and technological artefacts, as well as the theoretical impossibility of keeping them apart, Verbeek hints at the need for a post-anthropological turn that links humans to non-humans, but he is also very careful not to trespass certain limits. His analytic form of post-humanism is immediately qualified by a profoundly humanist and thus normative approach to technology itself. Verbeek's main argument is that 'technologies contribute actively to how humans do ethics' (2011: 5); a revised and updated form of humanist ethics gets superimposed on post-humanist technologies.

In order to defend the humanist principle at the heart of contemporary technologies, Verbeek emphasizes the moral nature of technological tools as agents that can guide human decision making on normative issues. He also introduces multiple forms of machinic intentionality, all of them indexed on non-human forms of moral consciousness. Only by taking seriously the morality of things, argues Verbeek, can we hope to integrate our technology into the wider social community and bring a posthuman brand of Humanism into the twenty-first century. This results in shifting the location of traditional moral intentionality from autonomous transcendental consciousness to the technological artefacts themselves.

The analytic post-humanism of science and technology studies is one of the most important elements of the contemporary posthuman landscape. In terms of critical theories of the subject, which is the focus of my position, however, this position falls wide of the mark, because it introduces selected segments of humanistic values without addressing the contradictions engendered by such a grafting exercise.

The pride in technological achievements and in the wealth that comes with them must not prevent us from seeing the great contradictions and the forms of social and moral inequality engendered by our advanced technologies. Not addressing them, in the name of either scientific neutrality or of a hastily reconstructed sense of the pan-human bond induced by globalization, simply begs the question.

In my eyes, what is striking about the science and technology studies approach, whether it relies theoretically on moral philosophy or on socio-cultural theory, is the high degree of political neutrality it expresses about the posthuman predicament. Both Rose and Franklin et al., for instance, make it clear that the focus of their research is analytic and aims to achieve a better, more thorough and in some ways intimate ethnographic understanding of how these new technologies actually function. Science and technology studies tend to dismiss the implications of their positions for a revised vision of the subject. Subjectivity is out of the picture and, with it, a sustained political analysis of the posthuman condition. In my view, a focus on subjectivity is necessary because this notion enables us to string together issues that are currently scattered across a number of domains. For instance, issues such as norms and values, forms of community bonding and social belonging as well as questions of political governance both assume and require a notion of the subject. Critical posthuman thought wants to re-assemble a discursive community out of the different, fragmented contemporary strands of posthumanism.

I cannot help noticing, moreover, a rather bizarre and highly problematic division of labour on the question of subjectivity between science and technology studies on the one hand, and political analyses of advanced capitalism on the other. For instance, Hardt and Negri (2000, 2004), or the Italian school of Lazzarato (2004) and Virno (2004), tend to avoid science and technology and not to treat it with anything like the depth and sophistication that they devote to the analysis of subjectivity. I think we may need to review this segregation of discursive fields and work towards a re-integrated posthuman theory that includes both scientific and technological complexity and its implications for political subjectivity, political economy and forms of governance. I will develop this project gradually in the chapters that follow.

There is another fundamental problem with the residual humanism of the analytically posthuman attempts to moralize technology and sideline experiments with new forms of subjectivity, namely their over-confidence about the moral intentionality of the technology itself. More specifically, they neglect the current state of autonomy reached by the machines. The complexity of our smart technologies lies at the core of the post-anthropocentric turn that will be the theme of the next chapter. For now, let us consider just one aspect of our technological smartness.

A recent issue of the weekly magazine *The Economist* (2 June 2012) on 'Morals and the machine' raises some pertinent issues about the degree of autonomy reached by robots and calls for society to develop new rules to manage them. The analysis is significant: in contrast to the modernist idea of the robot as subservient to the human, as exemplified by Isaac Asimov's 'three laws of robotics' formulated in 1942,[7] we are now confronted by a new situation, which makes

[7] These three laws are: (1) A robot may not injure a human being or, through inaction, allow a human being to come to harm. (2) A robot must obey the orders given to it by human beings, except where such orders would conflict with the First Law. (3) A robot must protect its own existence as long as such protection does not conflict with the First or Second Laws. These rules were set up by Isaac Asimov in a short story in 1942 and then re-printed in the world best-seller: *I, Robot*, in 1950. They became foundational notions in cyber-studies. Later, Asimov added a fourth law which precedes all others: (0) A robot may not harm humanity, or, by inaction, allow humanity to come to harm.

human intervention rather peripheral if not completely irrel-evant. *The Economist* argues (2012: 11):

> As robots become more autonomous, the notion of computer-controlled machines facing ethical decisions is moving out of the realm of science fiction and into the real world.

Most of these new robots are military in purpose and I will return to them in chapter 3, but many others are used for perfectly reasonable civilian purposes. All of them share a crucial feature: they have made it technologically feasible to by-pass human decision making at both the operational and the moral levels. According to this report, humans will increasingly operate not 'in the loop' but 'on the loop', monitoring armed and working robots rather than fully controlling them. Only ethical and legal issues remain to be solved to grant responsibility to autonomous machines' deci-sion making, while the cognitive capacities are already in place.

As they become smarter and more widespread, autono-mous machines are bound to make life-or-death decisions and thus assume agency. Whether this high degree of autonomy, however, results in moral decision making is at best an open question. Against claims to the in-built moral intentionality of the technology, I would claim that it is normatively neutral. Take some burning issues, such as: should an unmanned flying vehicle, also known as a drone, fire on a house where a target is known to be hiding, which also shelters civilians? Should robots involved in disaster relief tell people the truth about their conditions, thus causing panic and pain? Such questions lead to the field of 'machine ethics', which aims to give machines the ability to make such choices appropri-ately, in other words, to tell right from wrong. And who is to decide?

According to *The Economist* (2012), a new ethical approach needs to be developed by active experiments. They should focus on three areas especially: firstly, the rule of Laws to determine whether the designer, the programmer, the man-ufacturer, or the operator is at fault if a machine goes wrong. To allocate responsibility, a detailed logs system is needed so that it can explain the reasoning behind the decision-making process. This has implications for design, with a preference for systems that obey pre-defined rules rather than decision-making systems. Secondly, when ethical systems are embedded in robots, the judgements they make need to be ones that seem right to most people. The techniques of experimental philosophy, which studies how people respond to ethical dilemmas, should be able to help. Thirdly, new interdisciplinary collaboration is required between engineers, ethicists, lawyers and policy-makers, all of whom would draw up very different rules if left to their own devices. They all stand to gain by working with each other.

What is posthuman about the situation outlined in *The Economist* is that it does not assume a human, individualized self as the deciding factor of main subject. It rather envisages what I would call a transversal inter-connection or an 'assemblage' of human and non-human actors, not unlike Latour's Actor Network Theory (Law and Hassard, 1999). It is significant that a rather cautious and conservative journal like *The Economist*, faced with the challenge of the posthuman powers of the technologies we have developed, does not call for a return to humanist values, but for pragmatic experimentation. This prompts three comments on my part: firstly, that I could not agree more that this is no time for nostalgic longings for the humanist past, but for forward-looking experiments with new forms of subjectivity. Secondly, I want to emphasize the normatively neutral structure of contemporary technologies: they are not endowed with intrinsic humanistic agency. Thirdly, I note that the advocates of advanced capitalism seem to be faster in grasping the creative potential of the posthuman than some of the well-meaning and progressive neo-humanist opponents of this system. I will return in the next chapter to the opportunist brand of the posthuman developed in the contemporary market economy.

Critical Posthumanism

The third strand of posthuman thought, my own variation, shows no conceptual or normative ambivalence towards posthumanism. I want to move beyond analytic posthumanism and develop affirmative perspectives on the posthuman subject. My inspiration for taking the jump into critical posthumanism comes from my anti-humanist roots, of course. More specifically, the current of thought that has gone further in unfolding the productive potential of the posthuman predicament can be genealogically traced back to the post-structuralists, the anti-universalism of feminism and the anti-colonial phenomenology of Frantz Fanon (1967) and of his teacher Aimé Césaire (1955). What they have in common in a sustained commitment to work out the implications of posthumanism for our shared understandings of the human subject and of humanity as a whole.

The work of post-colonial and race theorists displays a situated cosmopolitan posthumanism that is supported as much by the European tradition as by non-Western sources of moral and intellectual inspiration. The examples are manifold and deserve more in-depth analysis than I can grant them here; for now, let me pick out the main gist of it.[8]

Edward Said (1978) was among the first to alert critical theorists in the West to the need to develop a reasoned scholarly account of Enlightenment-based secular Humanism, which would take into account the colonial experience, its violent abuses and structural injustice, as well as post-colonial existence. Post-colonial theory developed this insight into the notion that ideals of reason, secular tolerance, equality under the Law and democratic rule, need not be, and indeed historically have not been, mutually exclusive with European practices of violent domination, exclusion and systematic and instrumental use of terror. Acknowledging that reason and barbarism are not self-contradictory, nor are Enlightenment and horror, need not result in either cultural relativism, or in moral nihilism, but rather in a radical critique of the notion of Humanism and its link with both democratic criticism and secularism. Edward Said defends the idea that:

[8] Significant examples are: Avtar Brah's diasporic ethics (1996) echoes Vandana Shiva's anti-global neo-Humanism (1997). African Humanism or Ubuntu is receiving more attention, from Patricia Hill Collins (1991) to Drucilla Cornell (2002). In a more nomadic vein, Edouard Glissant's politics of relations (1997) inscribed multi-lingual hybridity at the heart of the contemporary posthuman condition. Homi Bhabha's 'subaltern secularism' (1994) builds on the huge legacy of Edward Said.

It is possible to be critical of Humanism in the name of Humanism and that, schooled in its abuses by the experience of Eurocentrism and empire, one could fashion a different kind of Humanism that was cosmopolitan and text-and-language bound in ways that absorbed the great lessons of the past [. . .] and still remain attuned to the emergent voices and currents of the present, many of them exilic extraterritorial and unhoused. (2004: 11)

Fighting for such subaltern secular spaces is a priority for a posthuman quest for what is known in some quarters as a 'global ethic for global politics and economics' (Kung, 1998).

Paul Gilroy's planetary cosmopolitanism (2000) also proposes a productive form of contemporary critical posthumanism. Gilroy holds Europe and the Europeans accountable for our collective failure in implementing the ideals of the humanist Enlightenment. Like the feminists, race theorists are suspicious of deconstructing a subject-position, which historically they never gained the right to. Gilroy considers colonialism and fascism as a betrayal of the European ideal of the Enlightenment, which he is determined to defend, holding Europeans accountable for their ethical and political failings. Racism splits common humanity and disengages whites from any ethical sensibility, reducing them to an infrahuman moral status. It also reduces non-whites to a subhuman ontological status that exposes them to murderous violence. Taking a strong stand against the return of fundamentalist appeals to ethnic differences by a variety of white, black, Serbian, Rwandan, Texan and other nationalists, Gilroy denounces what Deleuze calls 'micro-fascisms' (Deleuze and Guattari, 1987) as the epidemics of our globalized times. He locates the site of the ethical transformation in the critique of each nationalistic category, not in the assertion of a new dominant one. He sets diasporic mobility and the transcultural interconnections up against the forces of nationalism. This is a theory of mixture, hybridity and cosmopolitanism that is resolutely non-racial. Against the enduring power of nation states, Gilroy posits instead the affirmative politics of transversal movements, such as anti-slavery, feminism, Médécins sans frontières and the like.

An altogether different and powerful source of inspiration for contemporary re-configurations of critical posthumanism is ecology and environmentalism. They rest on an enlarged sense of inter-connection between self and others, including the non-human or 'earth' others. This practice of relating to others requires and is enhanced by the rejection of self-centred individualism. It produces a new way of combining self-interests with the well-being of an enlarged community, based on environmental inter-connections.

Environmental theory stresses the link between the humanistic emphasis on Man as the measure of all things and the domination and exploitation of nature and condemns the abuses of science and technology. Both of them involve epistemic and physical violence over the structural 'others' and are related to the European Enlightenment ideal of 'reason'. The worldview which equated Mastery with rational scientific control over 'others' also militated against the respect for the diversity of living matters and of human cultures (Mies and Shiva, 1993). The environmental alternative is a new holistic approach that combines cosmology with anthropology and post-secular, mostly feminist spirituality, to assert the need for loving respect for diversity in both its human and non-human forms. Significantly, Shiva and Mies stress the importance of life-sustaining spirituality in this struggle for new concrete forms of universality: a reverence for the sacredness of life, of deeply seated respect for all that lives. This attitude is opposed to Western Humanism and to the West's investment in rationality and secularity as the pre-condition for development through science and technology. In a holistic perspective, they call for the 're-enchantment of the world' (1993: 18), or for healing the Earth and that which has been so cruelly disconnected. Instead of the emphasis on emancipation from the realm of natural necessity, Shiva pleads for a form of emancipation that occurs within that realm and in harmony with it. From this shift of perspective there follows a critique of the ideal of equality as the emulation of masculine modes of behaviour and also the rejection of the model of development that is built upon this ideal and is compatible with world-wide forms of market domination.

Although ecological posthumanists like Shiva take great care to distance themselves from anything that is even remotely related to 'post'-modernism, post-colonialism, or post-feminism, paradoxically, they share in the epistemic premises of posthuman critiques. For instance, they agree with the post-structuralist generation on the critique of the homogenization of cultures under the effects of globalized advanced capitalism. They propose as an alternative a robust type of environmentalism, based on non-Western neo-humanism. What matters for Mies and Shiva is the reassertion of the need for new universal values in the sense of interconnectedness among humans, on a worldwide scale. Thus, universal needs are amalgamated to universal rights and they cover as much basic and concrete necessities, such as food, shelter, health, safety, as higher cultural needs, like education, identity, dignity, knowledge, affection, joy and care. These constitute the material grounding of the situated claims to new ethical values.

A new ecological posthumanism thus raises issues of power and entitlement in the age of globalization and calls for self-reflexivity on the part of the subjects who occupy the former humanist centre, but also those who dwell in one of the many scattered centres of power of advanced post-modernity (Grewal and Kaplan, 1994).

In my own work, I define the critical posthuman subject within an eco-philosophy of multiple belongings, as a relational subject constituted in and by multiplicity, that is to say a subject that works across differences and is also internally differentiated, but still grounded and accountable. Posthuman subjectivity expresses an embodied and embedded and hence partial form of accountability, based on a strong sense of collectivity, relationality and hence community building.

My position is in favour of complexity and promotes radical posthuman subjectivity, resting on the ethics of becoming, as we shall see in the next chapter. The focus is shifted accordingly from unitary to nomadic subjectivity, thus running against the grain of high humanism and its contemporary variations. This view rejects individualism, but also asserts an equally strong distance from relativism or nihilistic defeatism. It promotes an ethical bond of an altogether different sort from the self-interests of an individual subject, as defined along the canonical lines of classical Humanism. A posthuman ethics for a non-unitary subject proposes an enlarged sense of inter-connection between self and others, including the non-human or 'earth' others, by removing the obstacle of self-centred individualism. As we saw earlier, contemporary bio-genetic capitalism generates a global form of reactive mutual inter-dependence of all living organisms, including non-humans. This sort of unity tends to be of the negative kind, as a shared form of vulnerability, that is to say a global sense of inter-connection between the human and the non-human environment in the face of common threats. The posthuman recomposition of human interaction that I propose is not the same as the reactive bond of vulnerability, but is an affirmative bond that locates the subject in the flow of relations with multiple others.

As we shall see in the next chapter, for me there is a necessary link between critical posthumanism and the move beyond anthropocentrism. I refer to this move as expanding the notion of Life towards the non-human or *zoe*. This results in radical posthumanism as a position that transposes hybridity, nomadism, diasporas and creolization processes into means of re-grounding claims to subjectivity, connections and community among subjects of the human and the non-human kind. This is the next step of the argument, which I will outline in chapter 2.

Conclusion

This chapter has traced my own itinerary out of the multiple possible genealogies of the posthuman, including the rise of alternative forms of critical posthumanism. These new formations are postulated on the demise of that 'Man' – the former measure of all things. Eurocentrism, masculinism and anthropocentrism are exposed accordingly as complex and internally differentiated phenomena. This alone is in keeping with the highly complex character of the concept of Humanism itself. There are in fact many Humanisms and my own itinerary, generationally and geo-politically, struggles essentially with one specific genealogical line:

> The romantic and positivistic Humanisms through which the European bourgeoisies established their hegemonies over (modernity), the revolutionary Humanism that shook the world and the liberal Humanism that sought to tame it, the

Humanism of the Nazis and the Humanisms of their victims
and opponents, the antihumanist Humanism of Heidegger
and the humanist antihumanism of Foucault and Althusser,
the secularist Humanism of Huxley and Dawkins or the posthumanism of Gibson and Haraway. (Davies, 1997: 141)

The fact that these different humanisms cannot be reduced
to one linear narrative is part of the problem and the paradoxes involved in attempting to overcome Humanism. What
seems absolutely clear to me is the historical, ethical and
political necessity to overcome this notion, in the light of its
history of unfulfilled promises and unacknowledged brutality.
A key methodological and tactical measure to support this
process is to practise the politics of location, or situated and
accountable knowledge practices.

Let me conclude with three crucial remarks: firstly, that we
do need a new theory of the subject that takes stock of the
posthuman turn and hence acknowledges the decline of
Humanism. Secondly, as shown by the proliferation of critical
posthuman positions both within and outside the Western
philosophical tradition, the end of classical Humanism is not
a crisis, but entails positive consequences. Thirdly, advanced
capitalism has been quick in sensing and exploiting the
opportunities opened by the decline of western Humanism
and the processes of cultural hybridization induced by globalization. I will address the latter in the next chapter, so let
me say something briefly about the other two points.

Firstly, we need to work out the implications of the posthuman predicament in the sense of the decline of European
Humanism in order to develop a robust foundation for ethical
and political subjectivity. The posthuman era is ripe with
contradictions as we shall see in the next two chapters. These
call for ethical evaluation, political intervention and normative action. It follows therefore that the posthuman subject is
not postmodern, that is to say it is not anti-foundationalist.
Nor is it deconstructivist, because it is not linguistically
framed. The posthuman subjectivity I advocate is rather
materialist and vitalist, embodied and embedded, firmly
located somewhere, according to the feminist 'politics of location', which I have stressed throughout this chapter. Why do
I stress so much the issue of the subject? Because a theory

of subjectivity as both materialist and relational, 'nature-cultural' and self-organizing is crucial in order to elaborate critical tools suited to the complexity and contradictions of our times. A merely analytical form of posthuman thought does not go far enough. More especially, a serious concern for the subject allows us to take into account the elements of creativity and imagination, desire, hopes and aspirations (Moore, 2011) without which we simply cannot make sense of contemporary global culture and its posthuman overtones. We need a vision of the subject that is 'worthy of the present'.

This brings us to my second concluding remark: the issue of Eurocentrism in terms of 'methodological nationalism' (Beck, 2007) and its long-standing bond to Humanism. Contemporary European subjects of knowledge must meet the ethical obligation to be accountable for their past history and the long shadow it casts on their present-day politics.[9] The new mission that Europe has to embrace entails the criticism of narrow-minded self-interests, intolerance and xenophobic rejection of otherness. Symbolic of the closure of the European mind is the fate of migrants, refugees and asylum-seekers who bear the brunt of racism in contemporary Europe.

A new agenda needs to be set, which is no longer that of European or Eurocentric universal, rational subjectivity, but rather a radical transformation of it, in a break from Europe's imperial, fascistic and undemocratic tendencies. As I stated earlier on in this chapter, since the second half of the twentieth century, the crisis of philosophical Humanism – also known as the death of 'Man' – both reflected and amplified larger concerns about the decline of the geo-political status of Europe as an imperial world-power. Theory and world-historical phenomena work in tandem when it comes to the question of European Humanism. Because of this resonance between the two dimensions, critical theory has a unique contribution to make to the debate on Europe.

I believe that the posthuman condition can facilitate the task of redefining a new role for Europe in an age where global capitalism is both triumphant and clearly deficient in

[9] As Morin (1987), Passerini (1998), Balibar (2004) and Bauman (2004) have also argued.

terms of sustainability and social justice (Holland, 2011). This hopeful belief rests on the post-nationalist approach (Habermas, 2001; Braidotti, 2006) which expresses the decline of Eurocentrism as a historical event and calls for a qualitative shift of perspective in our collective sense of identity. Seyla Benhabib, in her brilliant work on alternative cosmopolitanism (2007), addresses the question of Europe as a site of transformation. Her emphasis on a pluralist cosmopolitan practice and her commitment to the rights of refugees and stateless people, as well as migrants, innovates on classical universalist notions of cosmopolitanism and calls for situated and context-specific practices. This resonates positively with my situated posthuman ethics. A primary task for posthuman critical theory therefore is to draw accurate and precise cartographies for these different subject positions as spring-boards towards posthuman recompositions of a pan-human cosmopolitan bond.

More specifically, I would like to push the case further than Habermas' social democratic aspiration and argue for a post-human project of 'becoming-minoritarian' or becoming-nomad of Europe (Deleuze and Guattari, 1987; Braidotti, 2008). This is a way of by-passing a number of binary pitfalls, for instance between a globalized and culturally diverse Europe on the one hand, and the narrow and xenophobic definitions of European identity on the other. The becoming-nomad of Europe entails resistance against nationalism, xenophobia and racism, bad habits of the old imperial Europe. As such, it is the opposite of the grandiose and aggressive universalism of the past, which is replaced by a situated and accountable perspective. It embraces a new political and ethical project, by taking a firm stand also against the 'Fortress Europe' syndrome and reviving tolerance as a tool of social justice (Brown, 2006).

The posthuman turn can support and enhance this project in so far as it displaces the exclusive focus on the idea of Europe as the cradle of Humanism, driven by a form of universalism that endows it with a unique sense of historical purpose. The process of becoming-minoritarian or becoming-nomad of Europe involves the rejection of the self-appointed missionary role of Europe as the alleged centre of the world. If it is the case that a socio-cultural mutation is taking place in the direction of a multi-ethnic, multi-media society, then the transformation cannot affect only the pole of 'the others'. It must equally dislocate the position and the prerogative of 'the same', the former centre. The project of developing a new kind of post-nationalist nomadic European identity is certainly challenging in that it requires dis-identification from established, nation-bound identities. This project is political at heart, but it has a strong affective core made of convictions, vision and active desire for change. We can collectively empower these alternative becomings.

My posthuman sensibility may come across as visionary and even impatient, but it is very pro-active or, to use my favourite term: affirmative. Affirmative politics combines critique with creativity in the pursuit of alternative visions and projects. As far as I am concerned, the challenge of the post-human condition consists in grabbing the opportunities offered by the decline of the unitary subject position upheld by Humanism, which has mutated in a number of complex directions. For instance: the cultural inter-mixity already available within our post-industrial ethno-scapes and the re-compositions of genders and sexualities sizzling under the apparently sedate image of equal opportunities, far from being indicators of a crisis, are productive events. They are the new starting points that bring into play untapped possibilities for bonding, community building and empowerment. Similarly, the current scientific revolution, led by contemporary bio-genetic, environmental, neural and other sciences, creates powerful alternatives to established practices and definitions of subjectivity. Instead of falling back on the sedimented habits of thought that the humanist past has institutionalized, the posthuman predicament encourages us to undertake a leap forward into the complexities and paradoxes of our times. To meet this task, new conceptual creativity is needed.

Chapter 2
Post-Anthropocentrism: Life beyond the Species

I loved George Eliot's prose well before I even knew that she actually translated Spinoza, my favourite philosopher, into English. Mary Evans was a woman of many talents and anyone who ever identified with Dorothea in *Middlemarch* (1973) or Maggie in *The Mill on the Floss* (2003) may not be cognitively aware of the fact that s/he stepped – surreptitiously and fatally – into a monistic universe of intersecting affective relations that simply make the world go round. George Eliot has authored my favourite sentence in the English language:

> If we had a keen vision and feeling of all ordinary human life, it would be like hearing the grass grow and the squirrel's heart beat, and we should die of that roar which lies on the other side of silence. As it is, the quickest of us walk around well wadded with stupidity. (Eliot, 1973: 226)

The roar which lies on the other side of the urbane, civilized veneer that allows for bound identities and efficient social interaction is the Spinozist indicator of the raw cosmic energy that underscores the making of civilizations, societies and their subjects. Vitalist materialism is a concept that helps us make sense of that external dimension, which in fact enfolds within the subject as the internalized score of cosmic vibrations (Deleuze, 1992; Deleuze and Guattari, 1994). It also constitutes the core of a posthuman sensibility that aims at overcoming anthropocentrism.

Let me spell out some of these rather dense ideas. A 'monistic universe' refers to Spinoza's central concept that matter, the world and humans are not dualistic entities structured according to principles of internal or external opposition. The obvious target of criticism here is Descartes' famous mind–body distinction, but for Spinoza the concept goes even further: matter is one, driven by the desire for self-expression and ontologically free. The absence of any reference to negativity and to violent dialectical oppositions caused intense criticism of Spinoza on the part of Hegel and the Marxist-Hegelians. Spinoza's monistic worldview was seen as politically ineffective and holistic at heart. This situation changed dramatically in the 1970s in France, when a new wave of scholars rehabilitated Spinozist monism precisely as an antidote to some of the contradictions of Marxism and as a way of clarifying Hegel's relationship to Marx.[1] The main idea is to overcome dialectical oppositions, engendering non-dialectical understandings of materialism itself (Braidotti, 1991; Cheah, 2008), as an alternative to the Hegelian scheme. The 'Spinozist legacy' therefore consists in a very active concept of monism, which allowed these modern French philosophers to define matter as vital and self-organizing, thereby producing the staggering combination of 'vitalist materialism'. Because this approach rejects all forms of transcendentalism, it is also known as 'radical immanence'. Monism results in relocating difference outside the dialectical scheme, as a complex process of differing which is framed by both internal and external forces and is based on the centrality of the relation to multiple others.

These monistic premises are for me the building blocks for a posthuman theory of subjectivity that does not rely on classical Humanism and carefully avoids anthropocentrism. The

---

[1] The group around Althusser started the debate in the mid-1960s; Deleuze's path-breaking study of Spinoza dates from 1968 (in English in 1990); Macherey's Hegel–Spinoza analysis came out in 1979 (in English in 2011); Negri's work on the imagination in Spinoza in 1981 (in English in 1991).

classical emphasis on the unity of all matter, which is central to Spinoza, is reinforced by an updated scientific understanding of the self-organizing or 'smart' structure of living matter. These ideas are supported by new advances in contemporary biosciences, neural and cognitive sciences and by the informatics sector. Posthuman subjects are technologically mediated to an unprecedented degree. For instance, a neo-Spinozist approach is supported and expanded today by new developments in the mind–body interrelation within the neural sciences (Damasio, 2003). In my view, there is a direct connection between monism, the unity of all living matter and post-anthropocentrism as a general frame of reference for contemporary subjectivity.

Global Warning

George Eliot's work is a good lead into at least some aspects of this materialist (or, as I will argue later in the chapter, 'matter-realist') worldview. The support is welcome, as many of the assumptions and premises of the post-anthropocentric universe are somewhat counter intuitive, although the term has acquired widespread currency nowadays. In mainstream public debates, for instance, the posthuman is usually coated in anxiety about the excesses of technological intervention and the threat of climate change, or by elation about the potential for human enhancement. In academic culture, on the other hand, the critique of anthropocentrism has even more shattering implications than the transformative agenda of posthumanism which I analysed in the previous chapter. The post-anthropocentric turn, linked to the compounded impacts of globalization and of technology-driven forms of mediation, strikes the human at his/her heart and shifts the parameters that used to define *anthropos*.

In this chapter I want to argue that the issue of the posthuman in relation to post-anthropocentrism is of an altogether different order than in post-humanism. For one thing, whereas the latter mobilized primarily the disciplinary field of philosophy, history, cultural studies and the classical Humanities in general, the issue of post-anthropocentrism enlists also science and technology studies, new media and digital culture, environmentalism and earth-sciences, bio-genetics, neuroscience and robotics, evolutionary theory, critical legal theory, primatology, animal rights and science fiction. This high degree of trans-disciplinarity alone adds an extra layer of complexity to the issue. The key question for me is: what understandings of contemporary subjectivity and subject-formation are enabled by a post-anthropocentric approach? What comes after the anthropocentric subject?

How one reacts to this change of perspective depends to a large extent on one's relationship to technology. Being rather technophilic myself, I am quite upbeat. I will always side firmly with the liberatory and even transgressive potential of these technologies, against those who attempt to index them to either a predictable conservative profile, or to a profit-oriented system that fosters and inflates individualism. I do think that one of the most pointed paradoxes of our era is precisely the tension between the urgency of finding new and alternative modes of political and ethical agency for our technologically mediated world and the inertia of established mental habits on the other. Donna Haraway put it with customary wit: the machines are so alive, whereas the humans are so inert! (Haraway, 1985). As if to mirror this, science and technology studies nowadays is a thriving area in academic institutions, whereas the Humanities are in serious trouble.

It may be useful to start by clarifying some aspects of the globalized context in which the decentring of anthropocentrism is taking place. As I argued elsewhere (Braidotti, 2002, 2006), advanced capitalism is a spinning machine that actively produces differences for the sake of commodification. It is a multiplier of deterritorialized differences, which are packaged and marketed under the labels of 'new, dynamic and negotiable identities' and an endless choice of consumer goods. This logic triggers a proliferation and a vampiric consumption of quantitative options. Many of them have to do with cultural 'others', from fusion cooking to 'world music'. Jackie Stacey, in her analysis of the new organic food industry (Franklin et al., 2000) argues that we literally eat the global economy. Paul Gilroy (2000) and Celia Lury (1998) remind us that we also wear it, listen to it and watch it on our many screens, on a daily basis.

The global circulation of goods, data, capital, bits and bytes of information frames the interaction of contemporary subjects on a daily basis. Multiple choices confront consumers at every step, but with varying degrees of actual freedom of choice. Take for instance the transformations incurred by the formerly elementary task of making a call to the local bank. What we have grown to expect nowadays is either an automated posthuman system of replies offering subsets of numbers that connect us to a further web of pre-recorded messages. Or else we welcome the relief of hearing a real-life human voice, knowing all along that it is emanating from some call centre miles away, in one of the emerging economies of the world. The end result is that phone calls are cheaper than ever but the actual length of the calls is definitely getting longer, as the caller wades through multiple new hurdles. Of course Internet communication is replacing all this, but my point is that the spinning differential force of our economic system is such that we have to run twice as fast, across automated replies or transcontinental phone lines, just to stay in the same place.

The most salient trait of the contemporary global economy is therefore its techno-scientific structure. It is built on the convergence between different and previously differentiated branches of technology, notably the four horsemen of the posthuman apocalypse: nanotechnology, biotechnology, information technology and cognitive science. The bio-genetic structure of contemporary capitalism is especially important and central to the discussion on the posthuman. This aspect involves the Human Genome project, stem cell research and bio-technological intervention upon animals, seeds, cells and plants. In substance, advanced capitalism both invests and profits from the scientific and economic control and the commodification of all that lives. This context produces a paradoxical and rather opportunistic form of post-anthropo-centrism on the part of market forces which happily trade on Life itself.

The commodification of Life by bio-genetic advanced capitalism, however, is a complex affair. Consider my argument: the great scientific advances of molecular biology have taught us that matter is self-organized (autopoietic), whereas monistic philosophy adds that it is also structurally relational and hence connected to a variety of environments. These insights combine in defining intelligent vitality or self-organizing capacity as a force that is not confined within feedback loops internal to the individual human self, but is present in all living matter. Why is matter so intelligent, though? Because it is driven by informational codes, which both deploy their own bars of information, and interact in multiple ways with the social, psychic and ecological environments (Guattari, 2000). What happens to subjectivity in this complex field of forces and data flows? My argument is that it becomes an expanded relational self, engendered by the cumulative effect of all these factors (Braidotti 1991, 2011a). The relational capacity of the posthuman subject is not confined within our species, but it includes all non-anthropomorphic elements. Living matter – including the flesh – is intelligent and self-organizing, but it is so precisely because it is not disconnected from the rest of organic life. I therefore do not work completely within the social constructivist method but rather emphasize the non-human, vital force of Life, which is what I have coded as *zoe*.

Post-anthropocentrism is marked by the emergence of 'the politics of life itself' (Rose, 2007). 'Life', far from being codified as the exclusive property or the unalienable right of one species, the human, over all others or of being sacralized as a pre-established given, is posited as process, interactive and open-ended. This vitalist approach to living matter displaces the boundary between the portion of life – both organic and discursive – that has traditionally been reserved for *anthropos*, that is to say *bios*, and the wider scope of animal and non-human life, also known as *zoe*. *Zoe* as the dynamic, self-organizing structure of life itself (Braidotti 2006, 2011b) stands for generative vitality. It is the transversal force that cuts across and reconnects previously segregated species, categories and domains. *Zoe*-centred egalitarianism is, for me, the core of the post-anthropocentric turn: it is a materialist, secular, grounded and unsentimental response to the opportunistic trans-species commodification of Life that is the logic of advanced capitalism. It is also an affirmative reaction of social and cultural theory to the great advances made by the other culture, that of the sciences. The relationship between the two will be addressed in chapter 4.

A posthuman theory of the subject emerges, therefore, as an empirical project that aims at experimenting with what contemporary, bio-technologically mediated bodies are capable of doing. These non-profit experiments with contemporary subjectivity actualize the virtual possibilities of an expanded, relational self that functions in a nature–culture continuum and is technologically mediated.

Not surprisingly, this non-profit, experimental approach to different practices of subjectivity is not exactly the spirit of contemporary capitalism. Under the cover of individualism, fuelled by a quantitative range of consumer choices, that system effectively promotes uniformity and conformism to the dominant ideology. The perversity of advanced capitalism, and its undeniable success, consists in reattaching the potential for experimentation with new subject formations back to an overinflated notion of possessive individualism (MacPherson, 1962), tied to the profit principle. This is precisely the opposite direction from the non-profit experimentations with intensity, which I defend in my theory of posthuman subjectivity. The opportunistic political economy of bio-genetic capitalism turns Life/*zoe* – that is to say human and non-human intelligent matter – into a commodity for trade and profit.

What the neo-liberal market forces are after, and what they financially invest in, is the informational power of living matter itself. The capitalization of living matter produces a new political economy, which Melinda Cooper (2008) calls 'Life as surplus'. It introduces discursive and material political techniques of population control of a very different order from the administration of demographics, which preoccupied Foucault's work on bio-political governmentality. The warnings are now global. Today, we are undertaking 'risk analyses' not only of entire social and national systems, but also of whole sections of the population in the world risk society (Beck, 1999). Data banks of bio-genetic, neural and mediatic information about individuals are the true capital today, as the success of Facebook demonstrates at a more banal level. 'Data-mining' includes profiling practices that identify different types or characteristics and highlights them as special strategic targets for capital investments. This kind of predictive analytics of the human amounts to 'Lifemining',[2] with visibility, predictability and exportability as the key criteria.

Cooper sums up lucidly the complications of this political economy (2008: 3):

> Where does (re)production end and technical invention begin, when life is out to work at the microbiological or cellular level? What is at stake in the extension of property law to cover everything from the molecular elements of life (biological patents) to the biospheric accident (catastrophe bonds)? What is the relationship between new theories of biological growth, complexity and evolution and recent neoliberal theories of accumulation? And how is it possible to counter these new dogmatisms without falling into the trap of neofundamentalist politics of life (the right-to-life movement or ecological survivalism, for example)?

It is significant to note the emphasis Cooper places on the risk of neo-fundamentalist positions, like the biological determinism of 'natural law' advocates, or ecological holism. This essentialist risk is high in our current socio-political context and it requires constant critical scrutiny on the part of scholars who start instead from the posthuman idea of the nature–culture continuum.

Patricia Clough pursues a similar line in her analysis of the 'affective turn' (2008). Because advanced capitalism reduces bodies to their informational substrate in terms of energy resources, it levels out other categorical differences, so that 'equivalencies might be found to value one form of life against another, one vital capacity against another' (Clough, 2008: 17). What constitutes capital value in our social system is the accumulation of information itself, its immanent vital qualities and self-organizing capacity. Clough provides an impressive list of the concrete techniques employed by 'cognitive capitalism' (Moulier Boutang, 2012) to test and monitor the capacities of affective or 'bio-mediated' bodies: DNA testing, brain fingerprinting, neural imaging, body heat detection and iris or hand recognition. All these are also immediately operationalized as surveillance techniques both in civil society and in the war against terror. This necro-political governmentality is the topic of the next chapter.

[2] With thanks to Jose van Dijck for this formulation.

For now, let me stress my main point: the opportunistic political economy of bio-genetic capitalism induces, if not the actual erasure, at least the blurring of the distinction between the human and other species when it comes to profiting from them. Seeds, plants, animals and bacteria fit into this logic of insatiable consumption alongside various specimens of humanity. The image of Da Vinci's Vitruvian Man on a Starbucks coffee cup (see figure 2.1) captures ironically the meretricious character of the posthuman connections engendered by global capital: 'I shop therefore I am!' may well be its motto.

The global economy is post-anthropocentric in that it ultimately unifies all species under the imperative of the market and its excesses threaten the sustainability of our planet as a whole. A negative sort of cosmopolitan interconnection is therefore established through a pan-human bond of vulnerability. The size of recent scholarship on the environmental

Figure 2.1   Vitruvian Man on Starbucks Coffee Cup
© Guardian News & Media Ltd 2011

crisis and climate change alone testifies to this state of emergency and to the emergence of the earth as a political agent. Post-anthropocentrism is especially thriving in popular culture and has been criticized (Smelik and Lykke, 2008) as a negative tendency to represent the transformations of the relations between humans and technological *apparatus* or machines in the mode of neo-gothic horror. The literature and cinema of extinction of our and other species, including disaster movies, is a successful genre of its own, enjoying broad popular appeal. I have labelled this narrow and negative social imaginary as techno-teratological (Braidotti, 2002), that is to say as the object of cultural admiration and aberration. This dystopian reflection of the bio-genetic structure of contemporary capitalism is crucial to explain the popularity of this genre.

The social theory literature on shared anxiety about the future of both our species and of our humanist legacy is also rich and varied. Important liberal thinkers like Habermas (2003) and influential ones like Fukuyama (2002) are very alert on this issue, as are social critics like Sloterdijk (2009) and Borradori (2003). In different ways, they express deep concern for the status of the human, and seem particularly struck by moral and cognitive panic at the prospect of the posthuman turn, blaming our advanced technologies for it. I share their concern, but as a posthuman thinker with distinct anti-humanist feelings, I am less prone to panic at the prospect of a displacement of the centrality of the human and can also see the advantages of such an evolution.

For instance: once these post-anthropocentric practices blur the qualitative lines of demarcation not only among categories (male/female, black/white, human/animal, dead/alive, centre/margin, etc.), but also within each one of them, the human becomes subsumed into global networks of control and commodification which have taken 'Life' as the main target. The generic figure of the human is consequently in trouble. Donna Haraway puts is as follows:

> our authenticity is warranted by a database for the human genome. The molecular database is held in an informational database as legally branded intellectual property in a national laboratory with the mandate to make the text publicly avail-

able for the progress of science and the advancement of industry. This is Man the taxonomic type become Man the brand.
(1997: 74)

We know by now that the standard which was posited in the
universal mode of 'Man' has been widely criticized (Lloyd,
1984) precisely because of its partiality. Universal 'Man', in
fact, is implicitly assumed to be masculine, white, urbanized,
speaking a standard language, heterosexually inscribed in a
reproductive unit and a full citizen of a recognized polity
(Irigaray, 1985b; Deleuze and Guattari, 1987). How non-
representative can you get? As if this line of criticism were
not enough, this 'Man' is also called to task and brought back
to its species specificity as *anthropos* (Rabinow, 2003;
Esposito, 2008), that is to say as the representative of a hierarchical, hegemonic and generally violent species whose centrality is now challenged by a combination of scientific
advances and global economic concerns. Massumi refers to
this phenomenon as 'Ex-Man': 'a genetic matrix embedded
in the materiality of the human' (1998: 60) and as such
undergoing significant mutations: 'species integrity is lost in
a bio-chemical mode expressing the mutability of human
matter' (1998: 60).

These analyses indicate in my view that the political
economy of bio-genetic capitalism is post-anthropocentric in
its very structures, but not necessarily or automatically posthumanistic. It also tends to be deeply inhuman(e), as we shall
see in the next chapter. The posthuman dimension of post-
anthropocentrism can consequently be seen as a deconstructive move. What it deconstructs is species supremacy, but it
also inflicts a blow to any lingering notion of human nature,
anthropos and *bios*, as categorically distinct from the life of
animals and non-humans, or *zoe*. What comes to the fore
instead is a nature–culture continuum in the very embodied
structure of the extended self, as I argued earlier. This shift
can be seen as a sort of 'anthropological exodus' from the
dominant configurations of the human as the king of creation
(Hardt and Negri, 2000: 215) – a colossal hybridization of
the species.

Once the centrality of *anthropos* is challenged, a number
of boundaries between 'Man' and his others go tumbling

down, in a cascade effect that opens up unexpected perspectives. Thus, if the crisis of Humanism inaugurates the posthuman by empowering the sexualized and racialized human 'others' to emancipate themselves from the dialectics of master–slave relations, the crisis of *anthropos* relinquishes the demonic forces of the naturalized others. Animals, insects, plants and the environment, in fact the planet and the cosmos as a whole, are called into play. This places a different burden of responsibility on our species, which is the primary cause for the mess. The fact that our geological era is known as the 'anthropocene'[3] stresses both the technologically mediated power acquired by *anthropos* and its potentially lethal consequences for everyone else.

Furthermore, the transposition of naturalized others poses a number of conceptual and methodological complications linked to the critique of anthropocentrism. This is due to the pragmatic fact that, as embodied and embedded entities, we are all part of nature, even though academic philosophy continues to claim transcendental grounds for human consciousness. How to reconcile this materialist awareness with the task of critical thought? As a brand of vital materialism, posthuman theory contests the arrogance of anthropocentrism and the 'exceptionalism' of the Human as a transcendental category. It strikes instead an alliance with the productive and immanent force of *zoe*, or life in its non-human aspects. This requires a mutation of our shared understanding of what it means to think at all, let alone think critically.

In the rest of this chapter I will develop this insight into a number of interrelated fields of post-anthropocentric enquiry. My focus is on the productive aspects of the posthuman predicament and the extent to which it opens up perspectives for affirmative transformations of both the structures of subjectivity and the production of theory and knowledge. I have labelled these processes as 'becoming-animal, becoming-earth and becoming-machine', with reference to Deleuze and Guattari's philosophy, though I am very independent in relation to them. Thus, the becoming-animal axis of transformation

---

[3] The term was coined by Nobel Prize winning chemist Paul Crutzen in 2002 and has become widely accepted.

entails the displacement of anthropocentrism and the recognition of trans species solidarity on the basis of our being environmentally based, that is to say embodied, embedded and in symbiosis with other species (Margulis and Sagan, 1995). The planetary or becoming-earth dimension brings issues of environmental and social sustainability to the fore, with special emphasis on ecology and the climate change issue. The becoming-machine axis cracks open the division between humans and technological circuits, introducing bio-technologically mediated relations as foundational for the constitution the subject. I will conclude by advancing an idea that will be central to chapter 4, namely that we need to apply the vitalist brand of 'matter-realism' as the foundation for a system of ethical values where 'life' stands central, not only to the Life Sciences, but also to the Humanities in the twenty-first century. Let us start by looking at each of these cases in turn.

The Posthuman as Becoming-animal

Post-anthropocentrism displaces the notion of species hierarchy and of a single, common standard for 'Man' as the measure of all things. In the ontological gap thus opened, other species come galloping in. This is easier done than said in the language and methodological conventions of critical theory. Is language not the anthropological tool *par excellence*? We saw in the previous chapter that the humanist image of thought also sets the frame for a self-congratulating relationship of Man to himself, which confirms the dominant subject as much in what he includes as his core characteristics as in what he excludes as 'other'.

The subject of Humanism makes an internally contradictory claim in order to support his sovereign position. He is simultaneously an abstract universal and very much the spokesman of an elite species: both Human and *anthropos*. This logically impossible claim rests on an assumed political anatomy, according to which the counterpart of the 'power of reason' is the notion of Man as 'rational animal'. As we saw in chapter 1, the latter is expected to inhabit a perfectly functional physical body, implicitly modelled upon ideals of white masculinity, normality, youth and health. The dialectics of otherness is the inner engine of humanist Man's power, who assigns difference on a hierarchical scale as a tool of governance. All other modes of embodiment are cast out of the subject position and they include anthropomorphic others: non-white, non-masculine, non-normal, non-young, non-healthy, disabled, malformed or enhanced peoples. They also cover more ontological categorical divides between Man and zoo-morphic, organic or earth others. All these 'others' are rendered as pejoration, pathologized and cast out of normality, on the side of anomaly, deviance, monstrosity and bestiality. This process is inherently anthropocentric, gendered and racialized in that it upholds aesthetic and moral ideals based on white, masculine, heterosexual European civilization.

Let us look more closely at the mechanisms involved in the dialectics of negative difference, from the angle of animals. The animal is the necessary, familiar and much cherished other of *anthropos*. This familiarity, however, is fraught with perils. In a Borges-like mock taxonomy, Deleuze classified animals into three groups: those we watch television with, those we eat and those we are scared of. These exceptionally high levels of lived familiarity confine the human–animal interaction within classical parameters, namely, an oedipalized relationship (you and me together on the same sofa); an instrumental (thou shalt be consumed eventually) and a fantasmatic one (exotic, extinct infotainment objects of titillation).

Let us now analyse briefly each of these. The oedipal relationship between humans and animals is unequal and framed by the dominant human and structurally masculine habit of taking for granted free access to and the consumption of the bodies of others, animals included. As a mode of relation, it is therefore neurotic in that it is saturated with projections, taboos and fantasies. It is also a token of the human subject's sense of supreme ontological entitlement. Derrida referred to the power of the human species over animals in terms of 'carno-phallogocentrism' (Derrida, 2006) and criticized it as an example of epistemic and material violence. In their commentary, Berger and Segarra (2011) argue that Derrida's work on animality is not peripheral but quite central to his analysis of the limits of the Enlightenment project. Derrida's attack on anthropocentrism is presented consequently as a necessary correlate of the critique of Humanism. The strong logical and historical connection between them frames a political critique of the damage inflicted by Western reason upon its multiple others. The recognition of shared ties of vulnerability can generate new forms of posthuman community and compassion (Pick, 2011). This familiar, oedipalized, and hence ambivalent and manipulative relationship between humans and animals expressed itself in a variety of ways that have become entrenched in our mental and cultural habits. The first is metaphorization.

Animals have long spelled out the social grammar of virtues and moral distinctions for the benefit of humans. This normative function was canonized in moral glossaries and cognitive bestiaries that turned animals into metaphorical referents for norms and values. Just think of the illustrious literary pedigree of the noble eagles, the deceitful foxes, the humble lambs and the crickets and bees that Livy and Moliere have immortalized. These metaphorical habits feed into the fantasmatic dimension of human–animal interaction, which in contemporary culture is best expressed by the entertainment value of non-anthropomorphic characters, ranging from King Kong to the hybrid blue creatures of Avatar, without forgetting Spielberg's Jurassic Park star-dinosaurs.

At the social level, the evidence for new human–animal interaction is strong and often it comes down to questions of representation. 'Companion species', as Haraway put it (2003), have been historically confined within infantilizing narratives that established affective kinship relations across the species. The most dominant spin-off of this narrative is the sentimental discourse about dogs' devotion and unconditional loyalty, which Haraway argues against with all her mighty passion. As a nature cultural compound, a dog – not unlike other products of techno science – is a radical other, albeit a significant other. It is as socially constructed as most humans, not only through genetic screening, but also via health and hygiene regulations and various grooming practices. Who has not struggled to suppress a giggle of recognition at the news of the success of pets' diet clinics in the glamorous suburbs of LA? Some surprising forms of material equivalence are found among different life-forms in these posthuman days. We need to devise, therefore, a system of representation that matches the complexity of contemporary non-human animals and their proximity to humans. The point now is to move towards a new mode of relation; animals are no longer the signifying system that props up the humans' self-projections and moral aspirations. They need to be approached in a neo-literal mode, as a code system or a 'zoontology' of their own (Wolfe, 2003).

The second major manifestation of the problematic and contradictory familiarity between humans and animals is linked to the market economy and labour force. Since antiquity, animals have constituted a sort of zoo-proletariat, in a species hierarchy run by the humans. They have been exploited for hard labour, as natural slaves and logistical supports for humans prior to and throughout the mechanical age. They constitute, moreover, an industrial resource in themselves, animal bodies being primary material products starting from milk and their edible meat, but think also of the tusks of elephants, the hides of most creatures, the wool of sheep, the oil and fat of whales, the silk of caterpillars, etc.

As indicated by the figures I presented in the second vignette of the general introduction, this political economy of full-scale discursive and material exploitation continues today, with animals providing living material for scientific experiment, for our bio-technological agriculture, the cosmetics industry, drugs and pharmaceutical industries and other sectors of the economy. Animals like pigs and mice are genetically modified to produce organs for humans in xeno-transplantation experiments. Using animals as test cases and cloning them is now an established scientific practice: Oncomouse and Dolly the sheep are already part of history (Haraway, 1997; Franklin, 2007). In advanced capitalism, animals of all categories and species have been turned into tradable disposable bodies, inscribed in a global market of post-anthropocentric exploitation. As I said earlier, traffic in animals constitutes the third largest illegal trade in the world today, after drugs and arms but ahead of women. This creates a new negative bond between humans and animals.

At the height of the Cold War, when dogs and monkeys were being launched into orbit as part of the budding space exploration programmes and escalating competition between the USA and the USSR, George Orwell ironically stated that 'all animals are equal, but some are more equal than others' (Orwell, 1946). At the dawn of the third millennium, in a world caught in indefinite and technologically mediated warfare, such metaphorical grandeur rings rather hollow. Post-anthropocentrism rather suggests the opposite: no animal is more equal than any other, because they are all equally inscribed in a market economy of planetary exchanges that commodifies them to a comparable degree and therefore makes them equally disposable. All other distinctions are blurred.

At the same time, the old mode of relation is currently being restructured. A *zoe*-egalitarian turn is taking place that encourages us to engage in a more equitable relationship with animals. Contemporary post-anthropocentric thought produces an anti-Oedipal animality within a fast-changing techno-culture that engenders mutations at all levels. In my view the challenge today is how to deterritorialize, or nomadize, the human–animal interaction, so as to by-pass the metaphysics of substance and its corollary, the dialectics of otherness. This also entails secularizing accordingly the concept of human nature and the life which animates it. Donna Haraway, a pioneer in post-anthropocentric thought and shrewd analyst of human–animal interaction, captured this fundamental shift in the ironical cartoons that depict companion species in the Vitruvian pose (see figures 2.2 and 2.3). Can a cat or a dog be the measure of at least some, if not exactly all things? Can it displace the genomic hierarchy that tacitly supported the humanists' self-representation? Here we see the contradictory effects of the post-anthropocentric politics of life itself, which I commented on earlier in the chapter.

The posthuman in the sense of post-anthropocentrism displaces the dialectical scheme of opposition, replacing well-established dualisms with the recognition of deep *zoe*-egalitarianism between humans and animals. The vitality of their bond is based on sharing this planet, territory or environment on terms that are no longer so clearly hierarchical, nor self-evident. This vital interconnection posits a qualitative shift of the relationship away from species-ism and towards an ethical appreciation of what bodies (human,

Figure 2.2   S. Harris, *Leonardo Da Vinci's Dog*
Source: www.cartoonstock.com

animal, others) can do. An ethology of forces based on Spinozist ethics emerges as the main point of reference for changing human–animal interaction. It traces a new political frame,
which I see as an affirmative project in response to the commodification of Life in all its forms, that is the opportunistic
logic of advanced capitalism.

This post-anthropocentric approach requires more efforts
of our imagination to ground our representations in real-life

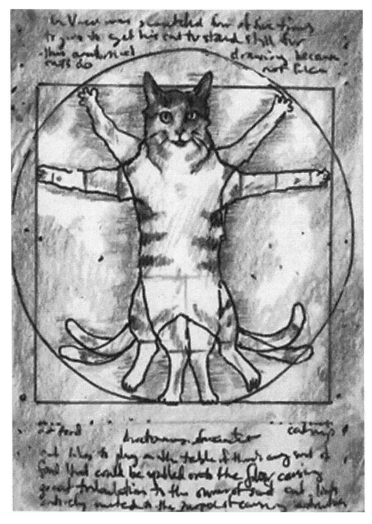

Figure 2.3 Maggie Stiefvater, *Vitruvian Cat*
Source: Maggie Stiefvater via Flickr

conditions and in an affirmative manner. In this respect, we need to rethink dogs, cats and other sofa-based companions today as cutting across species partitions not only affectively, but also organically, so to speak. As nature–cultural compounds, these animals qualify as cyborgs, that is to say as creatures of mixity or vectors of posthuman relationality. In many ways, Dolly the sheep is the ideal figuration for the complex bio-mediated temporalities and forms of intimacy that represent the new post-anthropocentric human–animal interaction. She/it is simultaneously the last specimen of her species – descended from the lineage of sheep that were conceived and reproduced as such – and the first specimen of a new species: the electronic sheep that Philip K. Dick dreamed of, the forerunner of the androids society of *Blade Runner* (1982). Cloned, not conceived sexually, heterogeneous mix of organism and machine, Dolly has become delinked from reproduction and hence divorced from descent. Dolly is no daughter of any member of her/its old species – simultaneously orphan and mother of her/itself. First of a new gender, she/it is also beyond the gender dichotomies of the patriarchal kinship system.

A copy made in the absence of one single original, Dolly pushes the logic of the postmodern simulacrum to its ultimate perversion. She/it spins Immaculate Conception into a biogenetic third-century version. The irony reaches a pathetic peak when we remember that Dolly died of a banal and all too familiar disease: rheumatism. After which, to add insult to injury, she suffered a last indignity, taxidermy, and was embalmed and exhibited in a science museum as a scientific rarity. She/it simultaneously inhabits the nineteenth century and as a media celebrity also strikes a chord with the twentieth century. Both archaic and hyper-modern, Dolly is a compound of multiple anachronisms, situated across different chronological axes. She/it inhabits complex and self-contradictory time zones. Like other contemporary techno-teratological animals or entities (oncomouse comes to mind), Dolly shatters the linearity of time and exists in a continuous present. This techno-electronic timeless time is saturated with asynchronicity, that is to say, it is structurally unhinged. Thinking about Dolly blurs the categories of thought we have inherited from the past – she/it stretches the longitude and latitude of thought itself, adding depth, intensity and contradiction. Because she/it embodies complexity, this entity which is no longer an animal but not yet fully a machine, is the icon of the posthuman condition.

Haraway also stresses the need for new images, visions and representations of the human–animal continuum. She proposes to start rethinking human–animal interaction from the hybrid figuration of oncomouse. As the first patented animal in the world, a transgenic organism created for the purposes of research, the oncomouse is posthuman in every possible sense of the term. It has been created for the purpose of profit-making trafficking between the laboratories and the marketplace, and thus navigates between patenting offices and the research benches. Haraway wants to establish a sense of kinship with this transgenic animal. Calling her 'my sibling [. . .] male or female, s/he is my sister' (1997: 79), Haraway stresses the extent to which oncomouse is both a victim and a scapegoat, a Christ-like figure that sacrifices herself in order to find the cure for breast cancer and thus save the lives of many women: a mammal rescuing other mammals. Because the oncomouse breaks the purity of lineage, she is also a spectral figure. Not unlike Dolly, it is the never dead that pollutes the natural order simply by being manufactured and not born. S/he is a cyber-teratological apparatus that scrambles the established codes and thus destabilizes but also reconstructs the posthuman subject. Figurations like Dolly and oncomouse are no metaphors, but rather vehicles to imaginatively ground our powers of understanding within the shifting landscapes of the present.[4]

I am quite aware that my cheerful endorsement of the post-anthropocentric turn may appear as over-enthusiastic and even triumphalist to some (Moore, 2011). As I said in the previous chapter, one's relation to the posthuman is affected in the first place by one's critical assessment of the human. My deep-seated anti-humanist leanings show in the glee with which I welcome the displacement of *anthropos*. My posthuman enthusiasm, however, does not blind me to the cruel contradictions and the power differences at work in contemporary human–animal interaction. The old patterns of instrumental behaviour are still operative, of course, with animals being used for food, wool and skin products, labour in agriculture, industry and science. If anything, the necro-political economy is exacerbated by the global conflicts and

---

[4] In this regard, these figurations fulfil the same function as Deleuze's *conceptual personae* (Deleuze and Guattari, 1994; Braidotti, 2011a, 2011b).

by the financial crisis. In so far as advanced capitalism markets and profits from the bio-genetic structures of life itself, it contributes to the displacement of anthropocentrism. Animals are caught in a double bind: on the one hand, they are more than ever the object of inhumane exploitation; on the other hand, they benefit from residual forms of reparative humanization. This conflicting situation leads me to conclude that post-anthropocentrism is for both humans and animals a mixed blessing. Allow me to explain.

Compensatory Humanism

Throughout the second half of the twentieth century, the issue of 'animal rights' has gathered momentum in most advanced liberal democracies. Political parties devoted entirely to the well-being of non-anthropocentric others – Green or Animal parties – sit in many Northern European parliaments. They rest on the critique of species-ism, that is to say the anthropocentric arrogance of Man as the dominant species whose sense of entitlement includes access to the body of all others. Animal rights activists defend the end of 'anthropolatry', the assumption of human superiority, and call for more respect and priority to be given to the interests of other species and life forms.

In animal rights theory, these post-anthropocentric analytic premises are combined with neo-humanism to reassess the validity of a number of humanist values. These concern anthropomorphic selves, who are assumed to hold unitary identity, self-reflexive consciousness, moral rationality and the capacity to share emotions like empathy and solidarity. The same virtues and capabilities are also attributed to non-anthropomorphic others. The epistemological and moral assumptions that underscore this position have been in place since the Enlightenment, but were previously reserved for humans only, to the detriment of all non-human agents such as animals and plants. Animal rights people, whom I define as post-anthropocentric neo-humanists, converge on the need to uphold and expand on these values across all species.

The best known champion of 'animal rights', Peter Singer, defends a utilitarian position in favour of the moral rationalism of animals. A liberal humanist like Nussbaum (2006) agrees to pursue species equity. Working within the classical liberal tradition, Mary Midgley (1996) does not even trust the term 'anthropocentrism', referring to it as 'human chauvinism; narrowness of sympathy, comparable to national, or race or gender-chauvinism. It could also be called exclusive humanism, as opposed to the hospitable, friendly, inclusive kind' (1996: 105). The alternative Midgley supports is to admit that 'we are not self-contained and self-sufficient, either as a species or as individuals, but live naturally in deep mutual dependence' (1996: 9–10). In her powerful analyses of the environmental crisis of reason, Val Plumwood (2003) also calls for a new dialogical interspecies ethics based on decentring human privilege.

For radical eco-feminists, both utilitarianism and liberalism are found wanting: the former for its condescending approach to non-human others, the latter in view of the hypocritical denial of humans' manipulative mastery over animals. This critique is expanded to the destructive side of human individualism that entails selfishness and a misplaced sense of superiority, which for feminists (Donovan and Adams, 1996, 2007) is connected to male privileges and the oppression of women and supports a general theory of male domination. Meat-eating is targeted as a legalized form of cannibalism by old and new feminist vegetarian and vegan critical theory (Adams, 1990; MacCormack, 2012). Speciesism is therefore held accountable as an undue privilege to the same degree as sexism and racism. The pervasiveness of a 'sex-species' hierarchical system tends to remain unacknowledged and uncriticized even in the framework of animal rights activism. The corrective influence of feminism is valued because it emphasizes both the political importance of the collectivity and of emotional bonding.

New analytic data on the status of animals is currently being analysed through the interdisciplinary tools of anthropology, primatology, palaeontology, science and technology studies. One of the most prominent post-anthropocentric neo-humanists in this field is Frans de Waal (1996), who extends classical humanist values, like empathy and moral responsibility, to the upper primates. On the basis of rigorous empirical observation of the great apes, de Waal transformed our thinking about evolution and evolutionary psychology by challenging the emphasis on aggression as the motor of species development. De Waal's groundbreaking work on 'our inner ape' and the bonobos located communication and sexual exchange at the core of community formation, striking also a note in support of the evolutionary role of the females of species. In his more recent work, de Waal (2009) stresses the importance of empathy as a form of emotional communication or emotionally mediated communication among non-human primates.

The emphasis on empathy accomplishes several significant goals in view of a posthuman theory of subjectivity. Firstly, it reappraises communication as an evolutionary tool. Secondly, it identifies in emotions, rather than in reason, the key to consciousness. Thirdly, it develops what Harry Kunneman has defined as 'a hermeneutical form of naturalism' which takes critical distance from the tradition of social constructivism and situates moral values as innate qualities. This is a significant addition to the theory of the nature–culture continuum. Our species, argues de Waal, is 'obligatorily gregarious' (2006: 4). Moreover, de Waal's view of the subject is materialist, as opposed to the transcendence of reason, and attracted to David Hume's approach to the emotions or passions as key to identity formation. Last but not least, I would suggest that Frans de Waal is a post-anthropocentric social democrat who is very committed to the creation of social infrastructures of generosity and reciprocal altruism and support. His idea that moral goodness is contagious is supported by the 'mirror neurons' theory of empathy. The emphasis falls on the ethical continuity between humans and upper primates, arguing that it is a bit too easy to project our aggressive tendencies onto the animals and reserve the quality of goodness as a prerogative of our species. De Waal (1996) argues that evolution has also provided the requisites for morality and attacks the 'anthropodenial' (2006: xvi) of human supremacists. Empathy as an innate and genetically transmitted moral tendency, or the naturalization of morals, is in fashion, whereas selfish genes and greed are definitely out. All these aspects are extremely relevant for a posthuman theory of the subject.

The reason why I am somewhat sceptical of post-anthropocentric neo-humanism, however, is that it is rather uncritical about Humanism itself. The compensatory efforts on behalf of animals generate what I consider as a belated kind of solidarity between the human dwellers of this planet, currently traumatized by globalization, technology and the 'new' wars, and their animal others. It is at best an ambivalent phenomenon, in that it combines a negative sense of cross-species bonding with classical and rather high-minded humanist moral claims. In this cross-species embrace, Humanism is actually being reinstated uncritically under the aegis of species egalitarianism.

In my work on the posthuman subject, I choose not to leave aside the critical acknowledgement of the limitations of Humanism, as outlined in the previous chapter. I am also sharply aware of the fact that we live in the era of the anthropocene, that is to say an age when the earth's ecological balance is directly regulated by humanity. I think that at such a time of deep epistemological, ethical and political crises of values in human societies, extending the privileges of humanist values to other categories can hardly be considered as a selfless and generous, or a particularly productive move. Asserting a vital bond between the humans and other species is both necessary and fine. This bond is negative in that it is the effect of shared vulnerability, which is itself a consequence of human actions upon the environment. Is it not the case then that the humans have spread to non-humans their fundamental anxiety about the future? The humanization of non-human animals may therefore come at a price, especially at a historical time when the very category of the 'human' has become challenged.

Anthropomorphizing them so as to extend to animals the principle of moral and legal equality may be a noble gesture, but it is inherently flawed, on two scores. Firstly, it confirms the binary distinction human/animal by benevolently extending the hegemonic category, the human, towards the others. Secondly, it denies the specificity of animals altogether, because it uniformly takes them as emblems of the trans-species, universal ethical value of empathy. In my view, the point about posthuman relations, however, is to see the inter-*relation* human/animal as constitutive of the identity of *each*. It is a transformative or symbiotic relation that hybridizes and alters the 'nature' of each one and foregrounds the middle grounds of their interaction. This is the 'milieu' of the human/

non-human continuum and it needs to be explored as an open experiment, not as a foregone moral conclusion about allegedly universal values or qualities. The middle ground of that particular interaction has to remain normatively neutral, in order to allow for new parameters to emerge for the becoming-animal of *anthropos*, a subject that has been encased for much too long in the mould of species supremacy. Intensive spaces of becoming have to be opened and, more importantly, to be kept open.

In an era when natural offspring are being replaced by corporate brands and manufactured and patented bio-products, the ethical imperative to bind to them and be accountable for their well-being remains as strong as ever. We need new genealogies, alternative theoretical and legal representations of the new kinship system and adequate narratives to live up to this challenge. I hope my vision of posthuman subjectivity can insert more conceptual creativity into critical theory and thus work towards an affirmative brand of posthuman thought. In the universe that I inhabit as a post-industrial subject of so-called advanced capitalism, there is a great deal of familiarity and hence much in common in the way of embodied and embedded locations, between female humans, oncomouse and the cloned sheep Dolly. I owe as much to the genetically engineered members of the former animal kingdom, as to humanistic ideals of the uniqueness of my species. Similarly, my situated position as a female of the species makes me structurally serviceable and thus closer to the organisms that are willing or unwilling providers of organs or cells than to any notion of the inviolability and integrity of the human species.

I know that this may sound impatient and even reckless, but I stand by it: that in me which no longer identifies with the dominant categories of subjectivity, but which is not yet completely out of the cage of identity, that is to say that which goes on differing, is at home with *zoe*, the post-anthropocentric subject. These rebellious components for me are related to the feminist consciousness of what it means to be embodied female. As such, I am a she-wolf, a breeder that multiplies cells in all directions; I am an incubator and a carrier of vital and lethal viruses; I am mother-earth, the generator of the future. In the political economy of phallogocentrism and of anthropocentric humanism, which predicates the sovereignty of Sameness in a falsely universalistic mode, my sex fell on the side of 'Otherness', understood as pejorative difference, or as being-worth-less-than. The becoming-posthuman speaks to my feminist self, partly because my sex, historically speaking, never quite made it into full humanity, so my allegiance to that category is at best negotiable and never to be taken for granted.

The Posthuman as Becoming-earth

The displacement of anthropocentrism results in a drastic restructuring of humans' relation to animals, but critical theory may be able to adjust itself to the challenge, mostly by building on the multiple imaginary and affective ties that have consolidated human–animal interaction. The post-anthropocentric shift towards a planetary, geo-centred perspective, however, is a conceptual earthquake of an altogether different scale than the becoming-animal of Man. This event is sending seismic waves across the field of the Humanities and critical theory. Claire Colebrook, with her customary wit, calls it a 'critical climate change'.[5]

In the age of anthropocene, the phenomenon known as 'geo-morphism' is usually expressed in negative terms, as environmental crisis, climate change and ecological sustainability. Yet, there is also a more positive dimension to it in the sense of reconfiguring the relationship to our complex habitat, which we used to call 'nature'. The earth or planetary dimension of the environmental issue is indeed not a concern like any other. It is rather the issue that is immanent to all others, in so far as the earth is our middle and common ground. This is the 'milieu' for all of us, human and non-human inhabitant of this particular planet, in this particular era. The planetary opens onto the cosmic in an immanent materialist dimension. My argument is that, again, this change of perspective is rich in alternatives for a renewal of subjectivity. What would a geo-centred subject look like?

[5] This is the title of the on-line book series that Colebrook edits for the Open Humanities Press.

The starting point for me remains the nature–culture continuum, but by now we need to insert into this framework the monistic insight that, as Lloyd put it, we are all 'part of nature' (1994). This statement, which she frames in a monistic ontology based on Spinoza's philosophy, is sobering as well as inspiring. It is further complicated, for us citizens of the third millennium, by the fact that we actually inhabit a nature–culture continuum which is both technologically mediated and globally enforced. This means that we cannot assume a theory of subjectivity that takes for granted naturalistic foundationalism, nor can we rely on a social constructivist and hence dualistic theory of the subject which disavows the ecological dimension. Instead, critical theory needs to fulfil potentially contradictory requirements.

The first is to develop a dynamic and sustainable notion of vitalist, self-organizing materiality; the second is to enlarge the frame and scope of subjectivity along the transversal lines of post-anthropocentric relations I outlined in the previous section. The idea of subjectivity as an assemblage that includes non-human agents has a number of consequences. Firstly, it implies that subjectivity is not the exclusive prerogative of *anthropos*; secondly, that it is not linked to transcendental reason; thirdly, that it is unhinged from the dialectics of recognition; and lastly, that it is based on the immanence of relations. The challenge for critical theory is momentous: we need to visualize the subject as a transversal entity encompassing the human, our genetic neighbours the animals and the earth as a whole, and to do so within an understandable language.

Let us pause on the latter for a minute, as it raises the issue of representation, which is crucial for the Humanities and for critical theory. Finding an adequate language for post-anthropocentrism means that the resources of the imagination, as well as the tools of critical intelligence, need to be enlisted for this task. The collapse of the nature–culture divide requires that we need to devise a new vocabulary, with new figurations to refer to the elements of our posthuman embodied and embedded subjectivity. The limitations of the social constructivist method show up here and need to be compensated by more conceptual creativity. Most of us who were trained in social theory, however, have experienced at least some degree of discomfort at the thought that some elements of our subjectivity may not be totally socially constructed. Part of the legacy of the Marxist Left consists, in fact, in a deeply rooted suspicion towards the natural order and green politics.

As if this mistrust of the natural were not enough, we also need to reconceptualize the relation to the technological artefact as something as intimate as close as nature used to be. The technological apparatus is our new 'milieu' and this intimacy is far more complex and generative than the prosthetic, mechanical extension that modernity had made of it. Throughout this change of parameters, I also want to be ever mindful of the importance of the politics of locations and keep investigating who exactly is the 'we' who is positing all these queries in the first place. This new scheme for rethinking posthuman subjectivity is as rich as it is complex, but it is grounded in real-life, world-historical conditions that are confronting us with pressing urgency.

Dipesh Chakrabarty (2009) addresses some of these concerns by investigating the consequences of the climate change debate for the practice of history. He argues that the scholarship on climate change causes both spatial and temporal difficulties. It brings about a change of scale in our thinking, which now needs to encompass a planetary or geo-centred dimension, acknowledging that humans are larger than a biological entity and now wield a geological force. It also shifts the temporal parameters away from the expectation of continuity which sustains the discipline of history, to contemplate the idea of extinction, that is to say, a future without 'us'. Furthermore, these shifts in the basic parameters also affect the content of historical research, by 'destroying the artificial but time honoured distinction between natural and human histories' (Chakrabarty, 2009: 206). Although Chakrabarty does not take the post-anthropocentric path, he comes to the same conclusion as I do: the issue of geo-centred perspectives and the change of location of humans from mere biological to geological agents calls for recompositions of both subjectivity and community.

The geo-centred turn also has other serious political implications. The first concerns the limitations of classical Humanism in the Enlightenment model. Relying on post-colonial theory, Chakrabarty points out that the 'philosophers of freedom were mainly, and understandably, concerned with how humans would escape the injustice, oppression, inequality or even uniformity foisted on them by other humans or human-made systems' (2009: 208). Their anthropocentrism, coupled with a culture-specific notion of Humanism, limits their relevance today. The climate change issue and the spectre of human extinction also affect 'the analytic strategies that postcolonial and postimperial historians have deployed in the last two decades in response to the postwar scenario of decolonization and globalization' (Chakrabarty, 2009: 198). I would add that the social constructivist approach of Marxist, feminist and post-colonial analyses does not completely equip them to deal with the change of spatial and temporal scale engendered by the post-anthropocentric or geo-centred shift. This insight is the core of the radical post-anthropocentric position I want to defend, which I see as a way of updating critical theory for the third millennium.

Many scholars are coming to the same conclusion, through different routes. For instance, post-anthropocentric neo-humanist traditions of socialist or of standpoint feminist theories (Harding, 1986) and of post-colonial theory (Shiva, 1997) have approached the issues of environmentalism in a post-anthropocentric, or at least non-androcentric, or non-male-dominated, manner, as we saw in the previous chapter. This critique of anthropocentrism is expressed in the name of ecological awareness, with strong emphasis on the experience of social minorities like women and of non-Western peoples. The recognition of multicultural perspectives and the critique of imperialism and ethnocentrism add a crucial aspect to the discussion on the becoming-earth, but nowadays they also fall in their own internal contradictions.

Let us take, for instance, the case of 'deep ecology'. Arne Naess (1977a, 1977b) and James Lovelock's 'Gaia' hypothesis (1979) are geo-centred theories that propose a return to holism and to the notion of the whole earth as a single, sacred organism. This holistic approach is rich in perspectives, but also quite problematic for a vitalist, materialist posthuman thinker. What is problematic about it is less the holistic part than the fact that it is based on a social constructivist dualistic method. This means that it opposes the earth to industrialization, nature to culture, the environment to society and comes down firmly on the side of the natural order. This results in a relevant political agenda that is critical of consumerism and possessive individualism, including a strong indictment of technocratic reason and technological culture. But this approach has two drawbacks. Firstly, its technophobic aspect is not particularly helpful in itself, considering the world we are living in. Secondly, it paradoxically reinstates the very categorical divide between the natural and the manufactured which it is attempting to overcome.

Why do I not agree with this position? Because of two interrelated ideas: firstly, because of the nature–culture continuum and the subsequent rejection of the dualistic methodology of social constructivism – the post-anthropocentric neo-humanists end up reinstating this distinction, albeit with the best of intentions in relation to the natural order; secondly, because I am suspicious of the negative kind of bonding going on in the age of anthropocene between humans and non-humans. The trans-species embrace is based on the awareness of the impending catastrophe: the environmental crisis and the global warm/ning issue, not to speak of the militarization of space, reduce all species to a comparable degree of vulnerability. The problem with this position is that, in flagrant contradiction with its explicitly stated aims, it promotes full-scale humanization of the environment. This strikes me as a regressive move, reminiscent of the sentimentality of the Romantic phases of European culture. I concur therefore with Val Plumwood's (1993, 2003) assessment that deep ecology misreads the earth–cosmos nexus and merely expands the structures of possessive egoism and self-interests to include non-human agents.

Significantly, while the holistic approach also makes reference to Spinoza's monism, it steers clear of contemporary re-readings of Spinoza by the likes of Deleuze and Guattari, Foucault, or other radical branches of Continental philosophy. Spinoza's idea of the unity of mind and soul is applied in support of the belief that all that lives is holy and the greatest respect is due to it. This idolatry of the natural order is linked to Spinoza's vision of God and the unity between man and nature. It stresses the harmony between the human and the ecological habitat in order to propose a sort of synthesis of the two. Deep ecology is therefore spiritually charged in an essentialist way. Because there are no boundaries and everything is interrelated, to hurt nature is ultimately to hurt ourselves. Thus, the earth environment as a whole deserves the same ethical and political consideration as humans. This position is helpful but it strikes me as a way of humanizing the environment, that is to say, as a well-meaning form of residual anthropomorphic normativity, applied to non-human planetary agents. Compensatory Humanism is a two-faced position.

In contrast with this position, but also building on some of its premises, I would like to propose an updated brand of Spinozism (Citton and Lordon, 2008). I see Spinozist monism, and the radical immanent forms of critique that rest upon it, as a democratic move that promotes a kind of ontological pacifism. Species equality in a post-anthropocentric world does urge us to question the violence and the hierarchical thinking that result from human arrogance and the assumption of transcendental human exceptionalism. In my view, monistic relationality stresses instead the more compassionate aspect of subjectivity. A Spinozist approach, re-read with Deleuze and Guattari, allows us to by-pass the pitfalls of binary thinking and to address the environmental question in its full complexity. Contemporary monism implies a notion of vital and self-organizing matter, as we saw in the previous chapter, as well as a non-human definition of Life as *zoe*, or a dynamic and generative force. It is about 'the embodiment of the mind and the embrainment of the body' (Marks, 1998).

Deleuze also refers to this vital energy as the great animal, the cosmic 'machine', not in any mechanistic or utilitarian way, but in order to avoid any reference to biological determinism on the one hand and overinflated, psychologized individualism on the other. Deleuze and Guattari (1987) also use the term 'Chaos' to refer to that 'roar' of cosmic energy which most of us would rather ignore. They are careful to point out, however, that Chaos is not chaotic, but it rather contains the infinite expanse of all virtual forces. These potentialities are real in so far as they call for actualization through pragmatic and sustainable practices. To mark this close connection between the virtual and the real, they turn to literature and borrow from James Joyce the neologism 'chaosmos'. This is a condensation of 'chaos' and 'cosmos' that expresses the source of eternal energy.

Again, the issue of language and representation comes up in this seemingly abstruse choice of terms. What I find praiseworthy on the part of my critical theory teachers is the extent to which they are willing to take the risk of ridicule by experimenting with language that shocks established habits and deliberately provokes imaginative and emotional reactions. The point of critical theory is to upset common opinion (*doxa*), not to confirm it. Although this approach has met with hostile reception in academia (as we shall see in chapter 4), I see it as a gesture of generous and deliberate risk-taking and hence as a statement in favour of academic freedom.

I consequently experiment with my own alternative figurations, ranging from the nomadic subject to other *conceptual personae* that help me navigate across the stormy waters of the post-anthropocentric predicament. Rigorously materialist, my own nomadic thought defends a post-individualistic notion of the subject, which is marked by a monistic, relational structure. Yet, it is not undifferentiated in terms of the social coordinates of class, gender, sexuality, ethnicity and race. Nomadic subjectivity is the social branch of complexity theory.

Where does this leave our becoming-earth? Actually, we are in the middle of it. Let us resume the argument from the idea of the posthuman subject. You may remember that the recomposition of a negatively indexed new idea of 'the human' as an endangered species, alongside other non-human categories, is currently celebrated by post-anthropocentric neo-humanists of all sorts, from animal rights activists to eco-feminists. They take the environmental crisis as evidence of the need to reinstate universal humanist values. I have no real quarrels with the moral aspiration that drives this process and share the same ethical longing. I am, however, seriously worried about the limitations of an uncritical reassertion of Humanism as the binding factor of this reactively assumed notion of a pan-human bond. I want to stress that the awareness of a new (negatively indexed) reconstruction of something we call 'humanity' must not be allowed to flatten out or dismiss all the power differentials that are still enacted and operationalized through the axes of sexualization/racialization/naturalization, just as they are being reshuffled by the spinning machine of advanced, bio-genetic capitalism. Critical theory needs to think simultaneously the blurring of categorical differences and their reassertion as new forms of bio-political, bio-mediated political economy, with familiar patterns of exclusion and domination. For instance, in his analysis of the double limitations of both classical Humanism and Marxist oriented and post-colonial theory, Dipesh Chakrabarty raises a very pertinent question: if you consider the difference in carbon print between richer and poorer nations, is it really fair to speak of the climate change crisis as a common 'human' concern? I would push this further and ask: is it not risky to accept the construction of a negative formation of humanity as a category that stretches to all human beings, *all other differences notwithstanding*? Those differences do exist and continue to matter, so what are we to make of them? The process of becoming-earth points to a qualitatively different planetary relation.

The question of differences leads us back to power and to the politics of locations and the necessity of an ethical-political theory of subjectivity, namely, who exactly is the 'we' of this pan-humanity bonded in fear of a common threat? Chakrabarty puts it lucidly: 'Species may indeed be the name of a pace-holder for an emergent, new universal history of humans that flashes up the moment of the danger that is climate change' (2009: 222). As a result, I would argue that critical theorists need to strike a rigorous and coherent note of resistance against the neutralization of difference that is induced by the perverse materiality and the tendentious mobility of advanced capitalism.

A more egalitarian road, in a *zoe*-centred way, requires a modicum of goodwill on the part of the dominant party, in this case *anthropos* himself, towards his non-human others. I am aware, of course, that this is asking a lot. The post-anthropocentric shift away from the hierarchical relations that had privileged 'Man' requires a form of estrangement and a radical repositioning on the part of the subject. The best method to accomplish this is through the strategy of de-familiarization or critical distance from the dominant vision of the subject. Dis-identification involves the loss of familiar habits of thought and representation in order to pave the way for creative alternatives. Deleuze would call it an active 'deterritorialization'. Race and post-colonial theories have also made important contributions to the methodology and the political strategy of de-familiarization (Gilroy, 2005). I have defended this method as a dis-identification from familiar and hence normative values, such as the dominant institutions and representations of femininity and masculinity, so as to move sexual difference towards the process of becoming-minoritarian (Braidotti, 1994, 2011a). In a similar vein, Spinozist feminist thinkers like Moira Gatens and Genevieve Lloyd (1999) argue that socially embedded and historically grounded changes require a qualitative shift of our 'collective imaginings', or a shared desire for transformations. The conceptual frame of reference I have adopted for the method of de-familiarization is monism. It implies the open-ended, inter-relational, multi-sexed and trans-species flows of becoming through interaction with multiple others. A posthuman subject thus constituted exceeds the boundaries of both anthropocentrism and of compensatory humanism, to acquire a planetary dimension.

The Posthuman as Becoming-machine

The issue of technology is central to the post-anthropocentric predicament and it has already come out several times in the previous sections. The relationship between the human and the technological other has shifted in the contemporary context, to reach unprecedented degrees of intimacy and intrusion. The posthuman predicament is such as to force a displacement of the lines of demarcation between structural differences, or ontological categories, for instance between the organic and the inorganic, the born and the manufactured, flesh and metal, electronic circuits and organic nervous systems.

As in the case of human–animal relations, the move is beyond metaphorization. The metaphorical or analogue function that machinery fulfilled in modernity, as an anthropocentric device that imitated embodied human capacities, is replaced today by a more complex political economy that connects bodies to machines more intimately, through simulation and mutual modification. As Andreas Huyssen (1986) has argued, in the electronic era, wires and circuitry exercise another kind of seduction than the pistons and grinding engines of industrial machinery. Electronic machines are, from this angle, quite immaterial: plastic boxes and metal wires that convey information. They do not 'represent' anything, but rather carry clear instructions and can reproduce clear information patterns. The main thrust of micro-electronic seduction is actually neural, in that it foregrounds the fusion of human consciousness with the general electronic network. Contemporary information and communication technologies exteriorize and duplicate electronically the human nervous system. This has prompted a shift in our field of perception: the visual modes of representation have been replaced by sensorial-neuronal modes of simulation. As Patricia Clough puts it, we have become 'biomediated' bodies (2008: 3).

We can therefore safely start from the assumption that the cyborgs are the dominant social and cultural formations that are active throughout the social fabric, with many economic and political implications. The Vitruvian Man has gone cybernetic (see figure 2.4). Let me qualify this statement by adding that all technologies can be said to have a strong biopolitical effect upon the embodied subject they intersect with. Thus, cyborgs include not only the glamorous bodies of high-tech, jet-fighter pilots, athletes or film stars, but also the anonymous masses of the underpaid, digital proletariat who fuel the technology-driven global economy without ever accessing it themselves (Braidotti, 2006). I shall return to this cruel political economy in the next chapter.

What I want to argue next is that technological mediation is central to a new vision of posthuman subjectivity and that it provides the grounding for new ethical claims. A posthuman notion of the enfleshed and extended, relational self keeps the techno-hype in check by a sustainable ethics of transformations. This sober position pleads for resistance to both the fatal attraction of nostalgia and the fantasy of transhumanist and other techno-utopias. It also juxtaposes the rhetoric of 'the desire to be wired', to a more radical sense of the materialism of 'proud to be flesh' (Sobchack, 2004). The emphasis on immanence allows us to respect the bond of mutual dependence between bodies and technological

Figure 2.4 Victor Habbick (Maninblack), *Robot in the style of Leonardo's Vitruvian Man*
Source: Clivia – Pixmac

others, while avoiding the contempt for the flesh and the trans-humanist fantasy of escape from the finite materiality of the enfleshed self. As we shall see in the next chapter, the issue of death and mortality will be raised by necessity.

I want to argue for a vitalist view of the technologically bio-mediated other. This machinic vitality is not so much about determinism, inbuilt purpose or finality, but rather about becoming and transformation. This introduces a process that Deleuze and Guattari call 'becoming-machine', inspired by the Surrealists' 'bachelor machines', meaning a playful and pleasure-prone relationship to technology that is not based on functionalism. For Deleuze this is linked to the project of releasing human embodiment from its indexation on socialized productivity to become 'bodies without organs', that is to say without organized efficiency. This is no hippy-like insurrection of the senses, but rather a carefully thought-through programme that pursues two aims. Firstly, it attempts to rethink our bodies as part of a nature–culture continuum in their in-depth structures. Secondly, it adds a political dimension by setting the framework of recomposition of bodily materiality in directions diametrically opposed to the spurious efficiency and ruthless opportunism of advanced capitalism. Contemporary machines are no metaphors, but they are engines or devices that both capture and process forces and energies, facilitating interrelations, multiple connections and assemblages. They stand for radical relationality and delight as well as productivity.

The 'becoming-machine' understood in this specific sense indicates and actualizes the relational powers of a subject that is no longer cast in a dualistic frame, but bears a privileged bond with multiple others and merges with one's technologically mediated planetary environment. The merger of the human with the technological results in a new transversal compound, a new kind of eco-sophical unity, not unlike the symbiotic relationship between the animal and its planetary habitat. This is not the holistic fusion that Hegel accused Spinoza of, but rather radical transversal relations that generate new modes of subjectivity, held in check by an ethology of forces. They sustain a vitalist ethics of mutual trans-species interdependence. It is a generalized ecology, also known as eco-sophy, which aims at crossing transversally the multiple layers of the subject, from interiority to exteriority and everything in between.

This process is what I mean by 'post-anthropocentric posthumanism', which I defend throughout this book. It involves a radical estrangement from notions like moral rationality, unitary identity, transcendent consciousness or innate and universal moral values. The focus is entirely on the normatively neutral relational structures of both subject formation and of possible ethical relations. The elaboration of new normative frameworks for the posthuman subject is the focus of collectively enacted, non-profit-oriented experimentations with intensity, that is to say with what we are actually capable of becoming. They are a *praxis* (a grounded shared project), not a *doxa* (common sense belief). My own concept of nomadic subject embodies this approach, which combines non-unitary subjectivity with ethical accountability by fore-grounding the ontological role played by relationality.

According to Felix Guattari, the posthuman predicament calls for a new virtual social ecology, which includes social, political, ethical and aesthetic dimensions, and transversal links between them. To clarify this vision, Guattari proposes three fundamental ecologies: that of the environment, of the social nexus, and of the psyche. More importantly, he empha-sizes the need to create transversal lines through all three of them. This clarification is important and I would connect it to the theoretical reminder I issued earlier, namely that we need to practise de-familiarization as a crucial method in posthuman critical theory and learn to think differently.

It is crucial, for instance, to see the interconnections among the greenhouse effect, the status of women, racism and xeno-phobia and frantic consumerism. We must not stop at any fragmented portions of these realities, but rather trace trans-versal interconnections among them. The subject is ontologi-cally polyvocal. It rests on a plane of consistency including both the real that is already actualized, 'territorialized exis-tential territories', and the real that is still virtual, 'deterrito-rialized incorporeal universes' (Guattari, 1995: 26). Guattari calls for a collective reappropriation of the production of subjectivity, through 'chaosmic' de-segregation of the differ-ent categories. You may remember that 'Chaosmos' is the universe of reference for becoming in the sense of the unfold-ing of virtualities, or transformative values. A qualitative step forward is necessary if we want subjectivity to escape the regime of commodification that is the trait of our historical era, and experiment with virtual possibilities. We need to become the sorts of subjects who actively desire to reinvent subjectivity as a set of mutant values and to draw our plea-sure from that, not from the perpetuation of familiar regimes.

The work of Humberto Maturana and Francisco Varela (1972) is a great source of inspiration in redesigning this type of environmentally bound post-anthropocentric and non-Kantian ethics of codetermination between self and other. The notion of codependence replaces that of recognition, much as the ethics of sustainability replaces the moral philosophy of rights. This reiterates the importance of grounded, situated and very specific and hence accountable perspectives in a move that I call *zoe*-centred egalitarianism.

In his analysis of the 'collective existential mutations' (1995: 2) currently taking place, Felix Guattari refers to Varela's distinction between autopoietic (self-organizing) and allopoietic systems. Guattari moves beyond the distinction proposed by Varela by extending the principle of autopoiesis (which for Varela is reserved for the biological organisms) to cover also the machines or technological others. Another name for subjectivity, according to Guattari, is autopoietic subjectivation, or self-styling, and it accounts both for living organisms, humans as self-organizing systems, and also for inorganic matter, the machines.

Guattari's machinic autopoiesis establishes a qualitative link between organic matter and technological or machinic artefacts. This results in a radical redefinition of machines as both intelligent and generative. They have their own temporality and develop through 'generations': they contain their own virtuality and futurity. Consequently, they entertain their own forms of alterity not only towards humans, but also among themselves, and aim to create meta-stability, which is the precondition of individuation. The emphasis on self-organization and metastability frames the project of becoming-machine of the posthuman subject. It helps us rethink transversal technologically mediated subjectivity while avoiding scientific reductionism. In his critique of the rhetoric of bio-technological vitalism (1997), Ansell Pearson warns us against the pernicious fantasy of a renaturalized notion of evolution mediated by advanced bio-technological capitalism. I think that the point of the posthuman predicament is to rethink evolution in a non-deterministic but also a post-anthropocentric manner. In opposition to classical, linear teleological ideas of evolution (Chardin de Teillard, 1959), I want to emphasize instead the collective project of seeking a more adequate understanding of the complexity of factors that structure the posthuman subject: the new proximity to animals, the planetary dimension and the high level of technological mediation. Machinic autopoiesis means that the technological is a site of post-anthropocentric becoming, or the threshold to many possible worlds.

The key notion is the transversality of relations, for a postanthropocentric and posthuman subject that traces transversal connections among material and symbolic, concrete and discursive lines of relation or forces. Transversality actualizes *zoe*-centred egalitarianism as an ethics and also as a method to account for forms of alternative, posthuman subjectivity. An ethics based on the primacy of the relation, of interdependence, values *zoe* in itself.

I also refer to these practices of becoming-machine as 'radical neo-materialism' (Braidotti, 1991), or as 'matter-realism' (Fraser et al., 2006). These ideas are supported by and intersect with changing understandings of the conceptual structure of matter itself (De Landa, 2002; Bennett, 2010), under the impact of contemporary bio-genetics and information technologies. The Spinozist switch to a monistic political ontology stresses processes, vital politics and non-deterministic evolutionary theories. Politically, the emphasis falls accordingly on the micro-politics of relations, as a posthumanist ethics that traces transversal connections among material and symbolic, concrete and discursive, lines or forces. The focus is on the force and autonomy of affect and the logistics of its actualization (Massumi, 2002). Transversality actualizes an ethics based on the primacy of the relation, of interdependence, which values non-human or a-personal Life. This is what I call posthuman politics (Braidotti, 2006).

Difference as the Principle of Not-One

Let me take stock of how far we have come in the complex debate opened by the demise of *anthropos*. Firstly, I have argued that contemporary capitalism is 'bio-political' in that it aims at controlling all that lives. It has already turned into a form of 'bio-piracy' (Shiva, 1997), because it exploits the generative powers of women, animals, plants, genes and cells. Secondly, this means that human and anthropomorphic others are relocated in a continuum with non-anthropomorphic, animal or 'earth' others. The categorical distinction that separated the Human from his naturalized others has shifted, taking the humanist assumptions about what constitutes the basic unit of reference for the 'human' into a spin. Thirdly, this anthropocentric process produces a negative category of the human as an endangered species bound by fear of extinction. It also forces a new unity among the human and other species, in the form of compensatory extension of humanist values and rights to the non-human others. Fourthly, the same system perpetuates familiar patterns of exclusion, exploitation and oppression. In order to ground my claim about the advantages of a posthuman subject position based on relationality and transversal interconnections across the classical axes of differentiation, the next step of the argument needs to address the question of difference. I will look critically at the status and function of difference in this new post-anthropocentric landscape.

As I argued in the previous chapter, the most striking feature of the current scientific redefinition of 'matter' is the dislocation of difference from binaries to rhizomatics; from sex/gender or nature/culture to processes of sexualization/racialization/naturalization that take Life itself, or the vitality of matter as the main target. This system engenders a deliberate blurring of dichotomous differences, which does not in itself resolve or improve the power differences and in many ways increases them. In other words, the opportunistic post-anthropocentric effects of the global economy engender a negative cosmopolitanism or a sense of reactive pan-human bonding by introducing the notion of 'Life as surplus' and of a common human vulnerability.

The political line of questioning has to start from this firm location to raise some key questions about subjectivity. For instance, Katherine Hayles argues, 'What do gendered bodies have to do with the erasure of embodiment and the subsequent merging of machine and human intelligence in the figure of the cyborg?' (Hayles, 1999: xii). In a similar vein, Balsamo, who believes that bodies are always and already marked by gender and race, asks (1996: 6), 'When the human body is fractured into organs, fluids and genetic codes, what happens to gender identity? When the body is fractured into functional parts and molecular codes, where is gender located?' Let us trust women, gays, lesbians and other alternative forces, with their historically 'leaky bodies' (Grosz, 1994) and not fully human rights, to both reassert the powers and enhance the potentiality of the posthuman organism as generative 'wetware'.

Genetic engineering and biotechnologies have seen to it that a qualitative conceptual dislocation has taken place in the contemporary classification of embodied subjects. As I argued previously, bodies are reduced to their informational substrate in terms of materiality and vital capacity. By implication, this means that the markers for the organization and distribution of differences are now located in micro instances of vital materiality, like the cells of living organisms and the genetic codes of entire species. We have come a long way from the gross system that used to mark difference on the basis of visually verifiable anatomical differences between the empirical sexes, the races and the species. We have moved from the bio-power that Foucault exemplified by comparative anatomy to a society based on the governance of molecular *zoe* power of today. We have equally shifted from disciplinary to control societies, from the political economy of the Panopticon to the informatics of domination (Haraway, 1990, 1992, 2003). The question of difference and power disparity, however, remains as central as ever.

This posthuman political landscape is not necessarily more egalitarian or less racist and heterosexist in its commitment to uphold, for instance, conservative gender roles and family values, albeit – in the case of the Hollywood blockbusters like *Avatar* (2009) – of the intergalactic and alien kind. The power of contemporary techno-culture to destabilize the categorical axes of difference exacerbates power relations and brings them to new necro-political heights, as we shall see in the next chapter. It also results in some misleading tendencies like techno-transcendence that, coupled with a consumer-oriented brand of liberal individualism, emerge as one of the traits of the social imaginary of global capitalism.

What are the consequences of the fact that technological apparatus is no longer sexualized, racialized or naturalized, but rather neutralized as figures of mixity, hybridity and interconnectiveness, turning transsexuality into a dominant posthuman *topos*? If the machine is both self-organizing and transgender, the old organic human body needs to be relocated elsewhere. Ever mindful of Lyotard's warning about the political economy of advanced capitalism, I think we should not trust the blurring effects and states of indeterminacy it engenders. However tempting, it would be misguided to assume that posthuman embodied subjects are beyond sexual or racialized difference. The politics of representation and hence the location of sexualized, racialized and naturalized differences are still strongly in place, though they have shifted significantly (Bukatman, 1993). In the electronic frontier, as we saw earlier, the technologically mediated point of reference is neither organic/inorganic, male/female, nor especially white. Advanced capitalism is a post-gender system capable of accommodating a high degree of androgyny and a significant blurring of the categorical divide between the sexes. It is also a post-racial system that no longer classifies people and their cultures on grounds of pigmentation (Gilroy, 2000), but remains nonetheless profoundly racist. A strong theory of posthuman subjectivity can help us to re-appropriate these processes, both theoretically and politically, not only as analytical tools, but also as alternative grounds for formations of the self.

Sexualized, racialized and naturalized differences, from being categorical boundary markers under Humanism, have become unhinged and act as the forces leading to the elaboration of alternative modes of transversal subjectivity, which extend not only beyond gender and race, but also beyond the human. In my view, posthuman eco-philosophy functions as an attempt to rethink in a materialist manner the intricate web of interrelations that mark the contemporary subjects' relationship to their multiple ecologies, the natural, the social and the psychic, as Guattari indicates. More importantly for the sake of the current argument, they do not abolish but profoundly restructure the processes of sexualization, racialization and naturalization which provided the pillars of biopolitical governmentality.

In terms of feminist politics, this means we need to rethink sexuality without genders, starting from a vitalist return to the polymorphous and, according to Freud, 'perverse' (in the sense of playful and non-reproductive) structure of human sexuality. We also need to reassess the generative powers of female embodiment. In this vision, gender is just a historically contingent mechanism of capture of the multiple potentialities of the body, including their generative or reproductive capacities. To turn it into *the* transhistorical matrix of power, as suggested by queer theory in the linguistic and social constructivist tradition (Butler, 1991), is quite simply a conceptual error. From the perspective of a posthuman monist political economy, power is a not a static given, but a complex strategic flow of effects which call for a pragmatic politics of intervention and the quest for sustainable alternatives (Braidotti, 2006). In other words, we need to experiment with resistance and intensity in order to find out what posthuman bodies can do. Because the gender system captures the complexity of human sexuality in a binary machine that privileges heterosexual family formations and literally steals all other possible bodies from us, we no longer know what sexed bodies can do. We therefore need to rediscover the notion of the sexual complexity that marks sexuality in its human and posthuman forms. A post-anthropocentric approach makes it clear that bodily matter in the human as in other species is always already sexed and hence sexually differentiated along the axes of multiplicity and heterogeneity.

I have argued that matter-realist or posthuman vitalist feminism, resting on a dynamic monistic political ontology, shifts the focus away from the sex/gender distinction, bringing sexuality as process into full focus. This means by extension that sexuality is a force, or constitutive element, that is capable of deterritorializing gender identity and institutions (Braidotti, 1994). Combined with the idea of the body as an incorporeal complex assemblage of virtualities, this approach posits the ontological priority of difference and its self-transforming force. Claire Colebrook (2000), for instance, argues that sexual difference is not a problem that needs a solution but a productive location to start from. Patricia MacCormack (2008) similarly draws attention to the need to return to sexuality as a polymorphous and complex, visceral force and to disengage it from both identity issues and all dualistic oppositions. Posthuman feminists look for subversion not in counter-identity formations, but rather in pure dislocations of identities via the perversion of standardized patterns of sexualized, racialized and naturalized interaction.

These experiments with what sexed bodies can do, however, do not amount to saying that in the social sphere differences no longer matter or that the traditional power relations have actually improved. On the contrary, on a world scale, extreme forms of polarized sexual difference are stronger than ever. They get projected onto geo-political relations, creating belligerent gendered visions of a 'clash of civilizations' that is allegedly predicated in terms of women's and GLBT people's rights, as I argued in the previous chapter. These reactionary manifestations of gender dichotomies are only part of the picture.

The broader picture indicates that the dislocation of the former system of marking differences makes it all the more urgent to reassert the concept of difference as both central and non-essentialistic. I have stressed difference as the principle of not-One, that is to say as differing (Braidotti, 2002), as constitutive of the posthuman subject and elaborate post-anthropocentric forms of ethical accountability to match it. In my view, posthuman ethics urges us to endure the principle of not-One at the in-depth structures of our subjectivity by acknowledging the ties that bind us to the multiple 'others' in a vital web of complex interrelations. This ethical principle breaks up the fantasy of unity, totality and one-ness, but also the master narratives of primordial loss, incommensurable lack and irreparable separation. What I want to emphasize instead, in a more affirmative vein, is the priority of the relation and the awareness that one is the effect of irrepressible flows of encounters, interactions, affectivity and desire, which one is not in charge of.

This humbling experience of not-Oneness, which is constitutive of the non-unitary subject, anchors the subject in an ethical bond to alterity, to the multiple and external others that are constitutive of that entity which, out of laziness and habit, we call the 'self'. Posthuman nomadic vital political theory stresses the productive aspects of the condition of not-One, that is to say a generative notion of complexity. At the beginning, there is always already a relation to an affective, interactive entity endowed with intelligent flesh and an embodied mind: ontological relationality. A materialist politics of posthuman differences works by potential becomings that call for actualization. They are enacted through collectively shared, community-based *praxis* and are crucial to support the process of vitalist, non-unitary and yet accountable recomposition of a missing people. This is the 'we' that is evoked and actualized by the postanthropocentric creation of a new pan-humanity. It expresses the affirmative, ethical dimension of becoming-posthuman as a gesture of collective self-styling. It actualizes a community that is not bound negatively by shared vulnerability, the guilt of ancestral communal violence, or the melancholia of unpayable onto-logical debts, but rather by the compassionate acknowledge-ment of their interdependence with multiple others most of which, in the age of anthropocene, are quite simply not anthropomorphic.

Conclusion

In this chapter I have pursued a dual aim: I provided an answer to the question of what the posthuman might be in a post-anthropocentric perspective and argued the case for a posthuman theory that takes into account subjectivity.

The most serious political problems in post-anthropocen-tric theory arise from the instrumental alliance of bio-genetic capitalism with individualism, as a residual humanist defini-tion of the subject. My view of posthuman thought is instead profoundly anti-individualistic and it consists in working within the belly of the beast, resisting the myth of organicism and holistic harmony, but also capitalist opportunism. Kath-erine Hayles (1999: 286) makes a powerful intervention on contemporary posthuman bodies:

> But the posthuman does not really mean the end of humanity. It signals instead the end of a certain conception of the human [. . .]. What is lethal is not the posthuman as such but the grafting of the posthuman onto a liberal humanist view of the self [. . .] Located within the dialectic of pattern/randomness and grounded in embodied actuality rather than disembodied information, the posthuman offers resources for rethinking the articulation of humans with intelligent machines.

Hayles attacks the classical humanistic notion that subjectiv-ity must coincide with conscious agency, in such a way as to avoid some of the mistakes of the humanist past, notably the liberal vision of an autonomous subject whose 'manifest destiny is to dominate and control nature' (Hayles, 1999: 288).

One of the risks of the 'hype' that surrounds the post-anthropocentric body-machines is indeed that of recreating a hard core, unitary vision of the subject, under the cover of pluralistic fragmentation. We run the risk of reasserting transcendence via technological meditation and of proposing a neo-universal machinic *ethos*. In the language of posthuman critical theory, this would produce the deception of a quantitative multiplicity which does not entail any qualitative shifts. To avoid this pitfall, which fits in with the neo-liberal euphoria, and in order to enact qualitative transformations instead, we need to be equally distanced from both hyped-up disembodiment and fantasies of trans-humanist escape, and from re-essentialized, centralized notions of liberal individualism. I propose to reinscribe posthuman bodies into radical relationality, including webs of power relations at the social, psychic, ecological and micro-biological or cellular levels. The post-anthropocentrism of our science and our globalized and technologically mediated times makes it urgent to work towards 'a new techno-scientific democracy' (Haraway, 1997: 95).

The status and the location of Humanism, which was the theme of the previous chapter, are central to this discussion of post-anthropocentrism. I tend to resist the political neutrality of critical, social and science theorists who support an analytic form of post-anthropocentrism and avoid or dismiss the question of subjectivity. I maintain that the post-anthropocentric subject rests also on the anti-humanist project, which means that I want to keep an equal distance from both the humanistic assumptions of the universal value of the unitary subject and the extreme forms of science-driven post-humanism which dismiss the need for a subject altogether.

One needs at least *some* subject position: this need not be either unitary or exclusively anthropocentric, but it must be the site for political and ethical accountability, for collective imaginaries and shared aspirations. Philosophical investigations of alternative ways of accounting for the embedded and embodied nature of the subject are relevant to develop an approach to subjectivity worthy of the complexities of our age. As I will argue more extensively in chapter 4, this discussion reopens the question of the relationship between the two cultures, the Humanities and Science. My point is that the social studies of science (Latour, 1993) are not the only, or even the most useful, tools of analysis for the complex phenomena surrounding the postanthropocentric technobodies of advanced capitalism.

Let me get to this from another angle. I have argued that *zoe*-egalitarianism expresses the simultaneously materialist and vitalist force of life itself, *zoe* as the generative power that flows across all species. The new transversal alliance across species and among posthuman subjects opens up unexpected possibilities for the recomposition of communities, for the very idea of humanity and for ethical forms of belonging. These are not confined to negative bonding in terms of sharing the same planetary threats: climate change, environmental crisis or even extinction. What I propose is a more affirmative approach to the redefinition of posthuman subjectivity, as in the counter models of transversal, relational nomadic assemblages we saw earlier in this chapter or the extended nature–cultural self as an alternative to classical Humanist subjectivity in the previous chapter. Many more models are thinkable and feasible, if we collectively choose to experiment systematically with the project of what 'we', the differently located posthuman subjects of the anthropocene era, might be capable of becoming.

We all stand to gain by the acknowledgment of a postanthropocentric, transversal structural link in the position of these embodied non-human subjects that were previously known as the 'others' of the anthropocentric and humanistic 'Man'. The ethical part of the project concerns the creation of a new social nexus and new forms of social connection with these techno-others. What kinds of bonds can be established within the nature–culture continuum of technologically mediated organisms and how can they be sustained? Both kinship and ethical accountability need to be redefined in such a way as to rethink links of affectivity and responsibility not only for non-anthropomorphic organic others, but also for those technologically mediated, newly patented creatures we are sharing our planet with.

In opposition to the nostalgic trend that is so dominant in contemporary politics, but also opposing a tendency to melancholia on the part of the progressive Left (Derrida, 2001b; Butler, 2004a; Gilroy, 2005), I want to argue that the posthuman emphasis on life/*zoe* itself can engender affirmative politics. Critical post-anthropocentrism generates new perspectives that go beyond panic and mourning and produce a more workable platform. For one thing, it produces a more adequate cartography of our real-life conditions because it focuses with greater accuracy on the complexities of contemporary technologically mediated bodies and on social practices of human embodiment. Furthermore, this type of vital materialism, unconstrained by clear-cut distinctions between species composes the notion of *zoe* as a non-human yet generative life-force. This posthuman approach moves beyond 'high' cyber studies (Haraway, 1985; Hayles, 1999) into post-cyber materialism (Braidotti, 2002) and posthuman theory (Braidotti, 2006). A nomadic *zoe*-centred approach connects human to non-human life so as to develop a comprehensive eco-philosophy of becoming.

This posthuman and post-anthropocentric sensibility, which draws on deep affective as well as intellectual resources, also expresses my rejection of the principle of adequation to the *doxa*, or commonly received normative image of thought. The posthuman predicament, in both the post-humanist and the post-anthropocentric sense of the term, drives home the idea that the activity of thinking needs to be experimental and even transgressive in combining critique with creativity. As Deleuze and Guattari teach us, thinking is about the invention of new concepts and new productive ethical relations. In this respect, theory is a form of organized estrangement from dominant values. More clinical than critical, posthuman theory cuts to the core of classical visions of subjectivity and works towards an expanded vision of vitalist, transversal relational subjects. Theory today is about coming to terms with unprecedented changes and transformations of the basic unit of reference for what counts as human. This affirmative, unprogrammed mutation can help actualize new concepts, affects and planetary subject formations. Just as we do not know what posthuman bodies can do, we cannot even begin to guess what postanthropocentric embodied brains will actually be able to think up.

Chapter 3
The Inhuman:
Life beyond Death

One of my favourite films is Marcel L'Herbier's *L'Inhumaine* (1924). With sets designed by Fernand Léger and Robert Mallet-Stevens, it is a manifesto of expressionist elegance, constructivist exuberance and futurist self-confidence. What is 'inhuman' in this masterful artwork is symptomatic of its own historical moment. The film deals with the super-human capacity of the female of our species to manipulate and control the course of human history and evolution. A highly seductive alliance is struck between the female body and the accelerating powers of technology. The ambivalence of fear and desire towards technology is re-cast in the mode of an ancestral patriarchal suspicion towards powerful women and women in positions of power. The progressive promise as well as the destructive potential of the female body-machine is held in close and calculated balance.

The technological artefact and the mechanic 'other' are both gendered and eroticized in modernism and become the emblem of a technology-driven future (Huyssen, 1986). In yet another expressionist masterpiece, Fritz Lang's *Metropolis* (1927), the heroine Maria is the demonical robot that perverts the course of history. It is based on the futurist novel *L'Eve future* (*Future Eve*, Villiers de l'Isle-Adam, 1977), which depicts the mechanical body-other of the industrial revolution as an object of intense desire: flesh turns to metal to fuel capital growth. Progress is visualized as a fantasy-landscape where locomotives successfully drive the train of Western history through endless tunnels. Both machine-vamp and praying mantis, both virgin-mother and pregnant suicide-bomber, L'Herbier's character Claire in *L'Inhumaine* and Lang's Maria express the highly sexualized and deeply gendered relationship of the twentieth century to its industrial technology and machinery. This vision, however, is not only caught in an anthropomorphic frame, which locates the human at the centre of world evolution; it also upholds the distinction between the human and the technological, if only to redefine it as a new alliance. This produces a multi-faceted inhuman world.

The modernist era stressed the power of technology not as an isolated event, but as a crucial element in the assemblage of industrialization, which involved manufactured objects, money, power, social progress, imagination and the construction of subjectivity. As a critical analysis of this historical moment, Marxism and its socialist Humanism taught us that objectification is indeed a humiliating and demeaning experience for humans in that it denies their full humanity and can thus be truly called inhuman at a basic social level. The commodification process itself reduces humans to the status of manufactured and hence profit-driven technologically mediated objects. This insight constitutes the core of the humanist heart of Marxism, which I analysed in chapter 1. Subsuming human relations into the nexus 'money-power' is for Marxists a form of inhumanity and the key social injustice of capitalist modes of production. This normative stance is all the more striking as Marxism was, from the methodological angle, an anti-humanist theoretical movement that argued against natural essences and debunked the naturalization of differences as a power strategy. As we saw in chapter 1, Marxist social constructivism was a deeply anti-essentialist methodology, resting on a Hegelian philosophy of history, which firmly believed in technologically driven social progress. Even Lenin defined socialism, the motor of historical progress, as the soviets (local workers' councils) plus electricity.

The modernist delirium, and its Marxist off-shoot, did not entirely go up in smoke, though many of those railroad tracks did lead to disaster. To return to Marcel L'Herbier's film, the analogy between the cruelty of the seductress, on the one hand, and the ruthless energy of the mechanical engine, on the other, produced a notion of the inhuman as super-human that posed technology as a transcendent other. It also instilled cruelty as a salient element of the narrative of growth and progress, already aware that these new technologies cannot but alter the organic human body through new forms of wanted and unwanted intimacy.

There is consequently another aspect of the inhuman as it is invoked by the modernist canon, namely the function and structure of the imagination as expressed in art. Modernism located the issue of artistic practice at the core of industrialized modernity. Both the technological object and the artefact are manufactured and hence pertain to the realm of the unnatural. Their anti-naturalistic structure is precisely the common denominator between the machine and the perverse, as in non-procreative, sexuality of the 'femme fatale' of artworks like *L'Inhumaine* and *Metropolis*. Female sexuality is inscribed in this inhuman script as a threat but also as an irresistible attraction: techno-Eves of multiple temptations, pointing the way to unsettling futures.

The inhuman nature of the artistic object consists of a combination of non-functionalism and ludic seductiveness. This is precisely what the surrealists meant by the 'bachelor machines' – an idea that Deleuze and Guattari adopted and transformed in the theory of 'bodies without organs' or a-functional and un-organic frames of becoming. Art, not unlike critical philosophy, is for Deleuze an intensive practice that aims at creating new ways of thinking, perceiving and sensing Life's infinite possibilities (Deleuze and Guattari, 1994). By transposing us beyond the confines of bound identities, art becomes necessarily inhuman in the sense of non-human in that it connects to the animal, the vegetable, earthy and planetary forces that surround us. Art is also, moreover, cosmic in its resonance and hence posthuman by structure, as it carries us to the limits of what our embodied selves can do or endure. In so far as art stretches the boundaries of representation to the utmost, it reaches the limits of life itself and thus confronts the horizon of death. To this effect, art is linked to death as the experience of limits (Blanchot, 2000).

I will return to this point later on in the chapter, in my discussion of a posthuman philosophy of death.

To pursue the point about the inhumanity of techno-industrial culture, it should be added at this stage of the argument that scientific reason and the rational practices of scientific research are not at all alien to both the project of modernism and its inhuman aspects. Science shares the mixed legacy of this historical period and is central to the project of industrialized modernity. Mechanical 'others', from impressive industrial machinery to banal household appliances, are the coveted objects of collectively funded and socially empowered scientific practices. They are yet another expression of that mixture of fear and desire for technology that art and cinema make manifest. The inhuman aspects, including cruelty and violence, are a crucial component of the scientific *ratio* in the modernist era. As Paul Rabinow put it (2003: 103):

> The twentieth century witnessed the establishment of a potent and malign connection between knowledge and the military [. . .]. From the horrific effects of poison gas (and other gifts of the chemical industries), through the atom bomb (and other gifts of physics and engineering), through the Nazi nightmare of racial purification (and other gifts of anthropology and the bio-sciences), to the indigestible fact that close to three quarters of the spending on scientific research during the Cold War was devoted to military ends. The industries and science of Thanatos have had a glorious century.

The issue of death and of killing is raised here, this time in relation to the aims and structure of science itself. Jean-Francois Lyotard's work *The Inhuman* (1989) contributes a crucial chapter to this discussion. Pursuing the critical stance announced in his classical text *The Postmodern Condition* (1984), he defines the inhuman as the alienating and commodifying effect of advanced capitalism on the human. The technological intrusion and manipulation is such as to dehumanize this subject in the name of ruthless efficiency. Lyotard does not stop at this technophobic insight, but goes on to identify a deeper kind of inhumanity, which is specific to *anthropos* him/her-self. That inner core of structural strangeness or productive estrangement is, for Lyotard, the

non-rational and non-volitional core of the inhuman which
makes us quintessentially human.[1] It not only confirms the
non-unitary structure of the subject, but also functions as the
site of ultimate resistance by humanity itself against the de-
humanizing effects of technology-driven capitalism. In this
respect, for Lyotard the inhuman has a productive ethical and
political force, which points the way to posthuman ethical
relations.

In this chapter I defend the position that the current historical context has transformed the modernist inhuman into
a posthuman and post-anthropocentric set of practices.
The inhuman is not what it used to be. The relationship
between the human and the technological other, as well as
the affects involved in it, including desire, cruelty and pain,
change radically with the contemporary technologies of
advanced capitalism. For one thing, the technological construct now mingles with the flesh in unprecedented degrees
of intrusiveness, as we saw in the previous chapter. Moreover,
the nature of the human–technological interaction has shifted
towards a blurring of the boundaries between the genders,
the races and the species, following a trend that Lyotard
assesses as a distinctive feature of the contemporary inhuman
condition. The technological other today – a mere assemblage
of circuitry and feedback loops – functions in the realm of
an egalitarian blurring of differences, if not downright indeterminacy. The most eloquent cinematic expression of the
neo-androgynous character of advanced capitalism is a film
like *Avatar* (2009), which is as removed from *L'Inhumaine*
as an iPhone is from an icon. There is no doubt as to which
is more fashionable today, but this is not the point. The point
is the extraordinary evolution of technology and its unexpected side-effects.

From the modernist fantasy of eroticizing the human–
machine interaction, to the postmodernist dis-enchantment
or at least ironical distance from the technological object,
something fundamental shifted. A different political economy
of affects came into action; a colder sensibility entered our
system, paving the road to the posthuman. Zygmunt Bauman

---

[1] This entity is akin to the Freudian 'uncanny', the Lacanian 'real'
and Kristeva's 'abjection' (1982).

(1993, 1998) was among the first to comment on this cruel, colder approach. In response to the historical disasters and the pain incurred in the historical era which Eric Hobsbawm called 'the short twentieth century' (1994) and more specifically the Holocaust, Bauman stressed the toll that such awful events took upon the moral fibre and the ethical sensibility of the perpetrators, as well as the victims, of the violence. This results in the brutalization of our moral selves, or an increase of moral bestiality among humans. Anti-colonial and anti-racist thinkers like Aimé Césaire and Frantz Fanon also developed this insight into the dissociation of moral sensibility that takes place in the soul of the misogynists, the racists and the fascists. In comparison to this lowering of the ethical standards, the 'victims' of violence actually tread the moral high ground. This insight lies at the core of the post-colonial, non-Western neo-humanism, which I analysed in chapter 1.

The question now becomes: how does the moral crisis of modernity play out in the posthuman frame of reference? Does the posthuman condition innovate also on the plane of the inhuman(e) aspects of our planetary interaction? Does it introduce de-humanization on a global scale? If one considers the scale of the major issues confronting the contemporary world, from the financial crises and their consequences for employment and structural economic inequalities, to climate change and the ensuing environmental crises, not to mention geo-political conflicts, terrorism and humanitarian armed interventions, it is clear that the posthuman condition has engendered its own inhuman(e) dimension.

This chapter deals with the multi-layered issue of the inhuman by examining multiple modes of relation to death and dying. In an argument about life that constitutes the perfect counterpart of the idea of *zoe* as a posthuman continuum, I propose to look more closely at *Thanatos*, and to necro-politics, as a way of constructing an affirmative posthuman theory of death. I think that a conceptual shift towards 'matter-realist' vitalism, grounded in ontological monism, can assist us in this project of rethinking death and mortality in the contemporary bio-mediated context. Politically, we need to assess the advantages of the politics of vital affirmation. Ethically, we need to re-locate compassion and care of both human and non-human others in this new frame.

Ways of Dying

We saw in the previous chapter that the posthuman predicament understood as the bio-political management of living
matter is post-anthropocentric in character, raising the need
for a Life/*zoe*-centred approach. Now I want to go a step
further and argue that posthuman vital politics shifts the
boundaries between life and death and consequently deals not
only with the government of the living, but also with practices
of dying. Most of these are linked to inhuman(e) social and
political phenomena such as poverty, famine and homeless-
ness, which Zillah Eisenstein aptly labelled as 'global obscenities' (1998). Vandana Shiva (1997) stresses the extent to
which bio-power has already turned into a form of 'bio-
piracy', which calls for very grounded and concrete political
analyses. Thus, the bodies of the empirical subjects who
signify difference (woman/native/earth or natural others)
have become the disposable bodies of the global economy.
Contemporary capitalism is indeed 'bio-political' in that it
aims at controlling all that lives, as Foucault argues, but
because Life is not the prerogative of humans only, it opens
up a *zoe*-political or post-anthropocentric dimension. If
anxiety about extinction was common in the nuclear era, the
posthuman condition, of the anthropocene, extends the death
horizon to most species. Yet there is a very important difference, as Chakrabarty points out: 'A nuclear war would have
been a conscious decision on the part of the powers that be.
Climate change is an unintended consequence of human
actions as a species' (2009: 221). This not only inaugurates
a negative or reactive form of pan-human planetary bond,
which recomposes humanity around a commonly shared
bond of vulnerability, but also connects the human to the fate
of other species, as I argued in the previous chapter. Death
and destruction are the common denominators for this transversal alliance.

Let me give you some examples of contemporary ways of
dying to illustrate this political economy. The posthuman
aspects of globalization encompass many phenomena that,
while not being *a priori* inhumane, still trigger significant
destructive aspects. The postsecular condition, with the rise

of religious extremism in a variety of forms, including Christian fundamentalism, entails a political regression of the rights of women, homosexuals and all sexual minorities. Significant signs of this regression are the decline in reproductive rights and the rise of violence against women and GLBT people. The effect of global financial networks and unchecked hedge funds has been an increase in poverty, especially among youth and women, affected by the disparity in access to the new technologies. The status of children is a chapter apart; from forced labour, to the child-soldier phenomenon, childhood has been violently inserted in infernal cycles of exploitation. Bodily politics has shifted, with the simultaneous emergence of cyborgs on the one hand and renewed forms of vulnerability on the other. Thus, next to the proliferation of pandemics like SARS, Ebola, HIV, bird-flu and others, more familiar epidemics have also returned, notably malaria and tuberculosis, so much so that health has become a public policy issue as well as a human rights concern.

The point is that Life/*zoe* can be a threatening force, as well as a generative one. A great deal of health and environmental concerns as well as geo-political issues, simply blur the distinction between life and death. In the era of bio-genetic capitalism and nature–culture continuum, *zoe* has become an infra-human force and all the attention is now drawn to the emergency of disappearing nature. For instance, the public discourse about environmental catastrophes or 'natural' disasters – the Fukushima nuclear plant and the Japanese tsunami, the Australian bushfires, hurricane Katrina in New Orleans, etc. – accomplishes a significant double-bind: it expresses a new ecological awareness, while re-inserting the distinction between nature and culture. As Protevi argues (2009), this results in the paradoxical re-naturalization of our bio-technologically mediated environment. The geo-political forces are simultaneously re-naturalized and subjected to the old hierarchical power relations determined by the dominant politics of the anthropomorphic subject. Public discourse has become simultaneously moralistic about the inhuman forces of the environment and quite hypocritical in perpetuating anthropocentric arrogance. This position results in the denial of the man-made structure of the catastrophes that we continue to attribute to forces beyond our collective control, like the earth, the cosmos or 'nature'. Our public morality is simply not up to the challenge of the scale and the complexity of damages engendered by our techno-logical advances. This gives rise to a double ethical urgency: firstly, how to turn anxiety and the tendency to mourn the loss of the natural order into effective social and political action, and secondly, how to ground such an action in the responsibility for future generation, in the spirit of social sustainability that I have also explored elsewhere (Braidotti, 2006).

Another significant case in point is the posthuman digital universe that I analysed in the previous chapter and which engenders its own inhuman variables. They are best mani-fested by the proliferation of viruses, both computer-based and organic, some of which transit from animals to humans and back. Illness is clearly not only a prerogative of organic entities, but includes a widespread practice of mutual con-tamination between organic matter – anthropomorphic or not – and electronic circuitry. A rather complex symbiotic relationship has emerged in our cyber universe: a sort of mutual dependence between the flesh and the machine. This engenders some significant paradoxes, namely that the cor-poreal site of subjectivity is simultaneously denied, in prac-tices of human enhancement and in fantasies of escape via techno-transcendence, and it is also re-enforced as increased vulnerability. Balsamo (1996) argues that digital technology promotes dreams of immortality and control over life and death: 'And yet, such beliefs about the technological future "life" of the body are complemented by a palpable fear of death and annihilation from uncontrollable and spectacular body-threats: antibiotic-resistant viruses, random contamina-tion, flesh-eating bacteria' (Balsamo, 1996: 1–2). The inhuman forces of technology have moved into the body, intensifying the spectral reminders of the corpse-to-come. Our social imaginary has taken a forensic turn.

Popular culture and the infotainment industry are quick to pick up this contradictory trend that reflects the changing status of the demise of the human body, including illness, death and extinction. The corpse is not only a daily presence in global media and journalistic news, but also an object of entertainment in contemporary popular culture, notably in the successful genre of forensic detectives. Culture and the arts have been very sensitive in registering the rise in women who kill, as shown by the success of recent literary and stage renditions of classics like Hecuba and Medea. Not to mention, of course, the global appeal of sharp-shooting Lara Croft in the world of computer games.

The evolution of gender roles towards a more egalitarian participation by both sexes in the business of killing is one of the most problematic aspects of contemporary gender politics. They can be summarized as the shift from the universal Human Rights stance of the Mothers of the Plaza de Mayo, to the brutal interventionism of the Chechnya war widows, pregnant female suicide-bombers and the growing role of women in the military 'Humanism' of 'humanitarian' wars.

Spiritual death is part of the picture as well, if we take into account contemporary embodied social practices that are often pathologized and never addressed fully, such as addictions, eating disorders and melancholia, burn-out and states of apathy and disaffection. I propose not to simply classify these practices as self-destructive, but rather to see them as normatively neutral manifestations of interaction with and resistance to the political economy of commodification of all that lives. They exemplify the shifting social relations between living and dying in the era of the politics of 'life itself'. The currency granted to both legal (Ritalin, Prozac) and illegal drugs in contemporary culture blurs the boundaries between self-destruction and fashionable behaviour and forces a reconsideration of what is the value of 'life itself'. Last but not least, assisted suicide and euthanasia practices are challenging the Law to rest on the tacit assumption of a self-evident value attributed to 'Life'. As is often the case, advanced capitalism functions by schizoid or internally contradictory moves. Thus, a socially enforced ideology of fitness, health and eternal youth goes hand in hand with increased social disparities in the provision of health care and in mortality rates among infants and youth. The obsession with being 'forever young' works in tandem with and forms the counterpart of social practices of euthanasia and assisted death.

The moment one starts thinking about it, multiple ways of dying, of inflicting death and suffering losses are proliferating around us. And yet, when it comes to accounting for them, social theory tends to refer to this political economy as 'bio'-political. What does life (*bios*) have to do with it, though? Bio-political analyses since Foucault have transformed the field and introduced more precise understandings of what is involved in the management of the living. Why is not the same degree of analytical precision devoted to the analysis of the necro-political management of dying?

Both the quantity and the scale of the changes that have taken place in social and personal practices of dying, in ways of killing and forms of extinction, as well as the creativity of mourning rituals and the necessity of bereavement, are such as to support the expansion of the socio-cultural agenda. This includes the emergence of a new discursive domain. 'Death Studies' has become a new and much needed addition to the academic landscape, growing out of the 1970s counter-culture into a serious interdisciplinary area that includes moral and religious discussions about mortality, but also research in social, policy and health issues as well as the very practical aspect of professional training.[2] I shall return to this expansion of new 'studies' areas in chapter 4.

Beyond Bio-politics

Let us start again from the basic insight that the new practices of bio-political management of 'life' mobilize not only generative forces, but also new and subtler degrees of death and extinction. My argument is that a focus on the vital and self-organizing powers of Life/*zoe* undoes any clear-cut distinctions between living and dying. It composes the notion of *zoe* as a posthuman yet affirmative life-force. This vitalist materialism rests solidly on a neo-Spinozist political ontology of monism and radical immanence, engendering a transversal relational ethics to counteract the inhuman(e) aspects of the posthuman predicament.

[2] See, for instance, the 'Centre for Death and Society' at the University of Bath in the UK. Several journals also testify to the vitality of this field. See among others: *Death Studies* (Routledge, 1970, redesigned in 1985); *Journal of Death and Dying* (Baywood Publishing, 1970) and *Journal of Near-Death Studies* (1978).

I have argued so far that the posthuman predicament, in so far as it dislocates the traditional understandings of the human, also entails significant changes in the status and structure of the inhuman and of inhumane practices. The next question then is: how do these new formations of the inhuman impact on a theory of the subject and on social and cultural theory? Bio-political analysis is central to this discussion, but in the current context it has moved beyond the premises articulated by Foucault in his pioneering efforts. I perceive several new trends in thinking about the bio-political management of life and death. For instance, a school of bio-political citizenship has emerged, with emphasis on the ethical implications of 'bio power' as an instance of governmentality that is as empowering as it is confining (Rabinow, 2003; Rose, 2007; Esposito, 2008). This school of thought locates the political moment in the relational and self-regulating accountability of a bio-ethical subject that takes full responsibility for his/her genetic existence, including illness and other forms of responsibility for one's embodied self. As we saw in the previous chapter, this position allows for a residual type of Kantianism to emerge around the last phase of Foucault's work, with emphasis on individual responsibility for the self-management of one's health and life-style. The advantage of this position is that it calls for a higher degree of lucidity about posthuman bio-organic existence, which means that the naturalist paradigm is definitely abandoned. The disadvantage of this position, however, is that it perverts the notion of responsibility towards individualism, in a political context of neo-liberal dismantling of the national health service, a pillar of the welfare state and increasing privatization. Bio-ethical citizenship indexes access to and responsibility for the cost of basic social services like health care to an individual's manifest ability to act responsibly by reducing the risks and exertions linked to the wrong lifestyle. In other words, here bio-ethical agency means taking adequate care of one's own genetic capital. The recent government campaigns against smoking, excessive drinking and obesity constitute evidence of this neo-liberal normative trend that supports hyper-individualism.

The neo-Kantian take on Foucault raises also serious theoretical questions about the notion of bio-power. Considering the fast rate of progress and change undergone by contemporary bio-technologies and the challenges they throw to the status of the human, Foucault's work has been criticized, notably by Haraway (1997), for relying on an outdated vision of contemporary technology. Haraway suggests that Foucault's bio-power provides the cartography of a world that no longer exists and that we have now entered the age of the informatics of domination. Other critical theories come closer to the target, notably feminist, environmentalist and race theorists who have addressed the shifting status of embodiment and difference in advanced capitalism in a manner that reflects the complexity of global social relations.[3]

The central discrepancy between Foucault's notion of bio-power and contemporary posthuman structures has to do with the dis-placement of anthropocentrism. In chapter 2, I argued that the bio-genetic structure of advanced capitalism reduces bodies to carriers of vital information, which get invested with financial value and capitalized. They provide the material for new classifications of entire populations on the basis of the genetic predispositions and vital capacities for self-organization. There is a structural isomorphism between economic and biological growth, which makes the power relations of contemporary neo-liberal capitalism rawer and cruder than in the Fordist era (Cooper, 2008). This has important repercussions for the *zoe* dimension of the politics of dying.

Because genetic information, like psychological traits or neural features, is unevenly distributed, this system is not only inherently discriminatory, but also racist at some basic level of the term. Patricia Clough (2008) explores this aspect of the contemporary political economy by analysing the public debates on the availability of pharmaceutical drugs against HIV, or large-scale vaccines against malaria, to mention just a few contemporary examples of posthuman management of Life. A whole under-class of genetically over-exposed and socially under-insured disposable bodies is engendered both within the Western world and in the emerging global economies. This kind of population control goes beyond Foucault's

[3] See, especially, Gilroy (2000), Braidotti (2002), Barad (2003), Butler (2004b) and Grosz (2004).

analysis of the bio-political, as it does not function by techniques of discipline and control, but rather by bio-genetic farming of data, and by 'bio-piracy' (Shiva, 1997). As Mark Halsey put it: 'Where once the sole objective was to control the insane, the young, the feminine, the vagrant and the deviant, the objective in recent times has been to arrest the nonhuman, the inorganic, the inert – in short, the so-called "natural worlds"' (Halsey, 2006: 15). This is posthuman zoe-politics, not bio-political governmentality.

Again, monistic posthuman philosophy is of great assistance to think through these challenging new historical conditions. Reading Deleuze through the lens of Massumi, Clough studies the new mechanisms of capture not of liberal individuals, but bio-genetic 'dividuals':

> statistically reconfigured in populations that surface as profiles of bodily capacities, indicating what a body can do now and what capacities it might be able to unfold in the future. The affective capacity of bodies, statistically simulated as risk factors, can be apprehended as such without the subject, even without the individual subject's body. This results in bringing forth competing bureaucratic procedures of control and political command in terms of securing the life of the population. (2008: 18)

This way of linking forms of political control with the estimation of risk factors is a technique that Foucault defined as racism, as it configures – it engenders as 'raced' – entire populations in a hierarchical scale, this time not determined by pigmentation, but by other genetic characteristics. Because the aim of this political exercise is to estimate a given population's chance of survival or of extinction, the bio-political management of the living is not only transversal across species and zoe-driven, but also inherently linked to death. This is the death-bound or necro-political face of post-anthropocentrism and the core of its inhuman(e) character: 'it permits the healthy life of some populations to necessitate the death of others, marked as nature's degenerate or unhealthy ones' (Clough, 2008: 18).

The necro-political dimension also means that the political representation of embodied subjects nowadays can no longer be understood within the visual economy of bio-politics in

Foucault's (1978) sense of the term. The representation of embodied subjects is not visual in the sense of being scopic, as in the post-Platonic sense of the simulacrum. Nor is it specular, as in the psychoanalytic mode of redefining vision within a dialectical scheme of oppositional recognition of self and/as other. The representation of embodied subjects has been replaced by simulation and has become schizoid, or internally disjointed. It is also spectral: the body doubles up as the potential corpse it has always been, and is represented as a self-replicating system that is caught in a visual economy of endless circulation (Braidotti, 2002). The contemporary social imaginary is immersed in this logic of boundless circulation and thus is suspended somewhere beyond the life and death cycle of the imaged self. The bio-genetic imagination has consequently become forensic in its relationship to the body as corpse and in the quest for traces of a life that it no longer controls. Contemporary embodied subjects have to be accounted for in terms of their surplus value as bio-genetic containers on the one hand, and as visual commodities circulating in a global media circuit of cash flow on the other. Much of this information is not knowledge-driven, but rather media-inflated and thus indistinguishable from sheer entertainment. They are therefore doubly mediated by bio-genetic and by informational codes.

We see then that contemporary bio-politics intersects with the eco-philosophical dimension I analysed in the previous chapter and illuminates the negative face of current socio-political power relations. The challenge consists in turning these hybrid and slightly schizoid social phenomena into points of resistance to the inhuman aspects of the posthuman condition. The central insight of Foucault's political anatomy remains valid: bio-power also involves the management of dying. In other words, the question of the governance of life contains that of extinction as well. In order to deploy the full ethical and political potential of this brilliant insight, however, we do need to return to the early Foucault and not be misled by the neo-Kantian interpretation of his second phase.

In his earlier work, Foucault (1977) focuses explicitly on the critical analysis of the power mechanisms at work in the production of subjectivity. The latter is defined as a process of both discursive and material circulation of effects, which are productive and not only confining. This emphasis on power is crucial to make sense of the posthuman predicament.

Forensic Social Theory

Social and political theory after Foucault has been invested by these transformations in the status and the theory of the human, as shown, for instance, in one of the most significant responses to the forensic turn by Giorgio Agamben (1998). He defines 'Life/*zoe*' as the result of the lethal intervention of sovereign power onto the embodied subject, who is reduced to 'bare life', that is to say a non-human status of extreme vulnerability bordering on extinction. Bio-power here means Thanatos-politics and it results, for Agamben, in the indictment of the project of industrialized modernity, in view of its de-humanizing effects. The colonial plantation is the prototype of this political economy and the enslaved human almost the epitome of '*homo sacer*' (Agamben, 1998). This insight results in drawing intrinsic links between modernization and violence, modernity and terror, sovereignty and murder.

The inhuman for Agamben, not unlike Lyotard, is the effect of modernization, but he also learned from Hannah Arendt (1951) to look at the phenomenon of totalitarianism as the ultimate denial of the humanity of the other. Arendt, however, constructed a powerful alternative to these political extremes by stressing the necessity of human rights for all, even and especially the de-humanized 'others'. Arendt is, in Seyla Benhabib's brilliant formulation, 'a reluctant modernist' (1996). Agamben, on the other hand, is less innovative and perpetuates the philosophical habit that consists in taking mortality, or finitude, as the trans-historical horizon for discussions of 'life'. For him 'bare life' is not generative vitality, but rather the constitutive vulnerability of the human subject, which sovereign power can kill; it is that which makes the body into disposable matter in the hands of the despotic force of unchecked power. This is linked to Heidegger's theory of being as deriving its force from the annihilation of animal life. Finitude is introduced as a constitutive element within the framework of subjectivity, which also fuels an affective political economy of loss and melancholia at the heart of the subject.

I am perturbed by this fixation on *Thanatos* that Nietzsche criticized over a century ago and which is still very present in critical debates today. It often produces a gloomy and pessimistic vision not only of power, but also of the technological developments that propel the regimes of bio-power. My understanding of 'life' as *zoe* ethics of sustainable transformations differs considerably from what Agamben calls 'bare life' or negative *zoe*. I beg to differ from the habit that favours the deployment of the problem of *zoe* on the horizon of death, or of liminal state of non-life. This over-emphasis on the horizons of mortality and perishability is characteristic of the 'forensic turn' in contemporary social and cultural theory, haunted by the spectre of extinction and by the limitations of the project of western modernity. I find the over-emphasis on death as the basic term of reference inadequate to the vital politics of our era. I therefore turn to another significant community of scholars who work within a Spinozist framework[4] and prefer to emphasize the politics of life itself as a relentlessly generative force including and going beyond death. This requires an interrogation of the shifting interrelations between human and non-human forces.

Speaking from the position of an embodied and embedded female subject, capable of reproducing the future and the species, I find the metaphysics of finitude to be a myopic way of putting the question of the limits of what we call 'life'. We need to re-think death, the ultimate subtraction, as another phase in a generative process, as I will argue in the second half of this chapter. Too bad that the relentless generative powers of death require the suppression of that which is the nearest and dearest to me, namely myself, my own vital being-there. For the narcissistic human subject, as psychoanalysis teaches us, it is unthinkable that Life should go on without my being there (Laplanche, 1976). The process of confronting the thinkability of a Life that may not have 'me' or any 'human' at the centre is actually a sobering and instructive process. I see this post-anthropocentric shift as the neces-

---

[4] This includes Deleuze and Guattari (1977, 1987), Guattari (1995), Glissant (1997), Balibar (2002) and Hardt and Negri (2000).

sary start for an ethics of sustainability that aims at re-directing the focus towards the posthuman positivity of *zoe*. At the heart of my research project lies an ethics that respects vulnerability while actively constructing social horizons of hope.

On Contemporary Necro-politics

At this point in the book it is important to stress that affirmative politics, as the process of transmuting negative passions into productive and sustainable praxis, does not deny the reality of horrors, violence and destruction. It just proposes a different way of dealing with them. Contemporary politics has more than its fair share of cruelty to account for. New scholarship has concentrated on the brutality of today's wars and the renewed expressions of violence which target not only the government of the living, but also multiple practices of dying. Bio-power and necro-politics are two sides of the same coin, as Achille Mbembe (2003) brilliantly argues. The explosion of discursive interest in the politics of life itself, in other words, affects also the geo-political dimension of death and of killing. Mbembe expands Foucault's insight in the direction of a more grounded analysis of the bio-political management of survival. Aptly re-naming it 'necro-politics', he defines this power essentially as the administration of death: 'the generalized instrumentalization of human existence and the material destruction of human bodies and population' (Mbembe, 2003: 19). And *not* only human, I might add, but also planetary.

The post-Cold War world has seen not only a dramatic increase in warfare, but also a profound transformation of the practice of war as such. New forms of warfare entail simultaneously the breath-taking efficiency of 'intelligent', un-manned, technological weaponry on the one hand, and the rawness of dismembered and humiliated human bodies on the other. This is exemplified by Gaddafi's undignified end, which I evoked in the third vignette of the introduction. Posthuman wars breed new forms of inhumanity. The implications of this approach to necro-power are radical: it is not up to the rationality of the Law and the universalism of moral values to structure the exercise of power, but rather the unleashing of the unrestricted sovereign right to kill, maim, rape and destroy the life of others. This political economy structures the attribution of different degrees of 'humanity' according to hierarchies that are disengaged from the old dialectics and unhinged from bio-political logic. They fulfil instead a more instrumental, narrow logic of opportunistic exploitation of the life in you, which is generic and not only individual.

Contemporary necro-politics has taken the politics of death on a global regional scale. The new forms of industrial-scale warfare rest upon the commercial privatization of the army and the global reach of conflicts, which de-territorialize the use of and the rationale for armed service. Reduced to 'infrastructural warfare' (Mbembe, 2003), and to a large-scale logistical operation (Virilio, 2002), war aims at the destruction of all the services that allow civil society to function: roads, electricity lines, airports, hospitals and other necessities. The old-fashioned army has now mutated into 'urban militias; private armies; armies of regional lords; private security firms and state armies, all claim the right to exercise violence or to kill' (Mbembe, 2003: 32). As a result, as a political category, the 'population' has also become disaggregated into 'rebels, child soldiers, victims or refugees, or civilians incapacitated by mutilation or massacred on the model of ancient sacrifices, while the "survivors", after a horrific exodus, are confined to camps and zones of exception' (Mbembe, 2003: 34). Many contemporary wars, led by Western coalitions under the cover of 'humanitarian aid' are often neo-colonial exercises aimed at protecting mineral extraction and other essential geo-physical resources needed by the global economy. In this respect, the 'new' wars look more like privatized conflicts and guerrilla or terrorist attacks, than the traditional confrontation of enlisted and nationally indexed armies.

Arjun Appadurai (1998) has also provided incisive analyses of the new 'ethnocidal violence' of the new forms of warfare which involve friends, kinsmen and neighbours. He is appalled by the violence of these conflicts 'associated with brutality and indignity – involving mutilation, cannibalism, rape, sexual abuse, and violence against civilian spaces and populations. Put briefly the focus here is on bodily brutality perpetrated by ordinary persons against other persons with whom they may have – or could have – previously lived in relative amity' (Appadurai, 1998: 907). This is the specifically inhuman edge of the posthuman condition.

Chomsky commented shrewdly on this new situation, which he labelled 'the new military humanism' of the humanitarian interventions:

> Armed with the technology of global devastation and the jargon of pulp fiction, tabloid headlines and PlayStation games: 'the War on terror, the Clash of Civilisations, the Axis of Evil, Operation Shock and Awe'. Those adventures set out to save the civilized world ('*homo humanus*') from its enemies ('*homo barbarus*'), under the venerable banners of liberty, decency and democracy. (Quoted in Davies, 1997: 134)

This deployment of technologically mediated violence cannot be adequately described in terms of disciplining the body, fighting the enemy or even as the techniques of a society of control. We have rather entered the era of orchestrated and instrumental massacres, a new 'semiosis of killing', leading to the creation of multiple and parallel 'death-worlds' (Mbembe, 2003: 37). These necro-political modes of governance also circulate as infotainment in global media circuits, according to the logic of double mediation I mentioned before.

The special issue of the weekly magazine *The Economist* (2 June 2012, p. 13) on 'Morals and the Machine', which I mentioned in chapter 1, offers an impressive update on contemporary military technology. It argues that recent developments are producing an extraordinary new techno-bestiary. For instance, the 'Sand Flea', built by Boston Dynamics (a spin-off from MIT), can leap through a window or onto a roof nine metres high, while gyro-stabilizers allow smooth filming all the way. The 5 kg robot then rolls along on wheels until it needs to jump again. Then comes 'RISE', a six-legged robo-cockroach that can climb walls; a 'TerraMax' robotic kit made by Oshkosh Defense (Wisconsin) that turns military lorries or armoured vehicles into remotely controlled machines. 'LS3' is a dog-like robot that uses computer vision so that it trots behind a human over rough terrain, carrying up to 180 kg of supplies. 'SUGV', a briefcase-sized robot running on caterpillar tracks, can identify a man in a crowd, upload a mugshot and follow him. 'First Look', a military robot Made by iRobot, another MIT spin-off, is designed to be thrown through windows or over walls. 'Scout XT Throwbot', made by Recon Robotics in Minnesota, shaped like a two-headed hammer with wheels on each head, has the heft of a grenade and can be thrown through glass windows. Wheel spikes provide traction on steep or rocky surfaces. An aquatic version is in the making. This is indeed the stuff of science fiction come true.

As *The Economist* points out, by far the most effective new weapons, however, are the UGVs (unmanned ground vehicles), which started work in Afghanistan a decade ago, and the UAVs (unmanned aerial vehicles) – also known as drones or remotely piloted aircraft (RPA) – which are part of a large robot army that includes land and sea as well as air. In 2005, CIA drones struck targets in Pakistan three times; last year there were 76 strikes, one of them crucial to killing Gaddafi in Libya. Drones come in all sorts of sizes: 'DelFly', a dragonfly-shaped surveillance drone, built at the technical university in Delft, weighs less than a gold wedding ring, camera included. At the other end of the scale comes America's biggest and fastest drone, Avenger, at a cost of US$15 mn, which can carry up to 2.7 tonnes of bombs, sensors and other equipment, at more than 740 km/h.

Do drones make killing too easy? Not necessarily, answers *The Economist*. They process so much data that they fight 'warfare by committee'. Government lawyers and others in operating rooms monitor video feeds from robots to call off strikes that are illegal or 'would look bad on CNN'. These remote human observers, moreover, are working in more humane surroundings and are unaffected by combat stress. The 'FireShadow', a robotic missile designed by MEDA, a French company, is a 'loitering munition' capable of travelling 100 km more than twice the maximum range of a traditional artillery shell; it can circle in the sky for hours, using sensors to track a moving target. A human operator, viewing a video feed, can decide when and if to fire it, find a better target range or abort the mission altogether. As *The Economist* repeatedly stresses, however, by-passing the human decision maker is already technologically feasible. The Israeli army has robotic machineguns on their border and monitors them by remote control. The Samson Remote Weapon Station built by David Ishai of Rafael, an Israeli firm, could function without human intervention, spotting the target by sensors.

Questioned on this issue by *The Guardian* (Carroll, 2012), RPA or drone pilots argue that their jobs involve different types of courage from conventional warfare, not only because they have to take the consequences of possible mistakes, but also because a different degree of rigour and accuracy is needed to kill by remote control. These tele-thanatological warriors need sophisticated equipment, such as: 'multi-spectral targeting systems that integrate infrared sensors, enhanced TV camera and laser designators and illuminators into single packages' (Carroll, 2012: 2). Moreover, this complex multi-tasking structure of this kind of warfare often takes place under close scrutiny from an array of specialists and supervisors: officers, intelligence analysts and military lawyers included. Drones do not kill more 'easily' in any sense of the term.

Critics of these lethal technologies, who include former US President Jimmy Carter, think otherwise. They argue that the drone strikes are 'extrajudicial executions that violate nations' sovereignty, stain US moral standing and fuel extremism' (Carroll, 2012: 2). They maintain that the best way of dealing with these complex questions is to ban autonomous battlefield weapons altogether and require robots to have the full attention of humans all the time. In Berlin in 2012 a group of engineers, philosophers and activists formed the International Committee for Robot Arm Control (ICRAC) in order to try to control the effects of the autonomy reached by contemporary robotic weapon systems and especially drones. As the Obama administration pledges investments to the tune of US$15 bn for Predator and Reaper drones, however, there is no denying their growing importance as both offensive weapons and as policy instruments.

The Economist points out other advantages of posthuman warfare and argues that autonomous robot-soldiers could do more good than harm: they would not rape women, burn down civilian dwellings in anger or become erratic decision-makers under the emotional stress of combat. By analogy, driverless cars are likely to be safer than ordinary vehicles, just as auto-pilots have made planes safer. Furthermore, drones are increasingly being used for civilian purposes, not unlike other robots that have long been employed in nuclear plants, on the flight-deck of passenger aircraft and in driverless trains. A recent report by the newspaper *The Guardian* (Franklin, 2012) describes how a battery-operated drone with a range of 300 km and a cost of less than US$800 is used by environmental activists to spot and possibly stop Japanese whaling operations in the waters of Antarctica. What was once exclusive to Israeli spy forces and the US Air Force is now sent on missions ranging from the survey of marine mammals to crop inspections. The Federal Aviation Authority in the USA has just issued new directives for the use of these vehicles.

The readers can only marvel at the sophistication of these technological achievements, but also wonder about the inhuman risks involved in post-anthropocentric weaponry. It is also striking to note the role played by academic research in leading universities in the development of these killing robots. The time-honoured bond between academia and the military has entered a new, highly productive phase in our posthuman world.

Post-anthropocentric technologies are also re-shaping the practice of surveillance in the social field. Border control of immigration and the smuggling of people are major aspects of the contemporary inhuman condition and central players in the necro-political game. Diken (2004) argues that refugees and asylum seekers become another emblem of the contemporary necro-power, because they are the perfect instantiation of the disposable humanity that Agamben also calls '*homo sacer*' and thus constitute the ultimate necro-political subject. The proliferation of detention and high-security camps and prisons within the once civic-minded space of European cities is an example of the inhuman face of Fortress Europe. The camps – 'sterilized, monofunctional enclosures' (Diken, 2004: 91) – stand as the undignified monuments of posthuman inhumanity.

Duffield (2008) pushes the necro-political, socio-political analysis further and makes a distinction between developed or insured humans and under-developed or uninsured humans: 'Developed life is sustained primarily through regimes of social insurance and bureaucratic protection historically associated with industrial capitalism and the growth of welfare states' (Duffield, 2008: 149). The distinction and the tensions between these two categories constitute the terrain for the 'global civil war', which is Duffield's definition of globalized advanced capitalism. The link to colonialism is clear: de-colonization created nation-states whose people, once enslaved, are now free to circulate globally. These people constitute the bulk of the unwanted immigrants, refugees and asylum seekers who are contained and locked up across the developed world. In a twist not deprived of ironical force, world migration is perceived as a particular threat in Europe precisely because it endangers Europe's main social infrastructure: the welfare state. The growing range of warfare weapons and killing techniques raises critical questions about the status of death as an object of contemporary political analysis.

The scale and sophistication of technological mediation in contemporary necro-politics indicates that death as a concept remains caught in a contradiction. It is central to political theory and practice in terms of the new killing techniques within a fast-expanding technological context which increases human vulnerability. Death is also, however, under-examined as a term in critical theory and as established practice in socio-political governance and international relations. Death as a concept remains unitary and un-differentiated, while the repertoire of political thought around Life and bio-power proliferates and diversifies.

Fortunately, new posthuman theory is filling this vacuum and making important contributions. Patrick Hanafin (2010), for instance, suggests that renewed interest in necro-politics, coupled with a transversal vision of posthuman subjectivity, may help us provide a political and ethical counter-narrative to 'the imposed bounded subject of liberal legalism' (2010: 133). For Hanafin, this involves a move from the traditional location of mortality as the defining, quasi-metaphysical horizon of being. The majoritarian masculine legal social contract is built on the desire to survive. This is not a politics of empowerment, but one of entrapment in an imagined natural order that in our system translates into a bio-political regime of discipline and control of bodies. What this means is that we are recognized as full citizens only through the position of victims, loss and injury and the forms of reparation that come with it. Posthuman necro-political political and legal theory raises the question of what political theory might look like if it were not based on the negative instances of wound and loss.

Hanafin proposes to take the necro-political dimension seriously by shifting away from thinking of legal subjectivity as death-bound to thinking about singularities without identity who relate intimately to one another and the environment in which they are located. This points towards a posthuman critical politics of rights. We see here how another fundamental binary of Western philosophical thinking gets uncoupled: that of a political life qualified by death, as opposed to a political and legal philosophy which valorizes our mortal condition and creates a politics of survival. This is a post-identitarian position that encourages us, following Virginia Woolf, to adopt a mode of thinking 'as if already gone', that is to say, to think with and not against death. The emphasis on the death–life continuum may, according to Hanafin, constitute the ultimate threat to a legal system built on the confining horizon of the metaphysics of mortality.

William Connolly's 'politics of becoming' (1999) argues a similar case: against necro-political destruction, we need to develop an 'ethos of engagement' with existing social and political givens – including the horrors of our times – in order to bring about counter-effects, that is to say unexpected consequences and transformations. Critical theory needs to engage with the present, becoming 'worthy of the times', while resisting the violence, horror and injustices of the times (Braidotti, 2008). Affirmative ethics is based on the praxis of constructing positivity, thus propelling new social conditions and relations into being, out of injury and pain. It actively constructs energy by transforming the negative charge of these experiences, even in intimate relationships where the dialectics of domination is at work (Benjamin, 1988). For Deleuze and Guattari, the time-line for this political activity is that of *Aion*, the continuous tense of becoming, which is different from working within or against the *Chronos* of the hegemonic political order. We need to actively and collectively work towards a refusal of horror and violence – the inhuman aspects of our present – and to turn it into the construction of affirmative alternatives. Such necro-political thought aims to bring affirmation to bear on undoing existing arrangements so as to actualize productive alternatives. In the rest of this chapter, I will attempt to think the life–death continuum within this on-going engagement with the political accountability of posthuman subjectivity.

Posthuman Theory on Death

One of the obvious preliminary conclusions we can draw from all the above is that we need to think more rigorously about ways of dying, in the posthuman context of necro-politics on the one hand and the new forensic social sensibility on the other. How would a vitalist and materialist understanding of death work? Death is not a human prerogative, especially in the era of 'disappearing' nature. Having reached the antipodes of the rationalist idea of human stewardship of nature, the environmental question is how to prevent species extinction. This is a bio-political issue: which species are allowed to survive and which to die? And what are the criteria that would allow us to decide? Posthuman theory stresses the point that in order to develop adequate criteria, we need an alternative vision of subjectivity to support this effort and make it operational.

We should start by itemizing the different socially distributed and organized ways of dying: violence, diseases, poverty; accidents; wars and catastrophes. The persistence of political violence and notions of 'just wars' is part of this conversation, as is the analysis of the ways in which critical philosophers have dealt with death (Critchley, 2008). Then we may proceed by looking at internally produced and self-run ways of dying: suicide, burn-out, depression and other psychosomatic pathologies. What does posthuman death theory look like? It provides a fuller understanding of how bio-politics actually works in the contemporary context marked by the 'new' wars and by remote-controlled techno-thanatological weaponry. A necro-political approach produces a more accurate cartography of how contemporary embodied subjects are interacting and inter-killing. In turn, this approach offers new analytical tools for an ethics that respects both the horror and the complexity of our times and attempts to deal with them affirmatively. Quite an agenda, which I regret that I cannot do full justice to here.

One's view on death depends on one's assumptions about Life. In my vitalist materialist view, Life is cosmic energy, simultaneously empty chaos and absolute speed or movement. It is impersonal and inhuman in the monstrous, animal sense of radical alterity: *zoe* in all its powers. This does not mean that *zoe*, or life as absolute vitality, is not above negativity, because it can hurt. *Zoe* is always too much for the specific slab of enfleshed existence that constitutes single subjects. The human is a step down for pure intensity, or the force of the virtual. It is a constant challenge for us to rise to the occasion, to be 'worthy of our times', while resisting them, and thus to practise *amor fati* affirmatively. It is quite demanding to catch the wave of life's intensities in a secular manner and ride on it, exposing the boundaries or limits as we transgress them. No wonder that most of us, as George Eliot astutely observed, turn our back on that roar of cosmic energy. We often crack in the process of facing life and just cannot take it anymore. Death is the ultimate transposition, though it is not final, as *zoe* carries on, relentlessly.

Death is the inhuman conceptual excess: the unrepresentable, the unthinkable, and the unproductive black hole that we all fear. Yet, death is also a creative synthesis of flows, energies and perpetual becoming. Gilles Deleuze (1983, 1990b, 1995) suggests that to make sense of death, we need an unconventional approach that rests on a preliminary and fundamental distinction between personal and impersonal death. The former is linked to the suppression of the individualized ego. The latter is beyond the ego: a death that is always ahead of me and marks the extreme threshold of my powers to become. In other words, in a posthuman perspective, the emphasis on the impersonality of life is echoed by an analogous reflection on death. Because humans are mortal, death, or the transience of life, is written at our core: it is the event that structures our time-lines and frames our time-zones, not as a limit, but as a porous threshold. In so far as it is ever-present in our psychic and somatic landscapes, as the event that has always already happened (Blanchot, 2000), death as a constitutive event is behind us; it has already taken place as a virtual potential that constructs everything we are. The full blast of the awareness of the transitory nature of all that lives is the defining moment in our existence. It structures our becoming-subjects, our capacity and powers of relation and the process of acquiring ethical awareness. Being mortal, we all are 'have beens': the spectacle of our death is written obliquely into the script of our temporality, not as a barrier, but as a condition of possibility.

This means that what we all fear the most, our being dead, the source of anguish, terror and fear, does not lie ahead but is already behind us; it has been. This death that pertains to a past that is forever present is not individual but impersonal; it is the precondition of our existence, of the future. This proximity to death is a close and intimate friendship that calls for endurance, in the double sense of temporal duration or continuity and spatial suffering or sustainability. Making friends with the impersonal necessity of death is an ethical way of installing oneself in life as a transient, slightly wounded visitor. We build our house on the crack, so to speak. We live to recover from the shocking awareness that this game is over even before it started. The proximity to death suspends life, not into transcendence, but rather into the radical immanence of 'just a life', here and now, for as long as we can and as much as we can take.

This does not mean, however, that Life unfolds on the horizon of death. As I argued before, this classical notion is central to the metaphysics of finitude that, especially in the Heideggerian tradition sacralizes death as the defining feature of human consciousness. I want to stress instead the productive differential nature of *zoe*, which means the productive aspect of the life–death continuum. It does not deny the reality of horrors, but rather to re-work it so as to assert the vital powers of healing and compassion. This is the core of posthuman affirmative ethics in a contemporary Spinozist mode (Braidotti, 2011b). An illuminating example is provided by Edouard Glissant (1997), whose work on colonialism and literature re-frames the horrors of modernity in an affirmative manner, starting from the world-historical experience of slavery. Glissant applies nomadic thought to the critique of dominant, nation-bound, mostly Eurocentric, 'mother-tongues'. Calling for hybridized poly-lingualism and creolization on a global scale is an affirmative answer to the coercive mono-culturalism imposed by the colonial and imperial powers. The ethics of productive affirmation is a different way of handling the issue of how to deal with pain and traumas and to operate in situations which are extreme, while working to bring out the generative force of *zoe* – life beyond the ego-bound human.

In this perspective, death is not the teleological destination of life, a sort of ontological magnet that propels us forward: I repeat that death is behind us. Death is the event that has always already taken place at the level of consciousness. As an individual occurrence it will come in the form of the physical extinction of the body, but as event, in the sense of the awareness of finitude, of the interrupted flow of my being-there, death has already taken place. We are all synchronized with death – death is the same thing as the time of our living, in so far as we all live on borrowed time. The time of death as event is the impersonal continuous present of *Aion*, perpetual becoming, not only the linear and individualized *Chronos*. The temporality of death is time itself, by which I mean the totality of time.

Some of these ideas may seem counter-intuitive to the secular critical theorists. I want to insist, however, on the necessity of re-thinking posthuman life beyond the old boundaries of death. We may do well to remember here the importance of the tactic of de-familiarization, which I outlined in the previous chapter. To approach death differently, we may want to start by introducing some critical distance from the allegedly self-evident value attributed to 'Life' in our culture. I live in a world where some people kill in the name of a sacralized 'Right to life'. I would like to refer to a more lucid tradition of thought that does not start from the assumption of the inherent, self-evident and intrinsic worth of 'life' and stresses instead the traumatic elements of this same life in their often unnoticed familiarity. 'Life', in other words, is an acquired taste, an addiction like any other, an open-ended project. One has to work at it. Life is passing and we do not own it; we just inhabit it, not unlike a time-share location.

Death of a Subject

My vitalist notion of death is that it is the inhuman within us, which frees us into life. Each of us is always already a 'has been', as we are mortal beings. Desire as the ontological drive to become (*potentia*) seduces us into going on living. If sustained long enough, life becomes a habit. If the habit becomes self-fulfilling, life becomes addictive, which is the opposite of necessary or self-evident. Living 'just a life' there-fore is a project, not a given, because there is nothing natural or automatic about it. One has to 'jump-start' into life regu-larly, by renewing the electro-magnetic charge of desire, though one often ends up going through the day on automatic pilot. Life is at best compelling, but it is not compulsive. Beyond pleasure and pain, life is a process of becoming, of stretching the boundaries of endurance.

Where does this vital notion of death leave critical theory? The experiment of de-familiarization consists in trying to think to infinity, against the horror of the void, in the wilder-ness of non-human mental landscapes, with the shadow of death dangling in front of our eyes. Thought then becomes a gesture of affirmation and hope for sustainability and endur-ance, of immanent relations and time-bound consistency. Moving beyond the paralysing effects of suspicion and pain, working across them is the key to ethics. Posthuman critical thought does not aim at mastery, but at the transformation of negative into positive passions.

Life is desire which essentially aims at expressing itself and consequently runs on entropic energy: it reaches its aim and then dissolves, like salmon swimming upstream to procreate and then die. The wish to die can consequently be seen as the counterpart and as another expression of the desire to live intensely. The corollary is more cheerful: not only is there no dialectical tension between Eros and Thanatos, but these two entities are really just one life-force that aims to reach its own fulfilment. Posthuman vital materialism displaces the bound-aries between living and dying. 'Life', or *zoe*, aims essentially at self-perpetuation and then, after it has achieved its aim, at dissolution. It can be argued, therefore, that Life as *zoe* also encompasses what we call 'death'. As a result, what we humans most deeply aspire to is not so much to disappear, but rather to do so in the space of our own life and in our own way (Phillips, 1999). It is as if each of us wishes to die in our own fashion. Our innermost desire is for a self-fashioned, a self-styled death. We thus pursue what we are ultimately trying to avoid and become virtual existential suicides, not from nihilism, but because it is our nature to die and our deepest desire to self-fashion our own death.

Of course it is a paradox; it is the paradox of the inhuman as analysed by Lyotard: something in the structure of the human that simply resists belonging to common humanity and stretches beyond. The ontological inhuman has often been rendered as the sacred, but for a secular materialist like myself this is not convincing. What we do stretch out towards is endless cosmic energy, which is as fierce as it is self-organizing. The awareness of the 'beyond' has to do with death as the experience that has always already happened, not as transcendental what-have-you. While at the conscious level all of us struggle for survival, at some deeper level of our unconscious structures all we long for is to lie silently and let time wash over us in the stillness of non-life. Self-styling one's death is an act of affirmation because it means cultivating an approach, a 'style' of life that progressively and continuously fixes the modalities and the stage for the final act, leaving nothing un-attended. Pursuing a sort of seduction into immortality, the ethical life is life as virtual suicide. Life as virtual suicide is life as constant creation. Life lived so as to break the cycles of inert repetitions that usher in banality. Lest we delude ourselves with narcissistic pretences, we need to cultivate endurance, immortality within time, that is to say death in life.

It bears repeating that the generative capacity of this life–death continuum cannot be bound or confined to the single, human individual. It rather transversally trespasses all boundaries in the pursuit of its aim, which is self-perpetuation as the expression of its potency. It connects us trans-individually, trans-generationally and eco-philosophically. Just as the life in me is not mine or even individual in the narrow, appropriative sense espoused by liberal individualism, so the death in me is not mine, except in a very circumscribed sense of the term. In both cases, all 'I' can hope for is to craft both my life and my death in a mode, at a speed and fashion which can sustain all the intensity 'I' is capable of. 'I' can self-style this gesture auto-poietically, thus expressing its essence as the constitutive desire to endure: I call it *potentia*.

Becoming-imperceptible

What we humans truly yearn for is to disappear by merging into this generative flow of becoming, the precondition for which is the loss, disappearance and disruption of the atomized, individual self. The ideal would be to take only memories and to leave behind only footsteps. What we most truly desire is to surrender the self, preferably in the agony of ecstasy, thus choosing our own way of disappearing, our way of dying to and as our self. This can be described also as the moment of ascetic dissolution of the subject; the moment of its merging with the web of non-human forces that frame him/her, the cosmos as a whole. We may call it death, but in a monistic ontology of vitalist materialism, it has rather to do with radical immanence. That is to say the grounded totality of the moment when we coincide completely with our body in becoming at last what we will have been all along: a virtual corpse.

Death, the inhuman within, marks the becoming-imperceptible of the subject as the furthest frontier of the processes of intensive transformation or becoming. This is no transcendence, but radical empirical immanence, that is to say a reversal of all that lives into the roar of the 'chaosmic' echoing chamber of becoming. It marks the generative force of *zoe*, the great animal-machine of the universe, beyond personal individual death. Remember that this is a secular discourse, generated by a critical theory that wants to think to the end the nature–culture continuum within a monistic ontology that considers all matter as intelligent and self-organizing. Recognizing this continuum makes us able to be worthy of all that happens to us: *amor fati* being the pragmatic acknowledgment that the posthuman subject is the expression of successive waves of becoming, fuelled by *zoe* as the ontological motor. It is neither human nor divine, but relentless material and vowed to multi-directional and cross-species relationality. Life does go on, relentlessly non-human in the vital force that animates it. Becoming-imperceptible marks the point of evacuation or evanescence of the bounded selves and their merger into the milieu, the middle grounds, the radical immanence of the earth itself and its cosmic resonance. Becoming-imperceptible is the event for which there is no representation, because it rests on the disappearance of the individuated self. Writing as if already gone, or thinking beyond the bounded self, is the ultimate gesture of de-familiarization. This process actualizes virtual possibilities in the present, in a time sequence that is somewhere between the 'no longer' and the 'not yet', mixing past, present and future into the critical mass of an event. The vital energy that propels the transmutation of values into affirmation is the *potentia* of life as perpetual becoming that expresses itself through the chaotic and generative void of positivity. The event enacts a seduction into Life that breaks from the spectral economy of negativity and involves making friends with impersonal death.

Posthuman death theory as a vital continuum could not be further removed from the notion of death as the inanimate and indifferent state of matter, the entropic state to which the body is supposed to 'return'. It rather spells desire as plenitude and over-flowing, not as lack. Death is the becoming-imperceptible of the posthuman subject and as such it is part of the cycles of becoming, yet another form of inter-connectedness, a vital relationship that links one with other, multiple forces. The impersonal is life and death as *bios/zoe* in us – the ultimate outside as the frontier of the incorporeal: becoming-imperceptible.

The paradox of affirming life as *potentia*, energy, even in and through the suppression of the specific slice of life that 'I' inhabit is a way of pushing both post-humanism and post-anthropocentrism to the point of implosion. It dissolves death into ever-shifting processual changes, and thus disintegrates the ego, with its capital of narcissism, paranoia and negativity. Death as process from the specific and highly restricted viewpoint of the ego is of no significance whatsoever. The kind of 'self' that is 'styled' in and through such a process is not-One, yet nor is it an anonymous multiplicity. The self is differential and constituted through embedded and embodied sets of interrelations. The inner coherence of this posthuman subject is held together by the immanence of his/her expressions, acts and interactions with others and by the powers of remembrance, or continuity in time. I refer to this process in terms of sustainability, so as to stress the idea of endurance which it entails. Sustainability does assume faith in a future, and also a sense of responsibility for 'passing on' to future generations a world that is liveable and worth living in. A present that endures is a sustainable model of the future. Against this self-glorifying image of a pretentious and egotistical, narcissistic and paranoid consciousness, posthuman critical theory unleashes the multiple dynamic forces of *zoe* that do not coincide with the human, let alone with consciousness. These non-essentialistic brands of vitalism frame the posthuman subject.

My vitalist brand of materialism could not be further removed from the Christian affirmation of Life or the transcendental delegation of the meaning and value system to categories higher than the embodied self. Quite the contrary, it is the intelligence of radically immanent flesh that states with every single breath that the life in you is not marked by any master signifier and it most certainly does not bear your name. The awareness of the absolute difference between intensive or incorporeal affects and the specific affected bodies that one happens to be is crucial to affirmative posthuman ethics. Death is the unsustainable, but it is also virtual in that it has the generative capacity to engender the actual. Consequently, death is but an obvious manifestation of principles that are active in every aspect of life, namely the impersonal power of *potentia*. The posthuman subject rests on the affirmation of this kind of multiplicity and the relational connection with an 'outside' that is cosmic and infinite.

Conclusion: On Posthuman Ethics

The posthuman predicament entails specific forms of inhuman(e) practices that call for new frames of analysis and new normative values. In this chapter, I have addressed the necro-political aspects on the posthuman condition through several inter-related issues. Firstly, I discussed the destructive aspects of the new forms of reactive or negative pan-humanity engendered by shared global risk societies and the general subsumption of all that lives to a political economy of capitalization of the informational capital of Life itself. Secondly, I focused on the pervasive forms of technological mediation and the extent to which global communication networks and bio-genetic intervention have re-structured the nature–culture relation into a complex continuum that is as destructive as it can be generative. Cases in point are the new wars, including humanitarian interventions and automated weaponry capable of human-free decision making. I have argued for the need to re-cast the life–death distinction in terms of a vital continuum based on internal differentiations. I presented it as the double overturning firstly of individualism, in favour of complex singularities, and secondly of anthropocentrism, in favour of multiplicities of non-human flows and assemblages. Throughout all these cases I stressed the inhumanity and the violence of our times and called for affirmative practices to counteract the necro-political economy we are caught in.

Let me summarize a number of features of this posthuman, necro-political turn. The first point is that the political and legal subject of this regime of life–death governmentality is a post-anthropocentric eco-sophical entity. This *zoe*-driven subject is marked by the interdependence with its environment through a structure of mutual flows and data transfer that is best configured as complex and intensive inter-connectedness.

Secondly, this environmentally bound subject is a finite collective entity, moving beyond the parameters of classical Humanism and anthropocentrism. The human organism is an in-between that is plugged into and connected to a variety of possible sources and forces. As such it is useful to define it as a machine, which does not mean an appliance or anything with a specifically utilitarian aim, but rather something that is simultaneously more abstract and more materially embedded. The minimalist definition of a body-machine is an embodied affective and intelligent entity that captures processes and transforms energies and forces. Being environmentally bound and territorially based, an embodied entity feeds upon, incorporates and transforms its (natural, social, human or technological) environment constantly. Being embodied in this high-tech ecological manner entails full immersion in fields of constant flows and transformations. Not all of them are positive, of course, because the inhuman aspects entail multiple forms of vulnerability, although in such a dynamic system they cannot be known or judged *a priori*. Thus we need to experiment with new practices that allow for a multiplicity of possible instances – actualizations and counter-actualizations – of the different lines of becoming, as I outlined in the previous chapter.

Thirdly, such a subject of *zoe*-power raises questions of ethical and political urgency. Given the acceleration of processes of change, how can we tell the difference among the different flows of changes and transformations? Transformative lines of flight or becoming need to be accounted for and mapped out as a collective assemblage of possible other paths of becoming. No monolithic or static model can provide an adequate answer: we need more pragmatic open-endedness and a diversification of possible strategies. The starting point is the relentless generative but also destructive force of *zoe* and the specific brand of trans-species egalitarianism which they establish as the grounds for posthuman ethics. It is a matter of forces as well as of ethology.

Fourthly, the specific temporality of the posthuman subject needs to be re-thought beyond the metaphysics of mortality. The subject is an evolutionary engine, endowed with her or his own embodied temporality, both in the sense of the specific timing of the genetic code and the more genealogical time of individualized memories. If the embodied subject of bio-power is a complex molecular organism, a bio-chemical factory of steady and jumping genes, an evolutionary entity endowed with its own navigational tools and an in-built temporality, then we need a form of ethical values and political agency that reflects this high degree of temporal complexity. My point is that by adopting a different vision of the subject and with it a new notion of the nature–culture interaction, critical theory may be able to move beyond modernist and rather reductive conceptions of the inhuman.

Fifthly, and last, this ethical approach cannot be dissociated from considerations of power. The *zoe*-centred vision of the technologically mediated subject of post-modernity or advanced capitalism is fraught with internal contradictions.

Accounting for them is the cartographic task of critical theory and an integral part of this project is to account for the implications they entail for the historically situated vision of the subject (Braidotti, 2002). The *zoe*-centred egalitarianism that is potentially conveyed by the current technological transformations has dire consequences for the humanistic vision of the subject. The potency of *zoe*, in other words, displaces the exploitative and necro-political gravitational pull of advanced capitalism. Both liberal individualism and classical humanism are disrupted at their very foundations by the social and symbolic transformations induced by our historical condition. Far from being merely a crisis of values, this situation confronts us with a formidable set of new opportunities. They converge, through different paths, upon a re-composition of our shared understanding of the human as a species. One of these is the negative bond of pan-human vulnerability I analysed in the previous chapter: the sense that 'we' are all in *this* mess together, all other differences notwithstanding. Another approach, much closer to my heart, is to start from those differences of location and, by accounting for them in terms of power, as both restrictive and productive (*potestas* and *potentia*), to experiment with different modes of posthuman subjectivity. I have argued that, as a possible response to this challenge, we should consider the posthumanistic brand of post-anthropocentric vitalism and have defined posthuman theory accordingly.

This conviction is supported by my historical and geopolitical location, which makes me aware of the schizoid coincidence of diametrically opposed social effects: overconsumption and depletion of the world's reserves of biodiversity in seeds, grains, plants and water supplies seem able to co-exist in a political economy of exploitation and celebration of Life itself. Similarly, the epidemic of anorexia/bulimia on the one hand, and poverty-induced starvation on the other, express the spasmodic waves of expansion and shrinking of the body-weight in the population of the opulent classes of the world and the thinning out and wilful destruction of many other peoples, by active intervention or sheer neglect.

The bio-political and the necro-political combine to relocate embodied subjectivity in a posthuman continuum that calls for new ethical coding. Thus, I also recognize that the status of embodied humans who become 'collateral damage' in high-tech wars that hit them from the sky with 'intelligent bombs' dropped by computer-driven drones is closer to that of the animals at Sarajevo zoo, which were forcefully freed as a result of NATO bombing and roamed the streets – terrorized and terrifying the humans till they succumbed to friendly fire – than it is to the Geneva Convention definition of 'casualties of war'. I want to confront the necro-political governmentality of bio-genetic capitalism and think from within the awareness that the market prices of exotic birds and quasi-extinct animals are comparable, often to the advantaged of the plumed species, to that of the disposable bodies of women, children and others in the global sex trade and industry. Conrad's terrifying dictum 'Exterminate the brutes!' knows no species boundaries today. This is the inhuman face of my location, the posthuman here and now in which I situate posthuman critical theory as the active quest for affirmative alternatives. It is also the framework within which I want to propose a creative alternative, through secular, non-essentialist, vital materialism and an affirmative theory of posthuman death as the generative inhuman within the subject, which makes us all too human.

Chapter 4
Posthuman Humanities: Life beyond Theory

How could the Humanities fail to be affected by the posthuman condition? The dislocations of the discursive boundaries and categorical differences triggered respectively by the explosion of humanism and the implosion of anthropocentrism causes an internal fracture within the Humanities that cannot be mended just by goodwill. Let us assess the damage on the basis of the analyses I provided in the three previous chapters.

In the first chapter I discussed the fallout of post-humanism. The idea of the 'Human' implied in the Humanities, that is to say the implicit assumptions about what constitutes the basic unit of reference for the knowing subject, is the Vitruvian model. It is the image of Man as a rational animal endowed with language. Anti-humanists over the last thirty years questioned both the self-representation and the image of thought implied in the Humanist definition of the Human, especially the ideas of transcendental reason and the notion that the subject coincides with rational consciousness. This flattering self-image of 'Man' is as problematic as it is partial in that it promotes a self-centred attitude. Furthermore, by organizing differences on a hierarchical scale of decreasing worth, this humanist subject defined himself as much by what he excluded from, as by what he included in, his self-representation, an approach which often justified a violent and belligerent relationship to the sexualized, racialized and naturalized 'others' that occupied the slot of devalued difference. Furthermore, claims to universalism were critiqued as being exclusive, androcentric and Eurocentric. They support masculinist, racist or racial supremacist ideologies that turn cultural specificity into a fake universal and normality into a normative injunction. This image of thought perverts the practice of the Humanities and in particular theory into an exercise of hierarchical exclusion and cultural hegemony.

Over the last thirty years, new critical epistemologies have offered alternative definitions of the 'human' by inventing interdisciplinary areas which call themselves 'studies', like: gender, feminism, ethnicity, cultural studies, post-colonial, media and new media and Human rights studies (Bart et al., 2003). Throughout this book I have foregrounded feminist theory as a major point of theoretical and methodological reference. According to James Chandler (2004) this proliferation of counter-discourses creates a condition of 'critical disciplinarity' which is a symptom of the posthuman predicament. Chandler argues that since Foucault's pertinent diagnosis of the death of 'Man', the traditional organization of the university in departmental structures has been challenged by the growth of these new discursive areas. This proliferation of discourses is both a threat and an opportunity in that it requires methodological innovations, such as a critical genealogical approach that by-passes the mere rhetoric of the crisis.

The fallout of post-anthropocentrism, which I outlined in chapter 2, sets a different agenda for the Humanities, and not only in terms of research priorities. The image of thought implied in the post-anthropocentric definition of the Human goes much further in the deconstruction of the subject, because it stresses radical relationality, that is to say non-unitary identities and multiple allegiances. As this shift occurs in a globalized and conflict-ridden world, it opens up new challenges in terms of both post-secular and post-nationalist perspectives, including a new European dimension marked by multi-lingualism and cultural diversity.[1] What is the place of the Humanities as a scientific enterprise in this globalized

[1] This aspect of global diversity is also known as 'vernacular cosmopolitanism' (Bhabha, 1996b; Nava, 2002; Gunew, 2004; Werbner, 2006).

network culture (Terranova, 2004) that no longer upholds the unity of space and time as its governing principle? In the era of citizens' science[2] and citizens' journalism, what can be the role of academic research institutions?

The displacement of anthropocentrism and the scrambling of species hierarchy leaves the Human un-moored and un-supported, which deprives the field of the Humanities of much-needed epistemological foundations. The question of the future of the Humanities, the issue of their renewal and the recurrent threat of death of the disciplines, is aggravated by one central factor: the new 'human–non-human linkages, among them complex interfaces involving machinic assemblages of biological "wetware" and non-biological "hardware"' (Bono et al., 2008: 3). We saw in chapter 2 that the dualistic distinction nature–culture has collapsed and is replaced by complex systems of data-feedback, interaction and communication transfer. This places the issue of the relationship between the two cultures at the centre of the agenda again. Against the prophets of doom, I want to argue that technologically mediated post-anthropocentrism can enlist the resources of bio-genetic codes, as well as telecommunication, new media and information technologies, to the task of renewing the Humanities. Posthuman subjectivity reshapes the identity of humanistic practices, by stressing heteronomy and multi-faceted relationality, instead of autonomy and self-referential disciplinary purity.

The profoundly anthropocentric core of the Humanities is displaced by this complex configuration of knowledge dominated by science studies and technological information, as I argued in chapters 2 and 3. Far from being a terminal crisis, however, this challenge opens up new global, eco-sophical dimensions. This posthuman enthusiasm on my part, which is not exactly devoid of impatient anticipation, stems from my anti-humanist and feminist background. It produces an energizing but nonetheless critical relationship to the contemporary field of the classical Humanities. It would be paradoxical to say the least, in fact, if the critical thinkers who entered the academic institutions in the aftermath of the 1970s cultural revolution, with the explicit aim of changing them from within, ended up having to simply restore those

[2] http://www.citizensciencealliance.org/

same disciplines and rescue them from institutional decline. As I pointed out in the previous chapters, things are never clear-cut when it comes to developing a consistent posthuman stance, and linear thinking may not be the best way to go about it. Sam Whimster analyses the dilemma lucidly (2006: 174):

> The Humanities, which are a celebration and expressive elucidation of the human condition as non-reducible to any materialist base, have been in retreat since the late 19th century with the emergence of Darwinism as the valid scientific account of the origin of all species of life. So a science of the human would seem either to have the capacity to be inhuman or, alternatively, to be humanistic but hardly scientific.

Whimster also reminds us that French philosophy had addressed the issue of post-anthropocentric Humanities and the status of the human in the strikingly original 1748 work by the philosopher Julien La Mettrie (1996). He was a materialist humanist in the grand tradition of French enlightened materialism, and constitutes a significant early modern precedent from the ancient archives of the Humanities. La Mettrie's theory of the inherently 'mechanical' or self-organizing structure of the human is path-breaking and highly relevant for our own situation.

Today, environmental, evolutionary, cognitive, bio-genetic and digital trans-disciplinary discursive fronts are emerging around the edges of the classical Humanities and across the disciplines. They rest on post-anthropocentric premises and technologically mediated emphasis on Life as a *zoe*-centred system of species egalitarianism (Braidotti, 2006), which are very promising for new research in the field. Probably the most significant example of the excellent health enjoyed by the post-anthropocentric Humanities is the recent explosion of scholarship in the fields of 'Animal Studies' and of 'Eco-criticism'. The fast-changing field of disability studies is almost emblematic of the posthuman predicament. Ever mindful that we do not yet know what a body can do, disability studies combine the critique of normative bodily models with the advocacy of new, creative models of embodiment (Braidotti and Groets, 2012). These areas are so rich and fast-growing that it is impossible to even attempt to summarize them.[3] Where do these developments leave the scholarship in the Humanities? Or rather: what's the human got to do with this shifting horizon? And what are the implications for the future of the Humanities today? A contemporary neo-vitalist thinker like Elizabeth Grosz pursues this line of research further, through a deconstructivist reappraisal of Charles Darwin. Grosz (2011) argues that evolutionary theory deflated humanist pretensions and was a precursor of the crisis of human 'exceptionalism', which has by now become manifest. Grosz calls accordingly for the development of 'inhuman Humanities', which consist in species-equality, an emphasis on genetically inscribed sexual difference, the primacy of sexual selection and a non-teleological approach to the evolution of the human alongside all other species. Although I find Grosz's emphasis on the genetic basis of sexual differentiation too rigid for my fluid nomadic vision of the subject, I agree on one important point. As a vitalist and self-organizing notion of 'matter' comes to the fore, the Humanities need to mutate and become posthuman, or to accept suffering's increasing irrelevance.

As if these post-anthropocentric challenges were not enough, last but not least comes the fallout of the inhuman(e) aspects of our historical condition which I discussed in chapter 3. According to the tenets of classical Humanism, the Humanities were defined by their capacity to humanize our social behaviour, values and civic interaction. This implies an implicit moral mission and concern for the well-being of academics, students and citizens alike. What happens to this claim in an era of posthuman and post-anthropocentric shifts of mass migration, wars on terror, robotized weapons and drones in technologically mediated conflicts?

[3] A companion to Animal Studies has just been published (Gross and Vallely, 2012), whereas a complete Eco-criticism reader has been available for a while (Glotfelty and Fromm, 1996). *The Journal of Ecocriticism* is quite established, while a recent issue of the prestigious *PMLA* papers (2009) was dedicated to the question of the animal. For an excellent historical analysis, see Joanna Bourke (2011). For the younger generation of scholars (Rossini and Tyler, 2009), the animal is the posthuman question *par excellence*. The field of disability studies is again too vast to be summarized adequately, with an established international Society for Disability Studies, which publishes a Quarterly, and a complete reader (Lenard, 1997).

A clear institutional response to the inhuman(e) structures of our times is the establishment and the proliferation of interdisciplinary areas of study that deal with the disasters of modern and contemporary history. Gender, feminist and postcolonial studies are the prototypes of these new experimental areas which have provided so much in terms of instruments as well as innovative concepts. More specifically, new multi-disciplinary research areas had to be set up to come to terms with the horrors of our times: from Holocaust studies to research on slavery and colonialism, through to work on the traumatic memories of multiple ideology-driven genocides. J.-F. Lyotard's idea of the 'differend' (1983) – a crime or moral lapse for which there cannot be adequate form of justice, let alone of retribution or compensation – is relevant to deal with the scale of the catastrophes of our era. The 'differend' is the ethical response to the tragedy of the intolerable, or the irreconcilable, but, given that much of this horror is unspeakable, how far can the Humanities delve into it? Again, radical epistemologies such as women's, gender, queer and feminist studies on the one hand, and post-colonial and race studies on the other, have played an innovative role in this regard. They provide themes and methods to handle the epistemic blast of such horrors and work through their consequence for the role of critical theory. They also fulfil a healing function in relation to the legacy of pain and hurt which they entail.

The proliferation of new discursive fields continues after the end of the Cold War, when we get the emergence of Centres for Conflict Studies and Peace Research; Humanitarian management; Human Rights-oriented medicine; trauma and reconciliation studies; Death Studies; and the list is still growing. These are institutional structures that combine pastoral care with a therapeutic function to deal with the inhumane and painful aspects of historical horrors. They perpetuate and update the transformative impact of the Humanities in an inhumane context, but they do so by exploding the boundaries of classical Humanities disciplines.

As a result of these multiple domino effects, the question of what happens to the Humanities, when their implicit assumptions about the Human and the process of humanization can no longer be taken for granted, is high on the social and academic agendas. Alongside the criticism voiced by posthuman critical thinkers, different strands of neo-humanism are at work within the contemporary Humanities, as we have examined in the previous chapters. Taking, for instance, the case of feminist and race theories as the main point of reference, the enduring legacy of Simone de Beauvoir's socialist Humanism plays a central role in bringing progressive humanism into the third millennium. Other feminist humanists have also proposed robust alternatives to the crisis of values – such as the neo-Kantian model of Seyla Benhabib (2002), adapted from Habermas' philosophy, and her re-appraisal of Hannah Arendt (1996). Residual forms of neo-humanism, already informed by non-Western assumptions, cultural traditions and values, come in through postcolonial theory, as we saw in chapter 1 (Hill Collins, 1991; Said, 2004). Contemporary science studies adopt compensatory Humanism both to the study of other species (de Waal 1996, 2006, 2009) and to the political analysis of environmental issues (Shiva, 1997).

The most vocal campaigner for a liberal humanist vision of the contemporary Humanities is Martha Nussbaum, who, as we saw in chapter 1, firmly rejects any critique or deconstruction of the field and turns classical humanism into a utopian project still to come (1999, 2006, 2010). *Not for Profit*, Nussbaum's impassioned defence of the classical Humanities, stands out in this context as a noble but also rather unrealistic plea for a *status quo ante*. The vision of the Humanities faculty as a haven of liberal education, based on the Kantian notion of the autonomy of rational judgement and the specific ethical and aesthetic criteria that go with it, is outdated to say the least. Moreover, because of its privately funded structure, it does not even apply to the state education model of the European Union. On the practical level, it fails to see to what extent faculties of the Humanities are actually profit-oriented and make a lot of money for their universities, mostly through high student enrolments and intensive teaching.

Furthermore, on the historical front, the university ceased to conform to this philosophical vision, primarily in the United States but also in the rest of the world, in the Cold War period. Concerns linked to national security, geopolitical conflicts and international prestige brought the university closer to the military and hence to government control, as we saw in chapter 3. After the cultural upheavals of the

1960s, the university lost its hegemonic function both as the standard referent for national culture and as the holder of a monopoly over fundamental research, which moved to the private sector or to joint enterprises. By the time Nussbaum wrote her pamphlet in favour of liberal education, the university had already become incorporated into the market economy as an important, but by no means unique, corporate structure (Readings, 1996).

Therefore, instead of turning backwards to a nostalgic vision of the Humanities as the repository and the executors of universal transcendental reason and inherent moral goodness, I propose to move forward into multiple posthuman futures. We need an active effort to reinvent the academic field of the Humanities in a new global context and to develop an ethical framework worthy of our posthuman times. Affirmation, not nostalgia, is the road to pursue: not the idealization of philosophical meta-discourse, but the more pragmatic task of self-transformation through humble experimentation. Let me expand on this project in the next section.

Institutional Patterns of Dissonance

The crises of self-definition and public perception of the Humanities have been building up, since the end of the 1970s, into an institutional debate framed by explicit political factors. A recent American study assesses the situation lucidly:

> In addition to the decline of federal funding, a shrinking job market, and the new pressures of globalization, the most significant internal challenges confronting the Humanities have emerged from the hegemony of techno science, the impact of the 'new media' revolution, the rise of expert cultures on the one hand and, on the other, the unprecedented democratic proliferation of new interdisciplinary fields, such as gender, ethnic, disability, and African-American studies, as well as studies of non-European cultures, all of which put the traditional canon and the 'common' mission of the Humanities into question. (Bono et al., 2008: 2)

The institutional crisis therefore grew beyond issues of self-representation, to question the dominant paradigm of what constitutes scientific knowledge for the contemporary humanists, within a university structure that is in flux to say the least.

During the conflict-ridden 1990s, 'science wars' – also known as 'theory' or 'culture' wars – broke out on the American campus (Arthur and Shapiro, 1995). The core of the dispute was precisely the question of differences of paradigm between the Humanities and the natural sciences. French Continental philosophy and especially post-structuralism were targeted for particular hostility, under the general charge of 'political correctness' (Bérubé and Nelson, 1995). Militant anti-post-structuralist scientists, like Socal and Bricmont (1998), accused the Humanities of scientific inadequacy and downright ignorance, with disastrous effects for the morale of the field.

They have encouraged the by-now familiar reaction of dismissal of the Humanities through the intellectually lazy charge of moral and cognitive relativism. This was definitely the lowest point in the contemporary relationship between the two cultures.

And yet, against these vulgar simplifications, I maintain that it is important to acknowledge the productive contribution that post-structuralism and other critical theories have made to a renewal of the field of the Humanities. Foucault argued back in the 1970s that the Humanities as we have come to know them are structured by an implicit set of humanistic assumptions about 'Man', which are historically framed and contextually defined, in spite of their universalistic pretensions. As an 'empirical-transcendental doublet', Man is framed by the structures of Life, Labour and Language, as constant work-in-progress. This is no manifesto for relativism, but rather, as Rabinow (2003: 114) puts it, a call for 'a renewed problematization of *anthropos*'.

The changing conditions of our historicity are responsible for the decline of humanist 'Man'. To blame post-structuralism for breaking the bad news is to mistake the messenger for the message. In Foucault's (1970) ironical terms, this 'death' is not a form of extinction, but rather a historically specific mode of endurance on the part of 'ex-Man', after the anthropological exodus we examined in chapter 2. With her customary insight and wit, Gayatri Spivak (1987) denounced this 'death' as the weakened but nonetheless hegemonic *modus vivendi* of Eurocentric 'ex-Man'. The fact that critical theory has been coming to terms with endless deaths since then, ranging from the death of Man to that of the universal, of the nation state, the end of history and of ideology down to the disappearance of the printed book, bears testimony to the sagacity of Spivak's remark.

What has emerged as a potentially fatal flaw at the core of the Humanities is their structural anthropomorphism and perennial methodological nationalism (Beck, 2007), as my hostile colleague from the natural sciences pointed out in the fourth vignette I quoted in the introduction. The former translates into sustained hostility towards, or genuine incompatibility with, the culture, practice and institutional existence of science and technology. The latter challenges the Humanities' ability to cope with two of the distinctive features of our times: firstly, the scientific rise of 'Life' sciences and technologically mediated communication and knowledge transfer and, secondly, the need to take into account cultural diversity, notably between different geo-political areas but also within each one of them.

This criticism hurts, especially in view of the political context. The European Union at present is dominated by a right-wing agenda of neo-liberal economics on the one hand and xenophobic, populist social and cultural agendas on the other. As a result, the university as an institution, and the Humanities especially, are under attack. They are accused of being unproductive, narcissistic and old-fashioned in their approach and also of being out of touch with contemporary science and technology culture. The Humanities are therefore experiencing at first hand the crisis of 'Man' that has been theorized by the very radical philosophies like post-structuralism and by feminist and post-colonial interdisciplinary 'studies', which were often marginalized in the university institutional settings. The Humanities are often forced into a defensive position.

The issue of methodological nationalism is crucial in that it is in-built into the European Humanities self-representation. Edward Said reminded us that Humanism must shed its smug Eurocentrism and become an adventure in difference and alternative cultural traditions. This shift of perspectives requires a prior consciousness-raising on the part of Humanities scholars: 'Humanists must recognize with some alarm that the politics of identity and the nationalistically grounded system of education remain at the core of what most of us actually do, despite changed boundaries and objects of research' (Said, 2004: 55). We shall see later how the changed institutional structure of the contemporary university both rests upon the decline of the nation-state as the horizon for research and has the potential to contribute to a post-national perspective.

To return to the main point of my current argument: I fully endorse the call for an epistemological turn in the Humanities, so as to enable them to clarify their own knowledge production processes and consequently become better equipped to help clarify those of others. There are, however, some serious obstacles to this worthy project. The first is the lack of a tradition of epistemological self-reflexivity in the field. Linked to this is the deplorable persistence of an introverted culture of disciplinary insularity, unthinking Eurocentrism and anthropocentrism. Few of these institutional habits of the Humanities are really conducive to epistemological self-scrutiny. The field furthermore tends to be unable to resist the fatal attraction of the gravitational pull back to Humanism. Only a serious mutation can therefore help the Humanities to grow out of some of their entrenched bad habits. This requires a number of new perspectives, but, over and above these formal criteria, I think the Humanities need to find the inspirational courage to move beyond an exclusive concern for the human, be it humanistic or anthropocentric Man, and to embrace more planetary intellectual challenges.

The Humanities in the Twenty-first Century

I have argued in the previous section that the identity crisis of the contemporary Humanities is related to the high levels of technological mediation and the multicultural structure of the globalized world. This places the issue of the relationship between the two cultures – the Humanities and the Sciences – at the centre of the debate.

In a critical evaluation of the contemporary situation, Roberts and Mackenzie (2006) argue for a variety of robust and constructive institutional alternatives to the rather unresolved and often conflict-ridden relationship between the Humanities and the Sciences in the third millennium. One useful strategy aims at identifying points of compatibility between the two cultures and points out the role played by cultural representation, images and literary devices – all of them drawn from the 'subtle' (a term that I find vastly preferable to the derogatory 'soft') sciences – in the making of publicly acclaimed science. For instance, Gillian Beer's (1983) study of evolutionary narratives was positively path-breaking in this respect, and it was brilliantly pursued by studies of literary Darwinism (Carroll, 2004). Working within scientific culture, Evelyn Fox Keller (1995, 2002) is a pioneer of a different kind, producing a series of key texts to illustrate the complementary nature of humanistic knowledge and empirical science. The study of Barbara McClintock's life and work (Keller, 1983) is especially relevant in that it demonstrates the contiguity between cultural insights, spiritual resources and experimental science.

Another angle of approach to the question of the two cultures today focuses on the function of visualization in science. Stephen Jay Gould and Rosamond Purcell (2000) pioneered the dialogue between art and science by a sophisticated interplay of images and scientific information. This tradition was brought to new heights by the collaborative interdisciplinary work on picturing science and the arts by Carrie Jones and Peter Galison (1998). The field is large and well-endowed with talents that range from the political analysis of the scientific gaze (Keller, 1985; Jordanova, 1989; Braidotti, 1994) to the cultural history of photography and new media (Lury, 1998; Zylinska, 2009). Cross-over studies of the visual arts in relation to the physical and biological sciences are also crucial, as Barbara Stafford has brilliantly demonstrated (1999, 2007).

Anthropology has played an inspirational role in the study of science, starting from agenda-setting pioneers like Marilyn Strathern (1992), to Paul Rabinow's Foucauldian take on the 'Life' sciences (2003) and Rayna Rapp's combination of political and epistemic elements in the analysis of bio-technologies (2000). Henrietta Moore's analyses of subject formations span across the decades of post-structuralism to provide the most consistent insights about the entanglements of bodies, psychic landscapes, cultures and technologies (1994, 2007, 2011).

Feminist epistemology and social studies of sciences posit feminist theory as the missing link between science studies and epistemological political subjectivity, with intellectual pioneers like Donna Haraway (1988), Sandra Harding (1991, 1993), Isabelle Stengers (1987, 2000), Lisa Cartwright (2001), Mette Bryld and Nina Lykke (1999) and Annemarie Mol (2002). The social studies of science also proved very innovative, as evidenced by the work of Fraser et al. (2006), Maureen McNeil's shrewd political analyses of technology (2007) and Sarah Franklin's path-breaking work on Dolly the sheep (2007). Cultural studies of science have also been crucial, as in Jackie Stacey's brilliant analysis of the social and therapeutic cultures of cancer (1997) and of the cinematic life of genetics (2010).

The field of media studies has produced an astonishing amount of high-quality research on science and technology, as testified by the work of Jonathan Crary (2001) and the Zone Books series, which brought French theory and philosophy of science to large American audiences. Jose van Dijck's analyses of digital culture are path-breaking (2007); Smelik and Lykke (2008) opened up the field to a variety of original interventions on the interdisciplinary structures of contemporary science and its embedded cultural and social aspects.

We are confronted, therefore, by a sort of embarrassment of riches in new discourses about the current relationship between the Sciences and the Humanities, and I regret that I cannot pursue a more detailed analysis of the fields I have outlined.

For the moment, apart from praising the range and quality of these new areas of scholarship, I want to draw several conclusions. Firstly, that such a wealth of innovative interdisciplinary scholarship in and across the Humanities is an expression of the vitality of this field, not of its crisis. Secondly, that much of this new research is conducted in those experimental interdisciplinary areas of 'studies' that I have highlighted throughout this book as a major source of inspiration. Thirdly, that they are epistemologically grounded and consequently they enable the contemporary Humanities to clarify their own methods and mechanisms of knowledge production. However, the very interdisciplinary nature of these new research areas does not facilitate the task of providing a new synthesis of the field. This wealth of approaches therefore re-opens the old question of the generic identity of the Humanities as a discipline.

Commenting on this lack of unity in the discursive practice of the Humanities, Rabinow remarks (2003: 4):

> No consensus has ever been reached about principles, methods and modes of problem specification, or [. . .] principles of verification, or about forms of narration in the human sciences.

It is important to stress, however, that this dis-unity points to over-abundance, not lack. As a result: '*anthropos* is that being who suffers from too many *logoi*' (2003: 6). This is especially true in the context of contemporary scientific and technological advances, which have contributed to even more heterogeneous discourses. Their heterogeneity is such that they are incapable of providing an over-arching theory of technological self-representation. They consequently push even further the disaggregation of the discursive unity of *anthropos*, which has proved very creative in adapting to this scientific exuberance. Perhaps the Humanities have a different relationship to complexity than the Natural and Life sciences.

Lorraine Daston (2004) acknowledges the range and quality of these resources and disciplinary precedents. She also emphasizes the importance of culture and interpretation to the making of science. Daston shows that hermeneutical frameworks are not only embedded in all sorts of disciplines close to the Humanities – notably the social sciences, law and the Life sciences – but are also playing a key role in society at large and are present in all decision-making processes. Daston therefore encourages humanists to make a bigger effort to explain to the outside world how we know what we know. Arguing that the scholarship on epistemology and philosophy of science is slanted in favour of the natural sciences, she calls for an epistemology of knowledge practices by humanists. This will result in explaining what counts as a scientific 'discovery' or just a 'finding' for the Humanities, with attention to process and praxis, as opposed to an exclusive focus on the objects of knowledge.

Although this is very important and necessary, I think that the very nature of data collection in the Humanities clashes with the methods of the natural or 'Life' sciences in that it is based on lived experience and tends towards complexity, not quantification. In a European context, moreover, other factors need to be factored in, for instance the multi-lingual structure of research and thinking in the Humanities. This means that research practice differs considerably in terms of not only geographical but also temporal locations across Europe and beyond. Is it then fair to ask this rich and internally differentiated field to conform to a different research paradigm?

While the calls for the Humanities to develop some 'bio-literacy' and cyber-nautical skills gather force, the resistance remains great, both in the Humanities and in the larger scientific community. In the meantime, the old citation indexes are fast being replaced by Google searches, and endless attempts to develop a metric system suited to the research culture of the Humanities is more urgent, but also more problematic, than ever. A new relationship is being established between arts and sciences under our very, but the question is whether the Humanities – which have so much to offer – are at all entitled to set the rules of this new institutional game, or whether they are merely asked to conform to rules that were not designed with their best interests in mind.

The missing links of this dialogue are manifold and they collide over the very definition of the posthuman. If we 'postanthropocentric posthumanists' (not hyphenated and non-unitary subjects) are to strike a note of resonance in both scientific communities, we need to insist on a culture of mutual respect. Cultural and social studies of science need to address their resistance to theories of the subject, while philosophies of the subject, on the other hand, would be advised to confront their mistrust and mis-cognition of bio-sciences. Posthuman times call for posthuman Humanities studies.

The issue of the status of theory is implicit in this discussion. In response to the current debate on the two cultures, Peter Galison (2004) welcomes the end of grand systematic theoretical discourse and, echoing Lyotard's point about the decline of master narratives, calls for 'specific theory'. This means a position between universalistic pretensions of standing outside space and time on the one hand, and narrow empiricism on the other. Specific theory is grounded, accountable but also shareable and hence open to generic applications. This approach offers both epistemic and ethical advantages which can be immediately put to good use. I think, for instance, that one of the most effective strategies developed by contemporary

Humanities scholars is to actually theorize via and with science. This methodological and strategic choice is based on the insight of post-structuralism about the parallelism of all discursive and textual practices. The textual egalitarianism which was introduced by the semiotic and linguistic 'turn' of the 1970s – and has shocked and irritated conservative scholars ever since – paved the way for new dialogues and interventions between the 'subtle' and the 'hard' sciences.

A new science theory has been perfected accordingly,[4] which I have referred to as the 'matter-realist' trend (in chapter 2). The 'matter-realists' combine the legacy of post-structuralist anti-humanism with the rejection of the classical opposition 'materialism/idealism' to move towards 'Life' as a non-essentialist brand of contemporary vitalism and as a complex system. I argue that the Humanities must adapt to the changing structure of materialism itself, notably the fact that it is based on a new concept of 'matter' and is both affective and auto-poietic or self-organizing.

Karen Barad's work on 'agential realism' (Barad, 2003, 2007) is an eminent example of this tendency. By choosing to by-pass the binary between the material and the cultural, agential realism focuses on the process of their interaction. The focus on material-cultural processes allows us to better interrogate the boundaries between them. This results in emphasizing an ethics of knowledge that reflects and respects complexity and also renews the practice of critical reflexivity.

Luciana Parisi (2004) also innovates on complexity theory, building on Felix Guattari's work. She emphasizes that the great advantage of vitalist monism is that it defines nature–culture as a continuum which evolves through ecology of differentiation. The non-semiotic codes (the DNA of all genetic material) intersect with complex assemblages of affects, embodied practices and other performances that include but are not confined to the linguistic realm. Parisi strengthens this case by cross-referring to the new epistemol-

---

[4] This trend includes thinkers like Ansell Pearson (1997, 1999), Massumi (2002), De Landa (2002), Barad (2007), Grosz (2004), Colebrook (2000, 2002), Bennett (2001, 2010), Clough (2008), Protevi (2009) and Braidotti (1994, 2011b).

ogy of Margulis and Sagan (1995), through the concept of endosymbiosis, which, like autopoiesis, indicates a creative form of evolution. This means that the genetic material is exposed to processes of becoming freed from ontological foundations for difference but is not confined by social constructivism.

In 'matter-realist' Humanities research, primacy is given to the relation over the terms, which foregrounds the transversal connections among material and symbolic, concrete and discursive entities or forces, which include non-human Life. This is what I call *zoe* itself (Braidotti, 2006 and chapters 2 and 3), which allows us to approach science as an object of humanistic study, and vice-versa, by transcending both fields in a transversal redefinition of what counts as the subject of posthuman scientific practice.

The theoretical advantage of the matter-realist monistic and vital approach is the ability to account for the fluid workings of power in advanced or cognitive capitalism, also known as information or network society, by grounding them in specific locations and immanent relations. This allows us to resist them by the same means. Posthuman thinkers embrace creatively the challenge of our historicity without giving in to cognitive panic. The argument is straightforward: if the proper study of mankind used to be Man and the proper study of humanity was the human, it seems to follow that the proper study of the posthuman condition is the posthuman itself. This new knowing subject is a complex assemblage of human and non-human, planetary and cosmic, given and manufactured, which requires major re-adjustments in our ways of thinking. This is not as abstract as it may sound at first. Let me give some concrete examples.

The first is the fast-growing field of environmental Humanities, inspired by the awareness that human activity has a geological influence. Also known as sustainable Humanities (Braidotti, 2006) and as 'anthropocene Humanities',[5] this interdisciplinary field of study introduces major methodological as well as theoretical innovations. For one thing, it spells the end of the idea of a de-naturalized social order discon-

---

[5] I am indebted to Debjani Ganguly and Poul Holm for this felicitous formulation.

nected from its environmental and organic foundations, and calls for more complex schemes of understanding the multilayered form of inter-dependence we all live in. Secondly, it stresses the specific contribution of the Humanities to the public debate on climate change, through the analysis of the social and cultural factors that underscore the public representation of these issues. Both the scale and the consequences of climate change are so momentous as to defy representation. Humanities and more specifically cultural research are best suited to fill in this deficit of the social imaginary and help us think the unthinkable.

The impact of the environmental Humanities is even further reaching. In his analysis of the implications of climate change research for the discipline of history, Dipesh Chakrabarty (2009) argues for a more conceptual shift towards 'Deep History'. This is an interdisciplinary combination of geological and socio-economic history that focuses both on the planetary or earth factors and on the cultural changes that have jointly created humanity over hundreds of thousands of years. It combines theories of historical subjectivity with 'species thinking'. This is, in my eyes, a post-anthropocentric configuration of knowledge that grants the earth the same role and agency as the human subjects that inhabit it. As I indicated in chapter 2, this involves changes in our understanding of the temporality of history, because we are contemplating the possibility of human and other species extinction and hence the end of recorded historical human time, and also the end of the future. The collapse of the divide between human and natural histories is a very recent phenomenon and, prior to this fundamental shift, geological time and the chronology of humans were unrelated, at least within the discipline of history. In fact, historians and climate change research ran parallel discussions without real interdisciplinary exchanges. All of this is changing under our very eyes.

The scale of these mental shifts is such as to almost defy representation, as I suggested above. Chakrabarty suggests further critical reflection on 'the difference between the present historiography of globalization and the historiography demanded by anthropogenic theories of climate change' (2009: 216). This forces us to bring together categories of thought which were until now kept apart not only by disciplinary boundaries – between the earth sciences and literature and history, for instance – but also by the anthropocentric bias that has sustained the Humanities. Far from being a crisis, this new development has enormous inspirational force for the field. It also calls into question some of the current ideas about the negative formation of a new sense of 'the human' as bound together by shared vulnerability in relation to the possibility of extinction. Chakrabarty's insights about a critical climate change-driven Deep History also challenge some of the given assumptions about post-colonial critiques of the Western universal. Quite a programme.

Another illuminating example of the advantages of a post-human scientific position is the 'One Health Initiative', which defines its mission in terms of Public Health as follows:[6]

> Recognizing that human health (including mental health via the human-animal bond phenomenon), animal health, and ecosystem health are inextricably linked, One Health seeks to promote, improve, and defend the health and well-being of all species by enhancing cooperation and collaboration between physicians, veterinarians, other scientific health and environmental professionals and by promoting strengths in leadership and management to achieve these goals.

The movement is inspired by Rudolf Virchow (1821–1902), who coined the term 'zoonosis', arguing that there should be no dividing lines between animal and human medicine. This position has been gathering momentum in the last fifteen years. The One Health Initiative is a rather daring interdisciplinary alliance that unites physicians, osteopaths, veterinarians, dentists, nurses and other scientific-health and environmentally related disciplines, on the basis of a simple hypothesis, which is the isomorphism of structures between humans and animals in immunology, bacteriology and vaccine developments.

This means that humans are both exposed and vulnerable to new diseases, like bird flu and other epidemics, which they share with animal species. Obviously a response to the new pandemics that have emerged in the global era, like Bovine

[6] http://www.onehealthinitiative.com/mission.php; with thanks to my colleague Anton Pijpers.

spongiform encephalopathy (BSE), better known as 'mad cow disease', the One Health Initiative stresses the variety of shared diseases that tie humans and animals. For instance, animals suffer from many of the same chronic diseases such as heart disease, cancer, diabetes, asthma and arthritis as humans. It follows, therefore, that we should develop comparative medicine as the study of disease processes across species and that therefore we should also connect doctors and veterinarians in their daily practices, both therapeutic and research-based. Environmentally embedded, the One Health Initiative pursues both ecological and social sustainability and has large social repercussions.

The common concerns about public health among humans and animals is intensified as a result of urbanization, globalization, climate change, wars and terrorism, and microbial and chemical pollution of land and water sources, which have created new threats to the health of both animals and humans.[7] Medical doctors and veterinarians need to join forces with environmental health scientists and practitioners to deal with disease outbreaks, prevent chronic disease caused by chemical exposure, and create healthier living environments. One Health is the perfect post-anthropocentric concept that brings together human health care practitioners, veterinarians, and public health professionals for the sake of environmental, social and individual sustainability.

Another significant example is the fast-growing field of the Digital Humanities – pioneered by Katherine Hayles – which deals with a rich agenda of thematic and methodological issues. One of them is the continuing relevance of the science of texts and the role of the press – from Gutenberg to 3D printing – in shaping human knowledge. Just as the Humanities led these discussions in the sixteenth century, when the printing press was introduced in the Western world, so they are at the forefront of contemporary frontiers of thought. And they are not alone.

The posthuman Humanities can create and evolve a new set of narratives about the planetary dimension of globalized humanity; the evolutionary sources of morality; the future of

---

[7] Source: Wikipedia: One Health Initiative, consulted on 26 April 2012.

our and other species; the semiotic systems of technological apparatus; the processes of translation underscoring the Digital Humanities; the role of gender and ethnicity as factors that index access to the posthuman predicament and the institutional implications of them all. This is a new and innovative agenda, which builds on but is not confined to either humanism or anthropocentrism – a genuinely new programme for the Humanities in the twentieth century.

At the experimental level, several new interdisciplinary posthuman studies research platforms have been set up across major universities and are running path-breaking experiments as this book goes to press.[8] As a consequence of this embarrassment of theoretical and research riches, the next question that arises is: how can the Humanities be inspired by these experiments in posthuman thought and new post-anthropocentric research? How can they adopt this approach to their own object of study?

Posthuman Critical Theory

The Humanities can be inspired by these new trans-disciplinary models of thought. The key to everything for me lies in the methodology and therefore I want to spell out the main criteria for posthuman theory, as a way of unfolding the new rules of the game, and try to apply them to the Humanities. My golden rules are: cartography accuracy, with the corollary of ethical accountability; trans-disciplinarity; the importance of combining critique with creative figurations; the principle of non-linearity; the powers of memory and the imagination and the strategy of de-familiarization. These methodological guidelines are valuable not only as building blocks for post-human critical theory but also because they can help redefine

[8] See, for instance, the Posthumanities Hub at the university of Linköping, funded by the Swedish government: http://www.tema. liu.se/tema-g/Posthuman/Network?l=en; research conducted at the Institute of Advanced Study in the Humanities and Social Sciences at the University of Bern, in Switzerland; experiments at the University of East London in the UK; and my work at the Centre for the Humanities at the University of Utrecht in the Netherlands.

the relationship between the Humanities and the Life sciences on the basis of mutual respect.

Let us begin with cartographic accuracy. A cartography is a theoretically based and politically informed reading of the present. Cartographies aim at epistemic and ethical account-ability by unveiling the power locations which structure our subject-position. As such, they account for one's locations in terms of both space (geo-political or ecological dimension) and time (historical and genealogical dimension). This stresses the situated structure of critical theory and it implies the partial or limited nature of all claims to knowledge. These qualifications are crucial to support the critique of both uni-versalism and of liberal individualism.

Critiques of power locations, however, are not enough. They work in tandem with the quest for alternative figura-tions or *conceptual personae* for these locations, in terms of power as restrictive (*potestas*) but also as empowering or affirmative (*potentia*). For example, figurations such as the feminist/the womanist/the queer/the cyborg/the diasporic, native, nomadic subjects, as well as oncomouse and Dolly the sheep are no mere metaphors, but signposts for specific geo-political and historical locations. As such, they express complex singularities, not universal claims (Braidotti, 2011a).

A figuration is the expression of alternative representations of the subject as a dynamic non-unitary entity; it is the dra-matization of processes of becoming. These processes assume that subject formation takes place in-between nature/technol-ogy; male/female; black/white; local/global; present/past – in the spaces that flow and connect the binaries. These in-between states defy the established modes of theoretical representation because they are zigzagging, not linear and process-oriented, not concept-driven. Critique and creation strike a new deal in actualizing the practice of *conceptual personae* or figura-tion as the active pursuit of affirmative alternatives to the dominant vision of the subject.

Zigzagging is indeed the operative word for the next build-ing block of posthuman critical theory, namely non-linearity. It would be self-defeating for the Humanities to stick to the traditional rule of visualization by automatically adopting linear thinking, considering the complexity of contemporary science and the fact that the global economy does not function in a linear manner, but is rather web-like, scattered and poly-centred. The heteroglossia of data we are confronted with demands complex topologies of knowledge for a subject structured by multi-directional relationality. We consequently need to adopt non-linearity to develop cartographies of power that account for the paradoxes of the posthuman era.

This issue gets even more complex in relation to time. Linearity is the dominant time of *Chronos*, as opposed to the dynamic and more cyclical time of becoming or *Aion*, as we saw in chapter 2. The former is the keeper of institutional time and practices – 'Royal' science; the latter the prerogative of marginal groups – 'minor' science. Official, *Chronos*-driven 'Royal science' is opposed to the process of 'becoming-minor of science', which is based on a different temporality. One is protocol-bound; the other is curiosity-driven and defines the scientific enterprise in terms of the creation of new concepts. Nomadic theory proposes a critique of the powers that dominant, linear memory-systems exercise over the Humanities and social sciences. Creativity and critique proceed together in the quest for affirmative alternatives which rest on a non-linear vision of memory as imagination, creation as becoming. Instead of deference to the authority of the past, we have the fleeting co-presence of multiple time zones, in a continuum that activates and de-territorializes stable identities and fractures temporal linearity (Deleuze, 1988). This dynamic vision of time enlists the creative resources of the imagination to the task of reconnecting to the past.

Non-linearity also affects scholarly practice in the Humanities disciplines – a method that replaces linearity with a more rhizomatic style of thinking, allows for multiple connections and lines of interaction that necessarily connect the text to its many 'outsides'. This method expresses the conviction that the 'truth' of a text is never really 'written' anywhere, let alone within the signifying space of the book. Nor is it about the authority of a proper noun, a signature, a tradition, a canon, or the prestige of an academic discipline. The 'truth' of a text requires an altogether different form of accountability and accuracy that resides in the transversal nature of the affects they engender, that is to say the outward-bound interconnections or relations they enable and sustain. George

Eliot pointed the way by writing with ears and mind open to that roar of energy that sustains Life. Virginia Woolf did the same by steering her writer's gaze towards the perfect stillness of Life defined as constant flow. Writing is a method for transcribing cosmic intensity into sustainable portions of being.

This has important implications for the task of criticism. As post-structuralism taught us (Barthes, 1975), the method of 'faithfulness to the text' and of citation is more than flat repetition without difference. What comes to the fore instead is the creative capacity that consists in being able to re-member and to endure the affective charges of texts as events.

To do so, loyalty is due neither to the spurious depth of the text, nor to the author's latent or manifest intentionality and even less to the sovereignty of the phallic Master signifier. A text, theoretical and scientific as well as literary, is a relay point between different moments in space and time, as well as different levels, degrees, forms and configurations of the thinking process. It is a mobile entity, a speed-jet. Thinking and writing, like breathing, are not held into the mould of linearity, or the confines of the printed page, but move out-wards, out of bounds, in webs of encounters with ideas, others, texts. The linguistic signifier is merely one of the points in a chain of effects, not its centre or its endgame. The source of intellectual inspiration comes from the never-ending flow of connections between the texts and their multiple 'outsides'. Creativity constantly reconnects to the virtual totality of a block of past experiences, memories and affects, which, in a monistic philosophy of becoming, get recomposed as action or praxis in the present. This approach to critical thinking is an exercise in synchronization, which sustains activity 'here and now' by making concrete or actual the virtual intensity. This intensity is simultaneously after and before us, both past and future, in a flow or process of muta-tion, differentiation or becoming. It is the 'matter-realist' core of critical thought.

Nomadic thought encourages an affective opening-out towards the geo-philosophical or planetary dimension of 'chaosmosis' (Guattari, 1995). It amounts to turning the thinking subject into the threshold of gratuitous (principle of non-profit), aimless (principle of mobility or flow) acts which express the vital energy of transformative becoming (principle of non-linearity). Loyalty is instead required to the intensity of the affective forces that compose a text or a concept, so as to account for what a text – or a concept or theory – can do, what it has done, how it has impacted upon one's self and others. Accounting for the affective impact of various items or data upon oneself is the process of remembering. In Bergson as in Deleuze, it has as much to do with the imagination, that is to say creative reworking, as with the passive repetition of chronologically prior, recorded and hence retrievable experiences.

Implicit in this process is the next key criterion for posthuman critical theory, which is the role of memory. Considering that posthuman time is a complex and non-linear system, internally fractured and multiplied over several time-sequences, affect and memory become essential elements. Freed from chronological linearity and the logo-centric gravitational force, memory in the posthuman nomadic mode is the active reinvention of a self that is joyfully discontinuous, as opposed to being mournfully consistent. Memories need the imagination to empower the actualization of virtual possibilities in the subject, which becomes redefined as a transversal relational entity inhabited by a vitalist and multi-directional memory (Rothberg, 2009). Memory works in terms of nomadic transpositions, that is to say as creative and highly generative inter-connections which mix and match, mingle and multiply the possibilities of expansion and relations among different units or entities (Braidotti, 2006).

The next methodological signpost is the practice of de-familiarization, which I discussed in chapters 2 and 3. This is a sobering process by which the knowing subject disengages itself from the dominant normative vision of the self he or she had become accustomed to, to evolve towards a post-human frame of reference. Leaving the Vitruvian frame once and for all, the subject becomes relational in a complex manner that connects it to multiple others. A subject thus constituted explodes the boundaries of humanism and anthropocentrism at skin level. We have seen in the previous chapters a series of concrete examples of how dis-identifications from dominant models of subject-formation can be productive and creative, drawn from feminist theory – which implies a radical dis-engagement from the dominant institutions and representations of femininity and masculinity (Braidotti, 1991; Butler, 1991). Post-colonial and race discourse disrupt white privilege and other racialized assumptions about accepted views of what constitutes a human subject.[9]

These dis-identifications occur along the axes of becoming-woman (sexualization) and becoming-other (racialization) and hence remain within the confines of anthropomorphism. Yet, a more radical shift is needed to break from the latter and develop post-anthropocentric forms of identification. The unbearable lightness of being falls upon us as soon as we start running with *zoe*; non-human life itself. Nomadic theory's vital geo-centrism – the love of *zoe* – is a parallel effort in the same direction. Becoming-earth or becoming-imperceptible are more radical breaks with established patterns of thought (naturalization) and introduce a radically imminent planetary dimension. This anthropological exodus is especially difficult, emotionally as well as methodologically, as it can involve a sense of loss and pain. Dis-identification involves the loss of cherished habits of thought and representation, a move which can also produce fear, sense of insecurity and nostalgia.

On the methodological front, de-familiarization shifts the relationship to the nonhuman others and requires dis-identification from century-old habits of anthropocentric thought and humanist arrogance, which is likely to test the ability and willingness of the Humanities. The 'hard' or experimental sciences, of course, are accomplishing this move away from anthropocentrism with relative ease, as we saw in the case of the Deep History or the One Health research movements. It may be worth taking seriously the critical charge that the Humanities' development towards complexity may be hampered by the anthropocentrism that underscores their practice. Will critical theory be able to connect to rich and complex post-Humanities to come?

My working definition of a posthuman scientific method in the Humanities as well as in the Life sciences cannot be dissociated from an ethics of inquiry that demands respect

[9] See Gilroy (2000), Hill Collins (1991), Ware (1992) and Griffin and Braidotti (2002).

for the complexities of the real-life world we are living in. Posthuman critical theory needs to apply a new vision of subjectivity to both the practice and the public perception of the scientist, which is still caught in the classical and outmoded model of the humanistic 'Man of reason' (Lloyd, 1984) as the quintessential European citizen. We need to overcome this model and move towards an intensive form of interdisciplinarity, transversality, and boundary-crossings among a range of discourses. This trans-disciplinary approach affects the very structure of thought and enacts a rhizomatic embrace of conceptual diversity in scholarship. The posthuman method amounts to higher degrees of disciplinary hybridization and relies on intense de-familiarization of our habits of thought through encounters that shatter the flat repetition of the protocols of institutional reason.

The 'Proper' Subject of the Humanities is not 'Man'

I have argued throughout this book that posthuman theory rests on a process ontology that challenges the traditional equation of subjectivity with rational consciousness, resisting the reduction of both to objectivity and linearity.[10] The nomadic vision of the posthuman knowing subject as a time continuum and a collective assemblage implies a double commitment, on the one hand to processes of change and on the other to a strong ethics of eco-sophical sense of community. Co-presence, that is to say the simultaneity of being in the world together, defines the ethics of interaction with both human and non-human others. A collectively distributed consciousness emerges from this, a transversal form of non-synthetic understanding of the relational bond that connects us. This places the relation and the notion of complexity at the centre of both the ethics and the epistemic structures and strategies of the posthuman subject (Braidotti, 2006).

This view has important implications for the production of scientific knowledge. The dominant vision of the scientific

[10] For an excellent critical account of the notion of objectivity, see Daston and Galison (2007).

enterprise is based on the institutional implementation of a number of Laws that discipline the practice of scientific research and police the thematic and methodological borders of what counts as respectable, acceptable, and fundable science. In so doing, the laws of scientific practice regulate what a mind is allowed to do, and thus they control the structures of our thinking. Posthuman thought proposes an alternative vision of both the thinking subject, of his or her evolution on the planetary stage, and the actual structure of thinking.

Deleuze and Guattari's idea that the task of thinking is to create new concepts is a great source of inspiration for the Humanities because it rests on the parallelism between philosophy, science and the arts. This is not to be mistaken for a flattening out of the differences between these intellectual pursuits, but rather a way of stressing the unity of purpose among the three branches of knowledge. Deleuze and Guattari take care to stress the differences between the distinctive styles of intelligence that philosophy, science and the arts respectively embody. They also argue that they remain indexed on a common plane of intensive self-transforming Life energy. This continuum sustains the ontology of becoming that is the conceptual motor of posthuman nomadic thought. In so far as science has to come to terms with the real physical processes of an actualized and defined world, it is less open to the processes of becoming or differentiation that characterize Deleuze's monistic ontology. Philosophy is at an advantage, being a subtler tool for the probing intellect, one that is more attuned to the virtual plane of immanence, to the generative force of a generative universe, or 'chaosmosis', which is nonhuman and in constant flux. Thinking is the conceptual counterpart of the ability to enter modes of relation, to affect and be affected, sustaining qualitative shifts and creative tensions accordingly, which is also the prerogative of art. Critical theory therefore has a major role to play.

Manuel De Landa (2002) analyses brilliantly the intensive mode of Deleuzian science and stresses the crucial importance of processes of actualization of virtual possibilities, over and above universal essence and linear realizations. De Landa points out that, apart from the anti-essentialism, intensive nomad science also aims to avoid typological thinking. The ruling principle of resemblance, identity, analogy and opposition has to be avoided in thinking about the virtual and intensive becoming. Deleuze demands 'that we give an account of that which allows making such judgements or establishing those relations' (De Landa, 2002: 42).

The important aspect of nomadic vitalism is that it is neither organicist nor essentialist, but pragmatic and immanent. In other words, vital materialism does not assume an over-arching concept of life, just practices and flows of becoming, complex assemblages and heterogeneous relations. As I argued in chapter 2, there is no idealized transcendental, but virtual multiplicity. The monistic ontology that sustains this vision of life as vitalist, self-organizing matter also allows the critical thinker to re-unite the different branches of philosophy, the sciences and the arts in a new alliance. I see this as a dynamic contemporary formula to redefine the relationship between the two cultures of the 'subtle' (Humanities) and 'hard' (Natural) sciences. They are different lines of approaching the vital matter that constitutes the core of both subjectivity and its planetary and cosmic relations.

Bonta and Protevi (2004) stress that Deleuze's 'geophilosophy' encourages the Humanities to engage with contemporary biology and physics in very creative ways. The emphasis falls on complexity in distinguishing between actualized states and virtual becoming – on the basis of a vision of matter as auto-poietic. The former constitute the object of 'Royal Science', the latter the frame for 'minor science'; both are necessary at different points in time, but only 'minor science' is ethically transformative and not bound to the economic imperatives of advanced capitalism and its cognitive excursions into living matter. As a consequence, one can venture the preliminary conclusion that the main implication of posthuman critical theory for the practice of science is that the scientific Laws need to be retuned according to a view of the subject of knowledge as a complex singularity, an affective assemblage and a relational vitalist entity.

It follows from all this that the Humanities in the posthuman era of anthropocene should not stick to the Human – let alone 'Man' – as its proper object of study. On the contrary, the field would benefit by being free from the empire of humanist Man, so as to be able to access in a post-anthropocentric manner issues of external and even planetary importance, such as scientific and technological advances, ecological and social sustainability and the multiple challenges of globalization. Such a change of focus requires assistance from other social and scientific actors as well.

The question is whether the Humanities are allowed to set their own agenda in relation to contemporary science and technology, or whether they are confined to places they did not choose to be in the first place. There is in fact a distinct tendency, for instance in the public debates about climate change or bio-technologies, to assign to the institutionally under-funded field of the Humanities all subjects related to the human component of these complex debates. This tendency has made the institutional fortunes of ethics, which is expected – and often claims itself the prerogative – to issue new meta-discourses and normative injunctions suited to the dilemmas of our age. This meta-discursive claim, however, is unsubstantiated. Moreover, it perpetuates the institutionalized habit of thought – reactive and sedentary – of erecting philosophy to the role of a master theory. The image of the philosopher as the legislator of knowledge and the judge of truth – a model rooted in the Kantian school – is the exact opposite of what posthuman critical theory is arguing for: post-identitarian, non-unitary and transversal subjectivity based on relations with human and non-human others.

Another discursive field that gets regularly evoked as the single responsibility of the Humanities is the controversial issue of the 'social and cultural aspects' of complex issues such as climate change or the impact of bio-technologies. In other words, the Humanities are actively confined to the anthropocentric corner, while being simultaneously blamed for this limitation, which is the perfect illustration of the paradox noted by Whimster (2006: 174): 'a science of the human would seem either to have the capacity to be inhuman or, alternatively, to be humanistic but hardly scientific'. Damned if you do, damned if you don't.

My point is that the Humanities need to embrace the multiple opportunities offered by the posthuman condition. The Humanities can set their own objects of enquiry, free from the traditional or institutional assignment to the human and its humanistic derivatives. We know by now that the field is richly endowed with an archive of multiple possibilities which equip it with the methodological and theoretical resources to set up original and necessary debates with the sciences and technologies and other grand challenges of today. The question is what the Humanities can become in the posthuman era and after the decline of the primacy of 'Man' and of *anthropos*.

The Global 'Multi'-versity

The question now is what is the institutional practice best suited to posthuman critical theory and to the twenty-first-century Humanities. The discussions about the Humanities' ability to cope with the challenges of the third millennium beg the question of the crisis of the university as idea and as representation.

A brief historical survey of the debate about the idea of the university can give an idea of the extent of this crisis. The Renaissance model of the Humanist academy defined by the scholar as an artist or artisan handcrafting his or her research patiently and without constraints, over a long period of time, is simply over. It has been replaced by a modern 'Fordist' model of the university as a chain-production unit mass-producing academic good. Nussbaum's claim (1999) that this model is still carried on today by the American Liberal Arts college is both elitist and nostalgic, as I mentioned in chapter 2. Immanuel Kant's classical text on 'The conflicts of the faculties', first published in 1789 (Kant, 1992) presents the blueprint for the modern university, based on the model of industrial production. Kant divided the university into 'higher' faculties – Law, Medicine and Theology – which are practically oriented and 'lower' faculties – the Arts, Humanities and Sciences – which are responsible for criticism and hence are withdrawn from markets and practical concerns.[11] This blueprint is still quite valid, in spite of several historical modifications. Probably the most significant is the nineteenth

---

[11] For a contemporary critical update on Kant's vision of the university, see Lambert (2001).

century von Humboldt model of the university as the place for training the highly selected, and until recently exclusively male, elites for leadership and intelligent citizenship. That model is still prevalent in Europe.

In his stimulating and at times devastating anatomy of the contemporary university, Bill Readings (1996) argues, however, that the institution has become 'post-historical', in that it has 'outlived itself, is now a survivor of the era in which it defined itself in terms of the project of the historical development, affirmation and inculcation of national culture' (1996: 6). All the previous models of the university I mentioned above: the Kantian, the von Humboldt and even the British colonial defended by Cardinal Newman (1907), have been destabilized by the global economy. In this respect, the decline of the nation-state has negative consequences for the university as a whole and especially for the Humanities. The central figure in academic life today is not the professor, argues Readings, but the administrator and the university is no longer a pillar of national identity, or an ideological arm of the nation-state and the state apparatus:

> The university is now no more of a parasitical drain, on resources, than the stock exchange or the insurance company are a drain on industrial production. Like the stock exchange, the university is a point of capital's self-knowledge, of capital's ability not just to manage risk or diversity, but to extract a surplus value from that management. In the case of the university, this extraction occurs as a result of speculation on differentials in information. (1996: 40)

In this context, the much-flaunted notion of 'excellence' means nothing substantial, but is a crucial factor in the transnational exchange of academic capital. A mere 'techno-bureaucratic ideal' (Readings, 1996: 14), it has no content reference. This 'de-referentialization' of academic standards has both negative and positive consequences.

On the negative front, the lack of specific referents means that 'excellence' is indexed on money, markets' demands and consumers' satisfaction. On a more positive note, 'de-referentialization' opens up the possibility for new spaces 'in which we can think the notions of country and community differently' (1996: 124). What can we do with these models of university today?

Let us start by looking at the classical conservative model, exemplified by John Searle in his defence of the key ideas in the Western rationalist tradition (1995), as the core values of Humanities research. Firmly grounded in a realist practice of truth, the rationalist tradition is text-based and deploys theory in a self-critical manner. It rests on linear thinking because it assumes that the function of language is to communicate effectively. Consequently, truth is a matter of the accuracy of representation – according to a correspondence theory of truth which grounds statements in observable factual realities. It follows that knowledge is expected to be objective – because it relies on representations of an independently existing reality and not on subjectivist interpretations. Rationality rules supreme and formal reason – as opposed to practical reason – has its own inner logic which provides standards of proof and validity. As a result, intellectual standards are non-negotiable and grounded in objective criteria of excellence.

The traditional idea of the university is supposed to embody and uphold these criteria. Searle opposes to this the 'postmodernist' university, influenced by imported anti-realist theories of truth which weaken the scientificity of the academic practice. The representativeness of the curriculum in terms of gender, race, and ethnicity – regrettably for Searle – becomes more important than its truth value, introducing a shallow intellectual egalitarianism under the guise of multiculturalism. This causes confusion between a domain to be studied and a cause to be defended, which disrupts the deployment of traditional Humanities methods and practices and erodes its self-confidence.

In an eloquent response to Searle, Richard Rorty (1996) criticizes the over-emphasis on rationalism as 'a secularized version of the Western monotheistic tradition' (1996: 33). Realism and the correspondence to reality are rather meaningless concepts, or rather 'a term without content' (1996: 26). The much-praised 'objectivity of science', argues Rorty, rests on active inter-subjectivity and social interaction.

Emphasizing the importance of socio-political factors in shaping meanings and truths, Rorty strikes a more pragmatic note:

> A healthy and free university accommodates generational change, radical religious and political disagreement and new social responsibilities as best it can. It muddles through. (1996: 28)

The question of theory and the aftermath of the 'theory wars' comes back to haunt this discussion. Searle's conservative remarks are accurate as the expression of his emotional involvement in the Humanities' self-defence. He is nonetheless ruthless in blaming the postmodern theorists for the situation. Contrary to the facile anti-postmodernism of his approach, I would stress the serious methodological challenges that this approach has thrown to the Humanities. Indeed, blaming the postmodern messengers for bringing the sobering message that the humanistic master narratives are in trouble is a sleight of hand that does not help further the cause of the Humanities today. It is a great pity that the serious debate about the future of humanistic higher education is caught up in the legacy of the 1990s 'theory wars' and the polemical in-fighting about feminism, postmodernism, multiculturalism and French philosophy. Joan Scott puts it brilliantly:

> As if postmodernists were the cause of all the problems of disciplinary uncertainty scholars are now facing; as if their banishment would end the questions about difference posed by demographic changes in university populations, by the emergence of postcolonial critiques of colonial assumptions, by developments in the history of philosophy that reach back to at least the nineteenth century, by the more recent end of the Cold War and by the extraordinary economic constraints of the last years. (Scott, 1996: 171)

Referring back to John Dewey's[12] notion of the university as a disciplinary community, Scott deplores the politicized

---

[12] Dewey played an important role in launching the American Association of University Professors in 1915.

contests about postmodernism and knowledge, which over-emphasize 'the presumed political implications of one's scholarly ideas, not the ideas themselves'. Louis Menand (1996) goes further and suggests that conservative political forces are manipulating 'theory wars' as a pretext to interfere in the internal academic affairs of the university, as evidence by the particularly targeted attacks against feminism, multi-culturalism and post-colonialism. This critical insight is picked up by Edward Said, who connects the identity crisis of the Humanities to the displacement of Eurocentric curri-cula in US universities and adds, quite ironically:

> Some critics have reacted as if the very nature of the University and academic freedom had been threatened because unduly politicized. Others have gone further: for them the critique of the Western canon, with its panoply of what its opponent have called Dead White European Males [. . .] has rather improbably signalled the outset of a new fascism, the demise of Western civilization itself, and the overturn of slavery, child marriage, bigamy and the harem. (Said, 1996: 214–15)

Irony left aside, it is quite clear that the real target of the conservatives' wrath is the threat that these new areas of studies pose to the power of corporate disciplines in two major ways: through their radical epistemologies and their methodological interdisciplinarity. The meltdown of disci-plinary boundaries and the subsequent loss of corporate power by the old disciplines is less of a theoretical than an administrative crisis. As Menand astutely observes, given that the disciplines are not timeless entities, but historically con-tingent discursive formations, their de-segregation is not itself a source of anxiety for the scholars, some of whom are even driving the process. It is, however, a major headache for the administrators in charge of the machinery of self-governance of Humanities faculties, who tend to 'take advantage of the state of flux to reduce spending and increase forceful retrench-ments' (1996: 19). But what does the posthuman have to do with any of this?

Instead of pursuing this polemic, I would rather start from the empirical imperative to think global, but act local, to develop an institutional frame that actualized a posthuman practice that is 'worthy of our times' (Braidotti, 2011b) while resisting the violence, the injustice and the vulgarity of the times. Confronting the historicity of our condition means moving the activity of thinking outwards, into the real world, so as to assume accountability for the conditions that define our location. The epistemic and the ethical walk hand in hand into the complicated landscapes of the third millennium. We need conceptual creativity and intellectual courage to rise to the occasion, as there is no going back.

Although the issues of pastoral care and intergenerational justice are more topical than ever in the academic classroom, it is also the case that, since the Cold War era, the function of the university has been mostly research and development for the sake of social development and industrial growth and technological advances, including but not only the military, as we saw in the previous chapter. This is especially true of the USA, but Europe and vast parts of Asia are also part of this model. According to Wernick, since the 1960s the university has mutated into a 'multi-versity', fulfilling a variety of social and economic functions, often linked to the Cold War militarization of the social space and geo-political conflicts. The term 'multi-versity' was coined in 1963 by the then Chancellor of the University of California system Clark Kerr (2001) to refer to the explosion of tasks and demands imposed on major universities. The university continued to mutate so that, over the next twenty years, 'universities have become corporate, oriented to performance and de-traditionalized. Under the aegis of professional managers they have become post-historical institutions without a memory' (Wernick, 2006: 561). As the professoriate and students' representative bodies lost their powers of governance to neo-liberal economic logic, the Humanities dispersed their foundational value to become a sort of luxury intellectual consumer good.

Can this trend be reversed? What is the most adequate model of the university for the globalized era? I want to argue that the posthuman predicament affects also an issue as crucial as the civic responsibility of the university today. How can the academic and civic space interact in our globalized, technologically mediated world? The digital revolution paves the way for at least a partial answer: the new campuses will be virtual and hence global by definition. This means that the universal ideal of transcendent values defended by Searle is over. It is being rapidly replaced by the infrastructural vision of the university as a hub of both localized knowledge production and global transmission of cognitive data. This need not necessarily result in either de-humanizing or disembedding the university, but in new forms of re-grounding and of accountability. Thus, in an article pointedly called 'The twenty kilometer university', an interdisciplinary team (Phillips et al., 2011) analyses the changing relationship between the university and the contemporary global city in China and draws some inspiring consequences for the mission of the academic institution today.

The global city space requires and depends upon intelligent spaces of high-technological interactivity and can thus be defined as a 'smart' city space with dense technological infrastructure. Ambient technology rests on infrastructural networks which, being non-hierarchical and user-friendly, defeat the traditional organization of both knowledge production and knowledge transfer. In some ways, the technologically smart urban space displaces and replaces the university, by inscribing knowledge and its circulation at the heart of the social order. What happens then to the formerly segregated and, at least in Europe, highly sacralized academic space? The authors argue that the academic needs to unfold onto the civic and become embedded in the urban environment in a radical new manner. The city as a whole is the science park of the future. The university consequently needs to transform itself into a 'multi-versity' (Wernick 2006: 561), capable of interacting with the city space so as to create 'a collective ethos of communal intelligence with a common goal of economic progress through the means that sustain and streamline city life' (Phillips et al., 2011: 299). The branding of cities and their universities – which was initiated in the Cold War era – enters a new phase of intensifying marketing practices, promotional efforts and a financial culture of private and public investments that are often unrelated to the actual content matter.

The global multi-versity is the place where technology and metaphysics meet, with explosive but also exhilarating consequences. This globalized, technologically mediated 'multi-versity' is a new entity: 'with its role in relation to citizen-formation and *bildung* fading into the background if not outright obscurity' (Phillips et al., 2011: 300). Stefan Collini (2012: 13) stresses the same point by arguing that we must stop thinking in terms of nineteenth-century European ideals and 'focus instead on how it is the Asian incarnation of the Americanized version of the European model, with schools of technology, medicine and management to the fore, which most powerfully instantiates the ideal of the university in the twenty-first century'.

In other words, the contemporary university needs to redefine its posthuman planetary mission in terms of a renewed relationship to the global city where it is situated. This implies both a revision of the urban space and a redefinition of civic responsibility. All the more so as, according to the United Nations, there will be 22 mega-cities in the world by 2015 and that by 2050 two-thirds of the world population will dwell in urban centres. In 2012 we officially registered the fact that 50 per cent of the world population now lives in cities. More Internet-backed interactivity will allow citizens to participate in all forms of planning, managing and assessing their urban environment. The key words are: open source, open governance, open data and open science, granting free access by the public to all scientific and administrative data. Contemporary twenty-first-century cities, as in the case of the Chinese study quoted above, are not only sprawled out or 'exploded' urban spaces. They are also – in the best of cases – technologically mediated, 'smart' urban surfaces. Just as in the past, in Europe, universities and their cities grew together, weaving a complex web of urban, social, economic, political and civic ties, so today a new network of relations is being set up. Because of the high degree of technological intervention involved in contemporary network societies, this new urban space can be considered as post-anthropocentric and well beyond the Vitruvian frame of reference of a humanist scale. Responding to local concerns and global challenges, the contemporary 'multi-versity' faces up to both the demands of a competitive labour market, global culture and the corporate world, while pursuing its century-old missions of scientific excellence and enlightened citizenship. The cities of tomorrow will be living centres of learning, information brokering and shared cognitive practice, based on intense social networking. After naval ports and airports, Internet ports will be the gateways to navigating the cities of the third millennium.

This takes me to the second aspect of the new covenant between the university and the city in the third millennium: the civic dimension. More than ever, the university needs to pursue its aim of ensuring independent research, constructive pedagogical practice and critical thinking. Compounded by the role that contemporary universities can play as major technological hubs and global centres of knowledge transfer, the mix of innovation and tradition can sustain the continuing relevance of the institution of the university in the contemporary world. The combination of technical skills and civic responsibility, a concern for social and environmental sustainability, and a discerning relationship to consumerism, are the core values of the contemporary multi-versity. Bill Readings (1996) was hinting at this when he referred to the possibility that the contemporary university may help redefine community and belonging away from classical nationalism on the one hand, and crass consumerism on the other. Referring to Blanchot's work, Readings call for a new model of the university as a community of post-identitarian, posthuman subjects. The model will be a community without steady identity or fixed unity, for a people and a multi-versity to come.

This has deep implications for the role and place of theory. I remember the day when this specific penny dropped inside my head. I was at a Laurie Anderson concert in Paris in the late 1980s. She is one of those conceptual artists who seamlessly unfold into a public intellectual, creating acoustic and aesthetic expressions for the transformations of our times. 'O Superman' was the first cyber song to become a global hit – a premonition of posthuman things to come – whereas 'Strange Angels' is a critical re-appraisal of Walter Benjamin's theses on the philosophy of History, hinting at a new continuum between the remembrance of things past and the sustainability of the future. At this particular concert, Anderson, who would soon embark on her artist residency with NASA, defined the work of people who used to call themselves 'intellectuals' as having become 'content-providers'. That was the late 1980s. Last week I received the announcement of a major conference on the future of European education in which an entire panel was devoted to papers by and about 'ideas brokers'. That entails marketing and advertising ideas, rather than fundamental research and experimentation; it does not even particularly require imaginative creativity. Academics are left to brokering ideas, while information networks do the content provision and are increasingly autonomous in decision making. All around, an exploded and expanded 'smart' city space distributes the knowledge products to students-users who are literate in infrastructural knowledge production. Welcome to the future!

That future has already started in the endless re-organizations and financial restrictions that plague the contemporary academic world and are particularly acute in the Humanities. Louis Menand argues that the modern research university is neither the embodiment of eternal truths and universal ideas, nor the paragon of truth, beauty and virtue. It is actually a rather cumbersome and expensive bureaucracy:

> [I]t is philosophically weak and it encourages intellectual predictability, professional insularity and social irrelevance. It deserves to be replaced. But if it is replaced, it is in the interests of everyone who values the continued integrity of teaching and inquiry to devise a new institutional structure that will perform the same function. Otherwise academic freedom will be killed by the thing that, in America, kills most swiftly and surely: not bad ideas, but lack of money. (Menand, 1996: 19)

This negative social and economic context of financial scarcity has caused a distinct deterioration of the working conditions of all staff in the average neo-liberal university worldwide. Stefan Collini comments on this issue with customary wit: 'The distracted, numbers-swamped, audit-crazed, grant-chasing life of most contemporary academics departments is far removed from classical ideals of the contemplative life' (Collini, 2012: 19). As a matter of fact, academics function more like mid-ranking executives in a business organization run by accountants and financial advisors than as independent scholars in a self-organized community. The more successful ones have become very skilful in obtaining external grants and funding. They are also known as the 'tender'-preneurs. Rosalind Gill (2010), on the other hand, not only deplores the working conditions in the academic world, but also attempts to assess the damage they cause to both individuals and the institutions where stress and competitiveness rule. The precariousness of younger staff members is a source of special concern. Collini concurs: 'the conditions of work of junior and temporary staff in some unfavoured institutions may, in limiting cases, suggest comparisons with those of staff in a call center' (2012: 19).

Yet, it does feel slightly incongruous to think about all this from my specific location, in the ancient city of Utrecht, in the heart of the old world. City and university here have become so interwoven over the span of centuries that it is difficult to tell the urban, civic structure apart from the academic one. *Civitas* and *Universitas* are two sides of the same coin and it may not be simple to shift the grounds of their interaction in the name of the posthuman predicament. What might the blueprint for the future look like? I want to resist the apocalyptic visions of the last professors as a dying species (Donoghue, 2008). Posthuman Humanities, marked by a new alliance between the arts and the sciences, and enriched by the ancient European academic and civic tradition, can sponsor multiple allegiances and new ecologies of belonging. They can redefine cosmopolitanism, fulfilling the posthuman definition of Europe as the place that is historically and morally bound to the critical re-elaboration of its own history.

By extension, we need a university that looks like the society it both reflects and serves, that is to say a globalized, technologically mediated, ethnically and linguistically diverse society that is still in tune with basic principles of social justice, the respect for diversity, the principles of hospitality and conviviality. I am aware but do not mind the residual Humanism of such aspirations, which I take at best as a productive contradiction. Against the social construction of wilful forgetfulness and of crass ignorance, I defend a fundamental aspiration to overarching principles of posthuman bonding. A university that is seriously committed to representing today's world needs to tackle these issues by instituting trans-disciplinary areas which explore the production of knowledge in a technologically mediated world; the new relationship between arts and sciences; and the poly-lingual realities engendered by global-

ization. In a new outpour of intellectual creativity, posthuman Humanities in the global multi-versity will include:
Humanistic Informatics, or digital Humanities; Cognitive or
neural humanities; Environmental or sustainable Humanities;
Bio-genetic and Global Humanities. They will also pursue the
project of investigating what kind of research methods and
insights are developed by literary and art practices. They will
continue to support 'the human mind's restless pursuit of
fuller understanding' (Collini, 2012: 27) which is the essential
mission of the Humanities.

In other words, I think the Humanities can and will survive
and prosper to the extent that they will show the ability and
willingness to undergo a major process of transformation in
the direction of the posthuman. To be worthy of our times,
we need to be pragmatic: we need schemes of thought and
figurations that enable us to account in empowering terms
for the changes and transformations currently on the way.
We already live in permanent states of transition, hybridization and nomadic mobility, in emancipated (post-feminist),
multi-ethnic societies with high degrees of technological intervention. These are neither simple, nor linear events, but
rather multi-layered and internally contradictory phenomena.
They combine elements of ultra-modernity with splinters of
neo-archaism: high-tech advances and neo-primitivism, which
defy the logic of the excluded middle.

Contemporary culture and institutional education are
often unable to represent these realities adequately. They
favour instead the predictably plaintive refrains about the end
of ideologies, run concurrently with the apology of the 'new'.
Nostalgia and hyper-consumerism join hands, under the hold
of neo-liberal restoration of possessive individualism. This
unitary vision of the humanist subject, however, cannot
provide an effective antidote to the processes of fragmentation, flows and mutations that mark our era. We need to start
from non-unitary, relational subject positions so as to learn
to think differently about ourselves and our systems of values,
starting with adequate cartographies of our embedded and
embodied posthuman locations.

A university that looks like the world of today can only be
a 'multi-versity', is an exploded and expanded institution that
will affirm a constructive post-humanity. As such it cannot

support education for the sole purpose of integration into the labour market, but also for its own sake. We do need to embrace non-profit as a key value in contemporary knowledge production, but this gratuitousness is linked to the construction of social horizons of hope and therefore it is a vote of confidence in the sheer sustainability of the future (Braidotti, 2006). The future is nothing more or less than inter-generational solidarity, responsibility for posterity, but it is also our shared dream, or a consensual hallucination.[13] Collini puts it beautifully (2012: 199): 'we are merely custodians for the present generation of a complex intellectual inheritance which we did not create, and which is not ours to destroy'. Posthuman Humanities are already at work in the global multi-versity, not only to fend off extinction, but also to actualize sustainable posthuman futures.

---

[13] This is William Gibson's definition of cyberspace.

Conclusion

Not all of us can say, with even a modicum of certainty, that we have actually become posthuman, or that we are only that. Some of us insist on feeling quite attached to the 'human', that creature familiar from time immemorial who, as a species, a planetary presence and a cultural formation, spells out specific modes of belonging. Nor could we explain, with any degree of accuracy, by which historical contingency, intellectual vicissitudes or twists of fate, we have entered the posthuman universe. And yet, the idea of the posthuman by now enjoys widespread currency in the era known as the anthropocene. It elicits elation in equal measure to anxiety and it stimulates controversial cultural representations. More importantly for the purposes of this book, the posthuman predicament enforces the necessity to think again and to think harder about the status of the human, the importance of recasting subjectivity accordingly, and the need to invent forms of ethical relations, norms and values worthy of the complexity of our times. This calls also for the re-definition of the aims and structures of critical thought and it ultimately comes to bear on the institutional status of the academic field of the Humanities in the contemporary university.

This book opened with four vignettes that illustrate the excitement as well as the horrors of our times: the undoing of the nature–culture divide and the high degrees of technological mediation that create a series of paradoxes, such as an electronically linked pan-humanity which also breeds intolerance and even xenophobic violence. Genetically recombined plants, animals and vegetables proliferate alongside computer and other viruses, while unmanned flying and ground armed vehicles confront us with new ways of dying. Humanity is re-created as a negative category, held together by shared vulnerability and the spectre of extinction, but also struck down by new and old epidemics, in endless 'new' wars, detention camps and refugee exodus. The appeals for new forms of cosmopolitan relations or a global *ethos* are often answered by the homicidal acts of the likes of Pekka Eric Auvinen or Anders Behring Breivik.[1]

This book has attempted to analyse in successive waves the alternation of fascination for the posthuman condition and the concern for its inhuman and even inhumane aspects. All along I have emphasized the importance of critical theory, in the sense of a mix of critique and creativity that makes it imperative for us to come to terms with the present in new, fundamental ways. My main concerns are: how to find adequate theoretical and imaginary representations for our lived conditions and how to experiment together with alternative forms of posthuman subjectivity. The four key questions I set out at the beginning have structured this book as a journey across the multi-faceted landscape of the posthuman: how can we account for the intellectual and historical itineraries that may have led us to the posthuman? Secondly, where does the posthuman condition leave humanity and, more specifically, what new forms of subjectivity does it engender? Thirdly, how can we stop the posthuman from becoming inhuman(e)? And last, what is the function of the Humanities and of theory in posthuman times? These questions are not linear but intertwined, and they trace a zigzagging route across a complex landscape. I adopted the speaking stance and the writing position of a tracker and a cartographer in order to account not only for the difficult transitions but also

---

[1] Anders Behring Breivik is the Norwegian mass murderer and the confessed perpetrator of the 2011 attacks in Oslo and on the island of Utoya, killing respectively eight and sixty-nine people, mostly Socialist youth.

for some of the contradictions inherent in our current predicament. Let us see how far we have come at the end of this
journey.

Posthuman Subjectivity

The posthuman subject is not postmodern, because it does
not rely on any anti-foundationalist premises. Nor is it post-
structuralist, because it does not function within the linguistic
turn or other forms of deconstruction. Not being framed by
the ineluctable powers of signification, it is consequently not
condemned to seek adequate representation of its existence
within a system that is constitutionally incapable of granting
due recognition. Being based on Lack and Law, the linguistic
signifier can at best distribute entrapment and withhold
empowerment. Its sovereign power builds on the negative
passions it solicits, making hungry where it most satisfies,
through envy, castration and by encouraging addictive patterns of consumption of material, discursive and cultural
goods.

The posthuman nomadic subject is materialist and vitalist,
embodied and embedded – it is firmly located somewhere,
according to the radical immanence of the 'politics of location' that I have stressed throughout this book. It is a multi-
faceted and relational subject, conceptualized within a
monistic ontology, through the lenses of Spinoza, Deleuze
and Guattari, plus feminist and post-colonial theories. It is a
subject actualized by the relational vitality and elemental
complexity that mark posthuman thought itself.

Vital politics breaks clearly from the notion, made canonical by post-structuralism and psychoanalysis, of the primacy
of culture and of signification over subject formation. There
is no originary and fatal capture of an allegedly 'unmarked'
subject by the matrix of power, be it the Phallus, the Logos,
Eurocentric transcendental reason or heterosexual normativity. Power is not a steady location operated by a single masterful owner. Monistic politics places differential mechanisms
of distribution of power effects at the core of subjectivity.
Multiple mechanisms of capture also engender multiple forms
of resistance. Power formations are time-bound and conse-

quently temporary and contingent upon social action and interaction. Movement and speed, lines of sedimentation and lines of flight are the main factors that affect the formation of a non-unitary, posthuman subject.

The nomadic vision of subjectivity is a good starting point, but we need to push it further, connecting it to two other crucial ideas: desire as plenitude and posthuman ethics. The idea of desire as plenitude and not as lack produces a more transformative and less negative approach to the nomadic relational subject than previously allowed, for instance by the split subject of psychoanalysis. The nomadic subject is a branch of complexity theory and it promotes a continuing emphasis on the radical ethics of transformation. This is not to deny the role that historical contingency and cultural codes play in subject formation, but rather to subject these very factors to a serious update in the light of their own changing structures and compositions. As Deleuze and Guattari argue in their critique of psychoanalysis (1977), Jacques Lacan's notion of the symbolic is as out-dated as a Polaroid shot of a world that has since moved on. It captures a frozen frame of family and other inter-subjective relations at a time in history when advanced capitalism is investing them with a thoroughly subversive spin. The bio-political nature of this system has grown exponentially since the 1970s, affecting radical new forms of intersubjective relationality. To state the contrary would be to embrace psychological essentialism and condemn our psychic life to step outside of history and social transformations. Our psyche – with its affective, fantasy-ridden, desire-driven complications – would then be forever static in an unhistorical limbo, framed by the self-replicating power of a despotic master signifier. For all vitalist 'matter-realists', this mournful vision of a subject desperately attached to the conditions of its own impotence is quite simply an inadequate representation of what we are in the process of becoming. We need to be 'worthy of the present' and thus be part of contemporary culture, embodying and embedding the subject of *this* particular world. Far from being a flight from the real, posthuman thought inscribes the contemporary subject in the conditions of its own historicity.

Life, by the same token, is neither a metaphysical notion, nor a semiotic system of meaning; it expresses itself in a multiplicity of empirical acts: there is nothing to say, but everything to do. Life, simply by being life, expresses itself by actualizing flows of energies, through codes of vital information across complex somatic, cultural and technologically networked systems. This is why I defend the idea of *amor fati* as a way of accepting vital processes and the expressive intensity of a Life we share with multiple others, here and now.

Posthuman Ethics

We are becoming posthuman ethical subjects in our multiple capacities for relations of all sorts and modes of communication by codes that transcend the linguistic sign by exceeding it in many directions. At this particular point in our collective history, we simply do not know what our enfleshed selves, minds and bodies as one, can actually do. We need to find out by embracing an ethics of experiment with intensities. The ethical imagination is alive and well in posthuman subjects, in the form of ontological relationality. A sustainable ethics for non-unitary subjects rests on an enlarged sense of inter-connection between self and others, including the non-human or 'earth' others, by removing the obstacle of self-centred individualism on the one hand and the barriers of negativity on the other.

In other words, to be posthuman does not mean to be indifferent to the humans, or to be de-humanized. On the contrary, it rather implies a new way of combining ethical values with the well-being of an enlarged sense of community, which includes one's territorial or environmental inter-connections. This is an ethical bond of an altogether different sort from the self-interests of an individual subject, as defined along the canonical lines of classical humanism, or from the moral universalism of the Kantians and their reliance on extending human rights to all species, virtual entities and cellular compositions (Nussbaum, 2006). Posthuman theory also bases the ethical relation on positive grounds of joint projects and activities, not on the negative or reactive grounds of shared vulnerability.

This process-oriented vision of the subject is capable of a universalistic reach, though it rejects moral and cognitive universalism. It expresses a grounded, partial form of accountability, based on a strong sense of collectivity and relationality, which results in a renewed claim to community and belonging by singular subjects. Lloyd refers to these locally situated micro-universalist claims as 'a collaborative morality' (Lloyd, 1996: 74). The stated criteria for this new ethics include: non-profit; emphasis on the collective; acceptance of relationality and of viral contaminations; concerted efforts at experimenting with and actualizing potential or virtual options; and a new link between theory and practice, including a central role for creativity. They are not moral injunctions, but dynamic frames for an ongoing experiment with intensities. They need to be enacted collectively, so as to produce effective cartographies of how much bodies can take, which is why I also call them 'thresholds of sustainability' (Braidotti, 2006). They aim to create collective bonds, a new affective community or polity.

The key notion in posthuman nomadic ethics is the transcendence of negativity. What this means concretely is that the conditions for renewed political and ethical agency cannot be drawn from the immediate context or the current state of the terrain. They have to be generated affirmatively and creatively by efforts geared to creating possible futures, by mobilizing resources and visions that have been left untapped and by actualizing them in daily practices of interconnection with others. This project requires more visionary power or prophetic energy, qualities which are neither especially in fashion in academic circles, nor highly valued scientifically in these times of coercive pursuit of globalized 'excellence'. Yet, the call for more vision is emerging from many quarters in critical theory. Feminists have a long and rich genealogy in terms of pleading for increased visionary insight. From the very early days, Joan Kelly (1979) typified feminist theory as a double-edged vision, with a strong critical and an equally strong creative function. That creative dimension has been central ever since (Haraway, 1997, 2003; Rich, 2001) and it constitutes the affirmative and innovative core of the radical epistemologies of feminism, gender, race and post-colonial studies. Faith in the creative powers of the imagination is an integral part of feminists' appraisal of lived embodied experience and the bodily roots of subjectivity, which would express the

complex singularities that feminist embodied females have
become. Conceptual creativity is simply unimaginable without
some visionary fuel.

Prophetic or visionary minds are thinkers of the future.
The future as an active object of desire propels us forth and
motivates us to be active in the here and now of a continuous
present that calls for both resistance and the counter-actual-
ization of alternatives. The yearning for sustainable futures
can construct a liveable present. This is not a leap of faith,
but an active transposition, a transformation at the in-depth
level (Braidotti, 2006). A prophetic or visionary dimension is
necessary in order to secure an affirmative hold over the
present, as the launching pad for sustainable becoming or
qualitative transformations of the negativity and the injustices of the present. The future is the virtual unfolding of the
affirmative aspect of the present, which honours our obliga-
tions to the generations to come.

Affirmative Politics

The pursuit of collective projects aimed at the affirmation of
hope, rooted in the ordinary micro-practices of everyday life,
is a strategy to set up, sustain and map out sustainable transformations. The motivation for the social construction of
hope is grounded in a sense of responsibility and inter-generational accountability. A fundamental gratuitousness and a
sense of hope is part of it. Hope is a way of dreaming up
possible futures: an anticipatory virtue that permeates our
lives and activates them. It is a powerful motivating force
grounded not only in projects that aim at reconstructing the
social imaginary, but also in the political economy of desires,
affects and creativity that underscore it.

Contemporary practices of posthuman subjectivity work
towards a more affirmative approach to critical theory.
Beyond unitary visions of the self and teleological renditions
of the processes of subject formation, posthuman thought can
sustain the contemporary subjects in the efforts to synchro-
nize themselves with the changing world in which they try to
make a positive difference. For instance, against the established tradition of methodological nationalism, a different

image of thought can be activated that rejects Euro-universalism and trusts instead in the powers of planetary diversity. We also need to enlist affectivity, memory and the imagination to the crucial task of inventing new figurations and new ways of representing the complex subjects we have become. Science itself is socially inscribed and ecologically integrated not along the nationalistic axis but in a nomadic web of posthuman earth-wide connections.

Becoming-posthuman consequently is a process of redefining one's sense of attachment and connection to a shared world, a territorial space: urban, social, psychic, ecological, planetary as it may be. It expresses multiple ecologies of belonging, while it enacts the transformation of one's sensorial and perceptual co-ordinates, in order to acknowledge the collective nature and outward-bound direction of what we still call the self. This is in fact a moveable assemblage within a common life-space that the subject never masters nor possesses but merely inhabits, crosses, always in a community, a pack, a group or a cluster. For posthuman theory, the subject is a transversal entity, fully immersed in and immanent to a network of non-human (animal, vegetable, viral) relations. The *zoe*-centred embodied subject is shot through with relational linkages of the contaminating/viral kind which inter-connect it to a variety of others, starting from the environmental or eco-others and include the technological apparatus.

This non-essentialist brand of vitalism reduces the hubris of rational consciousness, which far from being an act of vertical transcendence is rather re-cast and pushed downwards in a grounding exercise of radical immanence. It is an act of unfolding the self onto the world, while enfolding the world within. What if consciousness were, in fact, just another cognitive mode of relating to one's own environment and to others? What if, by comparison with the immanent know-how of animals, conscious self-representation were blighted by narcissistic delusions of transcendence and consequently blinded by its own aspirations to self-transparency? What if consciousness were ultimately incapable of finding a remedy to its obscure disease, this life, this *zoe*, an impersonal force that moves us without asking for our permission to do so? *Zoe* is an inhuman force that stretches beyond life, to new, vitalist ways of approaching death as an impersonal event. The process ontology centred on life leads the posthuman subject to confront this position lucidly, without making concessions to either moral panic or melancholia. It asserts a secular ethical drive to enter into modes of relation that enhance and sustain one's ability to renew and expand the boundaries of what transversal and non-unitary subjects can become. The ethical ideal is to actualize the cognitive, affective and sensorial means to cultivate higher degrees of empowerment and affirmation of one's interconnections to others in their multiplicity. The selection of the affective forces that propel the process of becoming posthuman is regulated by an ethics of joy and affirmation that functions through the transformation of negative into positive passions.

Very much a philosophy of the outside, of open spaces and embodied enactments, nomadic posthuman thought yearns for a qualitative leap out of the familiar, trusting the untapped possibilities opened by our historical location in the technologically mediated world of today. It is a way of being worthy of our times, to increase our freedom and understanding of the complexities we inhabit in a world that is neither anthropocentric nor anthropomorphic, but rather geo-political, ecosophical and proudly *zoe*-centred.

Posthuman, all too Human

I stated in the introduction that how one feels about the posthuman depends to a great extent on how one relates to the human in the first place. I have honestly stated my antihumanist propensities throughout this book; my interest in the posthuman is directly proportional to the sense of frustration I feel about the human, all too human, resources and limitations that frame our collective and personal intensity. There is anticipation as well as impatience in what I have been trying to write about in this book. Undeniably, the vitalist egalitarianism of *zoe* is likely to attract those who have become disenchanted with and disengaged from the anthropocentrism that is built into humanistic thought, even in what is left of the political Left, of feminism and post-colonial theory. I live at the tail end of bio-power, that is to say amidst the relentless necro-political consumption of all that lives. I am committed to starting from this, not from a nostalgic re-invention of an all-inclusive transcendental model, a romanticized margin or some holistic ideal. I want to think from here and now, from Dolly my sister and oncomouse as my totemic divinity; from missing seeds and dying species. But also, simultaneously and without contradiction, from the staggering, unexpected and relentlessly generative ways in which life, as *bios* and as *zoe*, keeps on fighting back. This is the kind of materialism that makes me a posthuman thinker at heart and a joyful member of multiple companion species in practice (Haraway, 2003). I have no nostalgia for that 'Man', alleged measure of all things human, or for the forms of knowledge and self-representation he engineered. I welcome the multiple horizons that have opened up since the historical downfall of andro-centric and Eurocentric Humanism. I see the posthuman turn as an amazing opportunity to decide together what and who we are capable of becoming, and a unique opportunity for humanity to re-invent itself affirmatively, through creativity and empowering ethical relations, and not only negatively, through vulnerability and fear. It is a chance to identify opportunities for resistance and empowerment on a planetary scale.

I am putting the finishing touches to this manuscript just as the 2012 London Olympics are in full swing. One of the sensations of these games is the performance by the Jamaican athlete Usain Bolt, who ran the men's 100 metre race in 9.63 seconds, at an average speed of 38 km/h; the 200 men's metre race in 19.32 seconds; and, with his team mates, the 4 × 100 metre relay race in a breath-taking world record of 36.84 seconds. The speed is such as to defy our powers of comprehension and it has ignited the imagination of the globally connected world. Although this extraordinary runner is expected to improve his personal best record by a couple of seconds more, it is generally acknowledged that Usain Bolt's 'superhuman' performance has stretched the boundaries of what the human body is capable of achieving at the present point in time. Whether this boundary turns out to be an insurmountable physiological limit, a collectively self-imposed limitation or rather the threshold of potential exploits by new bodies to come remains to be seen.

At the same Olympic Games, the South African athlete Oscar Pistorius made history as the first double amputee to compete. Although the struggle to qualify was long and controversial, and the athlete did not win any medals in the end, Pistorius was the first enhanced human to run on carbon fibre transtibial artificial limbs[2] and hold his ground valiantly against natural born fastidious bipeds. The extent to which Pistorius' 'otherwise human' performance sets the tone for posthuman things to come is now an open question. Whether the precedent he set has a future and what kind of scenarios it might enable remain to be seen.

Faced with transformations of this magnitude, it is urgent to set a new posthuman social agenda. The limits and limitations of posthuman bodies must become the object of collective discussions and decisions across the multiple constituencies of our polity and civil society, in a manner that does not assume the centrality, let alone the universality, of humanistic principles and anthropocentric assumptions. We now need to learn to think differently about ourselves and to experiment with new fundamental schemes of thought about what counts as the new basic unit of common reference for the human. This is why I insisted so much in this book on issues of subjectivity: we need new frameworks for the identification of common points of reference and values in order to come to terms with the staggering transformations we are witnessing. This book rests on the firm belief that we, early third millennium posthuman subjects in our multiple and differential locations, are perfectly capable of rising to the challenge of our times, provided we make it into a collective endeavour and joint project. Concrete, actualized praxis is the best way to deal with the virtual possibilities that are opening up under our very eyes, as a result of our collectively sustained social and scientific advances.

Human embodiment and subjectivity are currently undergoing a profound mutation. Like all people living in an age of transition, we are not always lucid or clear about where we are going, or even capable of explaining what exactly is happening to and around us. Some of these events strike us in awe and fear, while others startle us with delight. It is as if our current context kept on throwing open the doors of our collective perception, forcing us to hear the roar of cosmic energy that lies on the other side of silence and to stretch the

---

[2] They are Cheetah Flex-Foot devices by the firm Ossur.

measure of what has become possible. It is both exciting and
unsettling to be reminded, almost on a daily basis, that we
are, after all, such stuff as dreams are made of and that the
new possibilities are immense. No wonder so many of us turn
their backs on this, preferring to go about well wadded with
stupidity, as George Eliot prophetically put it.

And yet, Dolly the sheep is real, not a science fiction character but the result of our scientific research, an active social
imaginary and major financial investments. Although he is
popularly known as 'Blade Runner', Oscar Pistorius does not
dream of electric sheep. Conductor-free trains connecting
global transportation hubs to major metropolitan centres are
by now a familiar sight and our hand-held electronic devices
so powerful that we can barely keep up with them. Human,
all too posthuman, these extensions and enhancements of
what bodies can do are here to stay. Are we going to be able
to catch up with our posthuman selves, or shall we continue
to linger in a theoretical and imaginative state of jet-lag in
relation to our lived environment? This is not Huxley's *Brave
New World*, that is to say a dystopian rendition of the worst
modernist nightmares. Nor is it a trans-humanist delirium of
transcendence from the corporeal frame of the contemporary
human. This is a new situation we find ourselves in: the
immanent here and now of a posthuman planet. It is one of
the possible worlds we have made for ourselves, and in so far
as it is the result of our joint efforts and collective imaginings,
it is quite simply the best of all possible posthuman worlds.

References

Adams, Carol. 1990. *The Sexual Politics of Meat: A Feminist-Vegetarian Critical Theory*. New York: Continuum.

Adler, Rachel. 1998. Judaism. In: Alison M. Jaggar and Iris M. Young (eds.), *A Companion to Feminist Philosophy*. Oxford: Blackwell Publishers.

Agamben, Giorgio. 1998. *Homo Sacer: Sovereign Power and Bare Life*. Stanford, CA: Stanford University Press.

Ansell Pearson, Keith. 1997. *Viroid Life: Perspectives on Nietzsche and the Transhuman Condition*. London and New York: Routledge.

Ansell Pearson, Keith. 1999. *Germinal Life: The Difference and Repetition of Deleuze*. London and New York: Routledge.

Appadurai, Arjun. 1998. Dead certainty: Ethnic violence in the era of globalization. *Development and Change*, 29, 905–25.

Arendt, Hannah. 1951. *The Origins of Totalitarianism*. New York: Harcourt.

Arthur, John and Amy Shapiro. 1995. *Campus Wars: Multiculturalism and the Politics of Difference*. Boulder, CO: Westwood Press.

Asimov, Isaac. 1950. *I, Robot*. New York: Gnome Press.

Badiou, Alain and Slavoj Žižek. 2009. *Philosophy in the Present*. Cambridge: Polity Press.

Badmington, Neil. 2003. Theorizing Posthumanism. *Cultural Critique*, No. 53, pp. 10–27.

Balibar, Etienne. 2002. *Politics and the Other Scene*. London: Verso.

Balibar, Etienne. 2004. *We, the People of Europe? Reflections on Transnational Citizenship*. Princeton, NJ: Princeton University Press.

Balsamo, Anne. 1996. *Technologies of the Gendered Body: Reading Cyborg Women*. Durham, NC: Duke University Press.

Barad, Karen. 2003. Posthumanist performativity: toward an understanding of how matter comes to matter. *Signs*, 28 (3), 801–31.

Barad, Karen. 2007. *Meeting the Universe Half Way*. Durham, NC: Duke University Press.

Barrett, Michele. 1980. *Women's Oppression Today*. London: Verso Books.

Bart, Simon, Jill Didur and Teresa Heffernan (eds.) (2003) *Cultural Critique*, Special issue on Posthumanism, vol. 53.

Barthes, Roland. 1975. *The Pleasure of the Text*. New York: Hill and Wang.

Bauman, Zygmunt. 1993. *Postmodern Ethics*. Oxford: Blackwell.

Bauman, Zygmunt. 1998. *Globalization: The Human Consequences*. Cambridge: Polity Press.

Bauman, Zygmunt. 2004. *Europe: An Unfinished Adventure*. Cambridge: Polity Press.

Beauvoir, Simone de. 1973. *The Second Sex*. New York: Bantam Books.

Beck, Ulrich. 1999. *World Risk Society*. Cambridge: Polity Press.

Beck, Ulrich. 2007. The cosmopolitan condition: Why methodological nationalism fails. *Theory, Culture & Society*, 24 (7/8), 286–90.

Beer, Gillian. 1983. *Darwin's Plots: Evolutionary Narrative in Darwin, George Eliot and Nineteenth-Century Fiction*. London: Routledge & Kegan Paul.

Benhabib, Seyla. 1996. *The Reluctant Modernism of Hannah Arendt*. Thousand Oaks, CA: Sage.

Benhabib, Seyla. 2002. *The Claims of Culture: Equality and Diversity in the Global Era*. Princeton, NJ: Princeton University Press.

Benhabib, Seyla. 2007. *Another Cosmopolitanism*. Oxford: Oxford University Press.

Benjamin, Jessica. 1988. *The Bonds of Love. Psychoanalysis, Feminism and the Problem of Domination*. New York: Pantheon Books.

Bennett, Jane. 2001. *The Enchantment of Modern Life. Attachments, Crossings and Ethics*. Princeton, NJ: Princeton University Press.

Bennett, Jane. 2010. *Vibrant Matter. A Political Ecology of Things*. Durham, NC: Duke University Press.

Berger, Anne E. and Marta Segarra. 2011. *Demenageries. Thinking (of) Animals after Derrida*. Amsterdam: Rodopi.

Bérubé, Michael and Cary Nelson. 1995. *Higher Education under Fire. Politics, Economics and the Crisis of the Humanities*. New York and London: Routledge.

Bhabha, Homi K. 1994. *The Location of Culture*. London and New York: Routledge.

Bhabha, Homi K. 1996a. 'Unpacking my library . . . again'. In: Iain Chambers and Lidia Curti (eds.) *The Post-Colonial Question. Common Skies, Divided Horizons*. London and New York: Routledge.

Bhabha, Homi K. 1996b. Unsatisfied: Notes on vernacular cosmo-politanism. In: Laura Garcia Moreno and Peter C. Pfeiffer (eds.) *Text and Nation: Cross-Disciplinary Essays on Cultural and National Identities*. Columbia, SC: Camden House.

Blanchot, Maurice. 2000. *The Instant of My Death*. Stanford, CA: Stanford University Press.

Bono, James J., Tim Dean and Ewa Ziarek Plonowska. 2008. *A Time for the Humanities. Futurity and the Limits of Autonomy*. New York: Fordham University Press.

Bonta, Mark and John Protevi. 2004. *Deleuze and Geophilosophy. A Guide and Glossary*. Edinburgh: Edinburgh University Press.

Borradori, Giovanna. 2003. *Philosophy in a Time of Terror*. Chicago, IL: University of Chicago Press.

Bostrom, Nick. 2005. A history of transhuman thought. *Journal of Evolution and Technology*, 14 (1), 1–25.

Bourke, Joanna. 2011. *What It Means To Be Human*. London: Virago.

Brah, Avtar. 1996. *Cartographies of Diaspora: Contesting Identities*. New York and London: Routledge.

Braidotti, Rosi. 1991. *Patterns of Dissonance*. Cambridge: Polity Press.

Braidotti, Rosi. 1994. *Nomadic Subjects: Embodiment and Sexual Difference in Contemporary Feminist Theory*, 1st edn. New York: Columbia University Press.

Braidotti, Rosi. 2002. *Metamorphoses. Towards a Materialist Theory of Becoming*. Cambridge: Polity Press.

Braidotti, Rosi. 2006. *Transpositions: On Nomadic Ethics*. Cambridge: Polity Press.

Braidotti, Rosi. 2008. In spite of the times: the postsecular turn in feminism. *Theory, Culture & Society*, 25 (6), 1–24.

Braidotti, Rosi. 2011a. *Nomadic Subjects: Embodiment and Sexual Difference in Contemporary Feminist Theory*, 2nd edn. New York: Columbia University Press.

Braidotti, Rosi. 2011b. *Nomadic Theory. The Portable Rosi Braidotti*. New York: Columbia University Press.

Braidotti, Rosi and Roets, Griets. 2012. 'Nomadology and subjectivity: Deleuze, Guattari and critical disability studies'. In: Dan Goodley, Bill Hughes and Lennard Davis (eds.) *Disability and Social Theory. New Developments and Directions*. New York: Palgrave Macmillan, pp. 161–78.

British Humanist Association. 2007. *The Case for Secularism: A Neutral State in an Open Society*. London: British Humanist Association.

Brown, Wendy. 2006. *Regulating Aversion. Tolerance in the Age of Identity and Empire*. Princeton, NJ: Princeton University Press.

Bryld, Mette and Nina Lykke. 1999. *Cosmodolphins. Feminist Cultural Studies of Technologies, Animals and the Sacred*. London: Zed Books.

Bukatman, Scott. 1993. *Terminal Identity. The Virtual Subject in Post-Modern Science Fiction*. Durham, NC: Duke University Press.

Butler, Judith. 1991. *Gender Trouble*. London and New York: Routledge.

Butler, Judith. 2004a. *Precarious Life*. London: Verso.

Butler, Judith. 2004b. *Undoing Gender*. London and New York: Routledge.

Carroll, Joseph. 2004. *Literary Darwinism. Evolution, Human Nature and Literature*. London and New York: Routledge.

Carroll, Rory. 2012. US raises a new drone generation. *The Guardian Weekly*, 10–16 August, 1–2.

Cartwright, Lisa. 2001. *Practices of Looking*. Oxford: Oxford University Press.

Césaire, Aimé. 1955. *Discours sur le colonialisme*. Paris: Présence Africaine.

Chakrabarty, Dipesh. 2009. The climate of history: Four theses. *Critical Inquiry*, 35, 197–222.

Chandler, James. 2004. Critical disciplinarity. *Critical Inquiry*, 30 (2), 355–60.

Chardin de Teillard, Pierre. 1959. *The Future of Man*. New York: Harper and Row.

Cheah, Pheng. 2008. Nondialectical materialism. *Diacritics*, 38 (1), 143–57.

Citton, Yves and Frédéric Lordon. 2008. *Spinoza et les Sciences Sociales*. Paris: Editions Amsterdam.

Cixous, Hélène. 1997. Mon Algeriance. *Les Inrockuptibles*, 20 August, magazine archive nr. 115, p. 70.

Cixous, Helene. 2004. *Portrait of Jacques Derrida as a Young Jewish Saint*. New York: Columbia University Press.

Clough, Patricia. 2008. The affective turn: Political economy, biomedia and bodies. *Theory, Culture & Society*, 25 (1), 1–22.

Cohen, Tom, Claire Colebrook and J. Hillis Miller. 2012. *Theory and the Disappearing Future*. New York: Routledge.

Colebrook, Claire. 2000. Is sexual difference a problem? In: Ian Buchanan and Claire Colebrook (eds.) *Deleuze and Feminist Theory*. Edinburgh: Edinburgh University Press.

Colebrook, Claire. 2002. *Understanding Deleuze*. Crows Nest, NSW: Allen and Unwin.

Collini, Stefan. 2012. *What Are Universities For?* London: Penguin Books.

Connolly, William. 1999. *Why am I not a Secularist?* Minneapolis, MN: University of Minnesota Press.

Cooper, Melinda. 2008. *Life as Surplus. Biotechnology & Capitalism in the Neoliberal Era*. Seattle, WA: University of Washington Press.

Cornell, Drucilla. 2002. *The Ubuntu Project with Stellenbosch University*, www.fehe.org/index.php?id=281 (accessed 2 January 2007).

Coward, Rosalind. 1983. *Patriarchal Precedents*. London and New York: Routledge.

Coward, Rosalind and John Ellis. 1977. *Language and Materialism: Developments in Semiology and the Theory of the Subject*. London: Routledge & Kegan Paul.

Crary, Jonathan. 2001. *Suspensions of Perception: Attention, Spectacle and Modern Culture*. Boston, MA: MIT Press.

Crenshaw, Kimberle. 1995. Intersectionality and identity politics. Learning from violence against women of colour. In: Kimberle Crenshaw, Neil Gotanda, Gary Peller and Kendall Thomas (eds.) *Critical Race Theory*. New York: The New Press.

Critchley, Simon. 2008. *The Book of Dead Philosophers*. London: Granta.

Daly, Mary. 1973. *Beyond God the Father: Towards a Theory of Women's Liberation*. Boston, MA: Beacon Press.

Damasio, Antonio. 2003. *Looking for Spinoza*. Orlando, FL: Harcourt, Inc.

Daston, Lorraine. 2004. Whither *Critical Inquiry? Critical Inquiry*, 30 (2), 361–4.

Daston, Lorraine and Peter Galison. 2007. *Objectivity*. New York: Zone Books.

Davies, Tony. 1997. *Humanism*. London: Routledge.

Davis, Angela. 1981. *Women, Race and Class*. New York: Random House.

Davis, Lennard J., (ed.). 1997. *The Disability Studies Reader*. New York and London: Routledge.

Dawkins, Richard. 1976. *The Selfish Gene*. Oxford: Oxford University Press.

De Landa, Manuel. 2002. *Intensive Science and Virtual Philosophy*. London: Continuum.

Deleuze, Gilles. 1983. *Nietzsche and Philosophy*. New York: Columbia University Press.

Deleuze, Gilles. 1988. *Bergonism*. New York: Zone Books.

Deleuze, Gilles. 1990a. *Expressionism in Philosophy: Spinoza*. New York: Zone Books.

Deleuze, Gilles. 1990b. *The Logic of Sense*. New York: Columbia University Press.

Deleuze, Gilles. 1992. *The Fold: Leibniz and the Baroque*. Minneapolis, MN: University of Minnesota Press.

Deleuze, Gilles. 1994. *Difference and Repetition*. London: The Athlone Press.

Deleuze, Gilles. 1995. L'immanence: une vie . . . . *Philosophie*, 47, 3–7.

Deleuze, Gilles and Felix Guattari. 1977. *Anti-Oedipus. Capitalism and Schizophrenia*. New York: Viking Press/Richard Seaver.

Deleuze, Gilles and Felix Guattari. 1987. *A Thousand Plateaus: Capitalism and Schizophrenia*. Minneapolis, MN: University of Minnesota Press.

Deleuze, Gilles and Felix Guattari. 1994. *What is Philosophy?* New York: Columbia University Press.

Delphy, Christine. 1984. *Close to Home. A Materialist Analysis of Women's Oppression*. Amherst, MA: University of Massachusetts Press.

Derrida, Jacques. 1992. *The Other Heading: Reflections on Today's Europe*. Bloomington, IN: Indiana University Press.

Derrida, Jacques. 2001a. *Writing and Difference*. New York: Routledge.

Derrida, Jacques. 2001b. *The Work of Mourning*. Chicago, IL: University of Chicago Press.

Derrida, Jacques. 2006. Is there a philosophical language? In: Lasse Thomassen (ed.) *The Derrida–Habermas Reader*. Edinburgh: Edinburgh University Press.

Dijck, Jose, van. 2007. *Mediated Memories in the Digital Age*. Stanford, CA: Stanford University Press.

Diken, Bulent. 2004. From refugee camps to gated communities: Biopolitics and the end of the city. *Citizenship Studies*, 8 (1), 83–106.

Donoghue, Frank. 2008. *The Last Professors: The Corporate University and the Fate of the Humanities*. New York: Fordham University Press.

Donovan, Josephine and Carol J. Adams (eds.) 1996. *Beyond Animal Rights. A Feminist Caring Ethic for the Treatment of Animals*. New York: Continuum.

Donovan, Josephine and Carol J. Adams (eds.) 2007. *The Feminist Care Tradition in Animal Ethics*. New York: Columbia University Press.

Duffield, Mark. 2008. Global civil war: the non-insured, international containment and post-interventionary society. *Journal of Refugee Studies*, 21, 145–65.

Economist, The. 2012. Technology Quarterly: 'Robots on the frontline', 2 June, 4–20.

Eisenstein, Zillah. 1998. *Global Obscenities. Patriarchy, Capitalism and the Lure of Cyberfantasy*. New York: New York University Press.

Eliot, George. 1973. *Middlemarch*. London: Penguin Books.

Eliot, George. 2003. *The Mill on the Floss*. London: Penguin Books.

Esposito, Roberto. 2008. *Bios. Biopolitics and Philosophy*. Minneapolis, MN: University of Minnesota Press.

Fanon, Frantz. 1967. *Black Skin, White Masks*. New York: Grove Press.

Firestone, Shulamith. 1970. *The Dialectic of Sex*. New York: Bantam Books.

Foucault, Michel. 1970. *The Order of Things: An Archaeology of Human Sciences*. New York: Pantheon Books.

Foucault, Michel. 1977. *Discipline and Punish*. New York: Pantheon Books.

Foucault, Michel. 1978. *The History of Sexuality. Vol. I*. New York: Pantheon Books.

Foucault, Michel. 1985. *The History of Sexuality, Vol. II: The Use of Pleasure*. New York: Pantheon Books.

Foucault, Michel. 1986. *The History of Sexuality, Vol. III: The Care of the Self*. New York: Pantheon Books.

Franklin, Jonathan. 2012. Drones used by whaling's foes. *The Guardian Weekly*, 6 January, 14.

Franklin, Sarah. 2007. *Dolly Mixtures*. Durham, NC: Duke University Press.

Franklin, Sarah, Celia Lury and Jackie Stacey. 2000. *Global Nature, Global Culture*. London: Sage.

Fraser, Mariam, Sarah Kember and Celia Lury (eds.) 2006. *Inventive Life. Approaches to the New Vitalism*. London: Sage.

Freud, Sigmund. 1928. *The Future of an Illusion*. London: Hogarth Press.

Fukuyama, Francis. 1989. The end of history? *National Interest*, 16, 3–18.

Fukuyama, Francis. 2002. *Our Posthuman Future. Consequences of the BioTechnological Revolution*. London: Profile Books.

Galison, Peter. 2004. Specific theory. *Critical Inquiry*, 30 (2), 379–83.

Gatens, Moira and Genevieve Lloyd. 1999. *Collective Imaginings: Spinoza, Past and Present*. London and New York: Routledge.

Gill, Rosalind. 2010. Breaking the silence: the hidden injuries of the neoliberal universities. In: Rosalind Gill and Roisin Ryan Flood (eds.) *Secrecy and Silence in the Research Process: Feminist Reflections*. London and New York: Routledge.

Gilroy, Paul. 2000. *Against Race. Imaging Political Culture beyond the Colour Line*. Cambridge, MA: Harvard University Press.

Gilroy, Paul. 2005. *Postcolonial Melancholia*. New York: Columbia University Press.

Gilroy, Paul. 2010. *Darker than Blue*. Cambridge, MA: Harvard University Press.

Glissant, Edouard. 1997. *Poetics of Relation*. Ann Arbor, MI: University of Michigan Press.

Glotfelty, Cheryll and Harold Fromm (eds.) 1996. *The Ecocriticism Reader*. Athens, GA: University of Georgia Press.

Gould, Stephen Jay and Rosamond Wolff Purcell. 2000. *Crossing Over. Where Art and Science Meet*. New York: Three Rivers Press.

Gray, John. 2002. *Straw Dogs*. London: Granta Books.

Grewal, Inderpal and Caren Kaplan (eds.) (1994) *Scattered Hegemonies: Postmodernity and Transnational Feminist Practices*. Minneapolis, MN: University of Minnesota Press.

Griffin, Gabriele and Rosi Braidotti. 2002. *Thinking Differently. A Reader in European Women's Studies*. London: Zed Books.

Gross, Aaron and Anne Vallely. 2012. *Animals and the Human Imagination: A Companion to Animal Studies*. New York: Columbia University Press.

Grosz, Elizabeth. 1994. *Volatile Bodies. Towards a Corporeal Feminism*. Bloomington, IN: Indiana University Press.

Grosz, Elizabeth. 2004. *The Nick of Time*. Durham, NC: Duke University Press.

Grosz, Elizabeth. 2011. *Becoming Undone*. Durham, NC: Duke University Press.

Guattari, Felix. 1995. *Chaosmosis. An Ethico-aesthetic Paradigm*. Sydney: Power Publications.

Guattari, Felix. 2000. *The Three Ecologies*. London: The Athlone Press.

Gunew, Sneja. 2004. *Haunted Nations. The Colonial Dimension of Multiculturalisms*. London: Routledge.

Habermas, Jürgen. 2001. *The Post-National Constellation*. Cambridge: Polity Press.

Habermas, Jürgen. 2003. *The Future of Human Nature*. Cambridge: Polity Press.

Habermas, Jürgen. 2008. Notes on a post-secular society. *New Perspectives Quarterly*, 25 (4), 17–29.

Halberstam, Judith and Ira Livingston (eds.) 1995. *Posthuman Bodies*. Bloomington, IN: Indiana University Press.

Halsey, Mark. 2006. *Deleuze and Environmental Damage*. London: Ashgate.

Hanafin, Patrick. 2010. On reading 'Transpositions': a response to Rosi Braidotti's 'Transpositions: On nomadic ethics'. *Subjectivities*, 3, 131–6.

Haraway, Donna. 1985. A manifesto for cyborgs: Science, technology, and socialist feminism in the 1980s. *Socialist Review*, 5 (2), 65–107.

Haraway, Donna. 1988. Situated knowledges. The science question in feminism as a site of discourse on the privilege of partial perspective. *Feminist Studies*, 14 (3), 575–99.

Haraway, Donna. 1990. *Simians, Cyborgs and Women*. London: Free Association Press.

Haraway, Donna. 1992. The promises of monsters. A regenerative politics for inappropriate/d others. In: Lawrence Grossberg, Cary Nelson and Paula Treichler (eds.) *Cultural Studies*. London and New York: Routledge.

Haraway, Donna. 1997. *Modest_Witness@Second_Millennium. FemaleMan©_Meets_ OncoMouse™*. London and New York: Routledge.

Haraway, Donna. 2003. *The Companion Species Manifesto. Dogs, People and Significant Otherness*. Chicago, IL: Prickly Paradigm Press.

Haraway, Donna. 2006. When we have never been human, what is to be done? *Theory, Culture & Society*, 23 (7&8), 135–58.

Harding, Sandra. 1986. *The Science Question in Feminism*. Ithaca, NY: Cornell University Press.

Harding, Sandra. 1991. *Whose Science? Whose Knowledge?* Ithaca, NY: Cornell University Press.

Harding, Sandra. 1993. *The 'Racial' Economy of Science*. Bloomington, IN: Indiana University Press.

Harding, Sandra. 2000. *The Book of Jerry Falwell. Fundamentalist Language and Politics*. Princeton, NJ: Princeton University Press.

Hardt, Michael and Antonio Negri. 2000. *Empire*. Cambridge, MA: Harvard University Press.

Hardt, Michael and Antonio Negri. 2004. *Multitude: War and Democracy in the Age of Empire*. New York: Penguin Press.

Hartsock, Nancy. 1987. The feminist standpoint: developing the ground for a specifically feminist historical materialism. In: Sandra Harding (ed.) *Feminism and Methodology*. London: Open University Press.

Hayles, Katherine. 1999. *How We Became Posthuman. Virtual Bodies in Cybernetics, Literature and Informatics*. Chicago, IL: University of Chicago Press.

Hill Collins, Patricia. 1991. *Black Feminist Thought. Knowledge, Consciousness and the Politics of Empowerment*. New York and London: Routledge.

Hobsbawm, Eric. 1994. *The Age of Extremes: The Short Twentieth Century, 1914–1991*. New York: Vintage Books.

Holland, Eugene. 2011. *Nomad Citizenship*. Minneapolis, MN: University of Minnesota Press.

hooks, bell. 1981. *Ain't I a Woman*. Boston, MA: South End Press.

hooks, bell. 1990. Postmodern blackness. In: *Yearning: Race, Gender and Cultural Politics*. Toronto: Between the Lines.

Huntington, Samuel. 1996. *The Clash of Civilizations and the Remaking of World Order*. New York: Simon and Schuster.

Husserl, Edmund. 1970. *The Crisis of European Sciences and Transcendental Phenomenology*. Evanston, IL: Northwestern University Press.

Huyssen, Andreas. 1986. *After the Great Divide: Modernism, Mass Culture, Postmodernism*. Bloomington, IN: Indiana University Press.

Irigaray, Luce. 1985a. *Speculum of the Other Woman*. Ithaca, NY: Cornell University Press.

Irigaray, Luce. 1985b. *This Sex Which Is Not One*. Ithaca, NY: Cornell University Press.

Irigaray, Luce. 1993. *An Ethics of Sexual Difference*. Ithaca, NY: Cornell University Press.

Jones, Caroline A. and Peter Galison (eds.) 1998. *Picturing Science, Producing Art*. New York and London: Routledge.

Jordanova, Ludmilla. 1989. *Sexual Visions: Images of Gender in Science and Medicine between the Eighteenth and Twentieth Centuries*. London: Macmillan.

Judt, Tony. 2005. *Postwar: A History of Europe since 1945*. New York: Penguin Press.

Kant, Immanuel. 1992. *The Conflict of the Faculties*. Lincoln, NE: University of Nebraska Press.

Keller, Catherine. 1998. Christianity. In: Alison M. Jaggar and Iris M. Young (eds.) *A Companion to Feminist Philosophy*. Oxford: Blackwell.

Keller, Evelyn Fox. 1983. *A Feeling for the Organism*. New York: Henry Holt.

Keller, Evelyn Fox. 1985. *Reflections on Gender and Science*. New Haven, CT: Yale University Press.

Keller, Evelyn Fox. 1995. *Refiguring Life: Metaphors of Twentieth Century Biology*. New York: Columbia University Press.

Keller, Evelyn Fox. 2002. *Making Sense of Life*. Cambridge, MA: Harvard University Press.

Kelly, Joan. 1979. The double-edged vision of feminist theory. *Feminist Studies*, 5 (1), 216–27.

Kerr, Clark. 2001. *The Uses of the University*. Cambridge, MA: Harvard University Press.

Kristeva, Julia. 1982. *Powers of Horror*. New York: Columbia University Press.

Kristeva, Julia. 1991. *Strangers to Ourselves*. New York: Columbia University Press.

Kung, Hans. 1998. *A Global Ethic for Global Politics and Economics*. Oxford: Oxford University Press.

La Mettrie, Julien. 1996. *Machine Man and Other Writings*. Cambridge: Cambridge University Press.

Lambert, Gregg. 2001. *Report to the Academy*. Aurora, CO: The Davis Group Publisher.

Laplanche, Jean. 1976. *Life and Death in Psychoanalysis*. Baltimore, MD: Johns Hopkins University Press.

Latour, Bruno. 1993. *We Have Never Been Modern*. Cambridge, MA: Harvard University Press.

Latour, Bruno. 2004. Why has critique run out of steam? From matters of fact to matters of concern. *Critical Inquiry*, 30 (2), 225–48.

Law, John and John Hassard (eds.) 1999. *Actor Network Theory and After*. Oxford: Blackwell.

Lazzarato, Maurizio. 2004. *Les revolutions du capitalisme*. Paris: Seuil.

Lloyd, Genevieve. 1984. *The Man of Reason: Male and Female in Western Philosophy*. London: Methuen.

Lloyd, Genevieve. 1994. *Part of Nature: Self-knowledge in Spinoza's Ethic*. Ithaca, NY: Cornell University Press.

Lloyd, Genevieve. 1996. *Spinoza and the Ethics*. London and New York: Routledge.

Lorde, Audre. 1984. *Sister Outsider*. Trumansburg, NY: Crossing Press.

Lovelock, James. 1979. *Gaia: A New Look at Life on Earth*. Oxford: Oxford University Press.

Lury, Celia. 1998. *Prosthetic Culture. Photography, Memory and Identity*. London and New York: Routledge.

Lyotard, Jean-François. 1983. *The Differend. Phrases in Dispute*. Minneapolis, MN: University of Minnesota Press.

Lyotard, Jean-François. 1989. *The Inhuman: Reflections on Time*. Oxford: Blackwell.

Lyotard, Jean-François. 1984. *The Postmodern Condition*. Manchester: Manchester University Press.

MacCormack, Patricia. 2008. *Cinesexualities*. London: Ashgate.

MacCormack, Patricia. 2012. *Posthuman Ethics*. London: Ashgate.

MacPherson, Crawford B. 1962. *The Theory of Possessive Individualism*. Oxford: Oxford University Press.

McNeil, Maureen. 2007. *Feminist Cultural Studies of Science and Technology*. London: Routledge.

References *209*

Macherey, Pierre. 2011. *Hegel or Spinoza*. Minneapolis, MN: University of Minnesota Press.

Mahmood, Saba. 2005. *Politics of Piety. The Islamic Revival and the Feminist Subject*. Princeton, NJ: Princeton University Press.

Malraux, André. 1934. *Man's Fate*. New York: Modern Library.

Mandela, Nelson. 1994. *Long Walk to Freedom*. London and New York: Little Brown & Co.

Margulis, Lynn and Dorion Sagan. 1995. *What is Life?* Berkeley, CA: University of California Press.

Marks, John. 1998. *Gilles Deleuze. Vitalism and Multiplicity*. London: Pluto Press.

Massumi, Brian. 1992. Everywhere you want to be: Introduction to fear. *PLI – Warwick Journal of Philosophy*, 4 (1/2), 175–216.

Massumi, Brian. 1998. Requiem for our prospective dead! Toward a participatory critique of capitalist power. In: Eleanor Kaufman and Kevin Jon Heller (eds.) *Deleuze and Guattari. New Mappings in Politics, Philosophy and Culture*. Minneapolis, MN: University of Minnesota Press.

Massumi, Brian. 2002. *Parables for the Virtual. Movement, Affect, Sensation*. Durham, NC: Duke University Press.

Maturana, Humberto and Francisco Varela. 1972. *Autopoiesis and Cognition. The Realization of the Living*. Dordrecht: Reidel Publishing Company.

Mbembe, Achille. 2003. Necropolitics. *Public Culture*, 15 (1), 11–40.

Menand, Louis (ed.) 1996. *The Future of Academic Freedom*. Chicago, IL: University of Chicago Press.

Midgley, Mary. 1996. *Utopias, Dolphins and Computers. Problems of Philosophical Plumbing*. London and New York: Routledge.

Mies, Maria and Vandana Shiva. 1993. *Ecofeminism*. London: Zed Books.

Mitchell, Juliet. 1974. *Psychoanalysis and Feminism*. New York: Pantheon.

Mol, Annemarie. 2002. *The Body Multiple*. Durham, NC: Duke University Press.

Moore, Henrietta. 1994. *A Passion for Difference*. Cambridge: Polity Press.

Moore, Henrietta. 2007. *The Subject of Anthropology*. Cambridge: Polity Press.

Moore, Henrietta. 2011. *Still Life. Hopes, Desires and Satisfactions*. Cambridge: Polity Press.

Morin, Edgar. 1987. *Penser l'Europe*. Paris: Gallimard.

Moulier Boutang, Yann. 2012. *Cognitive Capitalism*. Cambridge: Polity Press.

Naess, Arne. 1977a. Spinoza and ecology. In: Siegfried Hessing (ed.) *Speculum Spinozanum, 1877–1977*. London: Routledge & Kegan Paul.

Naess, Arne. 1977b. Through Spinoza to Mahayana Buddhism or through Mahayana Buddhism to Spinoza? In: Jon Wetlesen (ed.) *Spinoza's Philosophy of Man*, Proceedings of the Scandinavian Spinoza Symposium. Oslo: Universitetsforlaget.

Nava, Mica. 2002. Cosmopolitan modernity. *Theory, Culture & Society*, 19 (1–2), 81–99.

Negri, Antonio. 1991. *The Savage Anomaly*. Minneapolis, MN: University of Minnesota Press.

Newman, John. 1907. *The Idea of a University*. London: Longmans, Green & Co.

Nussbaum, Martha C. 1999. *Cultivating Humanity: a Classical Defense of Reform in Liberal Education*. Cambridge, MA: Harvard University Press.

Nussbaum, Martha C. 2006. *Frontiers of Justice. Disability, Nationality, Species Membership*. Cambridge, MA: Harvard University Press.

Nussbaum, Martha. 2010. *Not for Profit. Why Democracy Needs the Humanities*. Princeton, NJ: Princeton University Press.

Orwell, George. 1946. *Animal Farm*. London: Penguin Group.

Parikka, Jussi. 2010. Insect Media. *An Archaeology of Animals and Technology*, Minneapolis, University of Minnesota Press.

Parisi, Luciana. 2004. *Abstract Sex. Philosophy, Bio-Technology, and the Mutation of Desire*. London: Continuum Press.

Passerini, Luisa (ed.) 1998. *Identità Culturale Europea. Idee, Sentimenti, Relazioni*. Florence: La Nuova Italia Editrice.

Patton, Paul. 2000. *Deleuze and the Political*. London and New York: Routledge.

Peterson, Christopher. 2011. The posthumanism to come. *Angelaki: Journal of the Theoretical Humanities*, 16 (2), 127–41.

Phillips, Adam. 1999. *Darwin's Worms*. London: Faber & Faber.

Phillips, John, Andrew Benjamin, Ryan Bishop, Li Shiqiao, Esther Lorenz, Liu Xiaodu and Meng Yan. 2011. The twenty-kilometer university. Knowledge as infrastructure. *Theory, Culture & Society*, 28 (7–8), 287–320.

Pick, Anat. 2011. *Creaturely Poetics: Animality and Vulnerability in Literature and Film*. New York: Columbia University Press.

Plumwood, Val. 1993. *Feminism and the Mastery of Nature*. London and New York: Routledge.

Plumwood, Val. 2003. *Environmental Culture*. London: Routledge.

PMLA (Publications of the Modern Language Association of America). 2009. Special issue on animal studies. *PMLA*, 124 (2).

Protevi, John. 2009. *Political Affect*. Minneapolis, MN: University of Minnesota Press.

Rabinow, Paul. 2003. *Anthropos Today*. Princeton, NJ: Princeton University Press.

Rapp, Rayna. 2000. *Testing Women, Testing the Foetus*. New York: Routledge.

Readings, Bill. 1996. *The University in Ruins*. Cambridge, MA: Harvard University Press.

Rich, Adrienne. 1987. *Blood, Bread and Poetry*. London: Virago Press.

Rich, Adrienne. 2001. *Arts of the Possible: Essays and Conversations*. New York: W.W. Norton.

Roberts, Celia and Adrian Mackenzie. 2006. Science: Experimental sensibilities in practice. *Theory, Culture & Society*, 23 (2–3), 157–82.

Rorty, Richard. 1996. Does academic freedom have philosophical presuppositions? In: Louis Menand (ed.) *The Future of Academic Freedom*. Chicago, IL: University of Chicago Press.

Rose, Nicholas. 2007. *The Politics of Life Itself: Biomedicine, Power and Subjectivity in the Twentieth-first Century*. Princeton, NJ: Princeton University Press.

Rossini, Manuela and Tom Tyler (eds.) 2009. *Animal Encounters*. Leiden: Brill.

Rothberg, Michael. 2009. *Multidirectional Memory: Remembering the Holocaust in the Age of Decolonization*. Stanford, CA: Stanford University Press.

Rowbotham, Sheila. 1973. *Women, Resistance and Revolution*. New York: Random House.

Russell, Bertrand. 1963. *Has Man a Future?* Harmondsworth: Penguin Books.

Said, Edward. 1978. *Orientalism*. Harmondsworth: Penguin Books.

Said, Edward. 1996. Identity, authority and freedom: The potentate and the traveller. In: Louis Menand (ed.) *The Future of Academic Freedom*. Chicago, IL: University of Chicago Press.

Said, Edward. 2004. *Humanism and Democratic Criticism*. New York: Columbia University Press.

Sartre, Jean-Paul. 1963. Preface. In: Frantz Fanon, *The Wretched of the Earth*. London: Penguin Books.

Schussler Fiorenza, Elizabeth. 1983. *In Memory of Her: A Feminist Theological Reconstruction of Christian Origins*. New York: Crossroads.

Scott, Joan. 1996. Academic freedom as an ethical practice. In: Louis Menand (ed.) *The Future of Academic Freedom*. Chicago, IL: University of Chicago Press.

Scott, Joan. 2007. *The Politics of the Veil*. Princeton, NJ: Princeton University Press.

Searle, John R. 1995. Postmodernism and the Western rationalist tradition. In: John Arthur and Amy Shapiro (eds.) *Campus Wars*. Boulder, CO: Westview Press.

Shiva, Vandana. 1997. *Biopiracy. The Plunder of Nature and Knowledge*. Boston, MA: South End Press.

Sloterdijk, Peter. 2009. *Rules for the Human Zoo*: a response to the 'Letter on Humanism'. *Environment and Planning D: Society and Space*, 27, 12–28.

Smelik, Anneke and Nina Lykke (eds.) 2008. *Bits of Life. Feminism at the Intersection of Media, Bioscience and Technology*. Seattle, WA: University of Washington Press.

Sobchack, Vivian. 2004. *Carnal Thoughts*. Berkeley, CA: University of California Press.

Socal, Alan and Jean Bricmont. 1998. *Fashionable Nonsense: Postmodern Intellectuals' Abuse of Science*. New York: Picador.

Solzhenitsyn, Alexandr. 1974. *The Gulag Archipelago*. New York: Harper & Row.

Soper, Kate. 1986. *Humanism and Anti-Humanism*. LaSalle, IL: Open Court Press.

Spivak, Gayatri Chakravorty. 1987. *In Other Worlds: Essays in Cultural Politics*. London: Methuen.

Spivak, Gayatri Chakravorty. 1999. *A Critique of Postcolonial Reason. Toward a History of the Vanishing Present*. Cambridge, MA: Harvard University Press.

Stacey, Jackie. 1997. *Teratologies. A Cultural Study of Cancer*. London and New York: Routledge.

Stacey, Jackie. 2010. *The Cinematic Life of the Gene*. Durham, NC: Duke University Press.

Stafford, Barbara. 1999. *Visual Analogy: Consciousness as the Art of Connecting*. Cambridge, MA: MIT Press.

Stafford, Barbara. 2007. *Echo Objects: The Cognitive Work of Images*. Chicago, IL: University of Chicago Press.

Starhawk. 1999. *The Spiral Dance*. San Francisco, CA: Harper Books.

Stengers, Isabelle. 1987. *D'une science à l'autre. Des concepts nomades*. Paris: Seuil.

Stengers, Isabelle. 1997. *Power and Invention. Situating Science*. Minneapolis, MN: University of Minnesota Press.

Stengers, Isabelle. 2000. *The Invention of Modern Science*. Minneapolis, MN: University of Minnesota Press.

Strathern, Marilyn. 1992. *After Nature. English Kinship in the Late Twentieth Century*. Cambridge: Cambridge University Press.

Tayyab, Basharat. 1998. Islam. In: Alison M. Jaggar and Iris M. Young (eds.) *A Companion to Feminist Philosophy*. Oxford: Blackwell.

Terranova, Tiziana. 2004. *Network Culture*. London: Pluto Press.

Todorov, Tzvetan. 2002. *Imperfect Garden. The Legacy of Humanism*. Princeton, NJ: Princeton University Press.

Verbeek, Peter Paul. 2011. *Moralizing Technology: Understanding and Designing the Morality of Things*. Chicago, IL: University of Chicago Press.

Villiers de l'Isle-Adam, Auguste. 1977. *L'Eve future*. Paris: José Corti.

Virilio, Paul. 2002. *Desert Screen: War at the Speed of Light*. London: Continuum.

Virno, Paolo. 2004. *A Grammar of the Multitude*. New York: Semiotext(e).

Waal, Frans de. 1996. *Good Natured*. Cambridge, MA: Harvard University Press.

Waal, Frans de. 2006. *Primates and Philosophers*. Princeton, NJ: Princeton University Press.

Waal, Frans de. 2009. *The Age of Empathy*. New York: Three Rivers Press.

Wadud, Amina. 1999. *Qur'an and Woman: Rereading the Sacred Text from a Woman's Perspective*. Oxford: Oxford University Press.

Walker, Alice. 1984. *In Search of Our Mother's Gardens*. London: Women's Press.

Ware, Vron. 1992. *Beyond the Pale. White Women, Racism and History*. London: Verso.

Werbner, Pnina. 2006. Vernacular cosmopolitanism. *Theory, Culture & Society*, 23 (2–3), 496–8.

Wernick, Andrew. 2006. University. *Theory, Culture & Society*, 23 (2–3), 557–79.

West, Cornell. 1994. *Prophetic Thought in Postmodern Times*. Monroe, ME: Common Courage Press.

Whimster, Sam. 2006. The human sciences. *Theory, Culture & Society*, 23 (2–3), 174–6.

Wolfe, Cary (ed.) 2003. *Zoontologies. The Question of the Animal*. Minneapolis, MN: University of Minnesota Press.

Wolfe, Cary. 2010a. Posthumanities. Available at: http:www.carywolfe.com/post_about.html (accessed 2 January 2012).

Wolfe, Cary. 2010b. *What is Posthumanism?* Minneapolis, MN: University of Minnesota Press.

Zylinska, Joanna. 2009. *Bioethics in the Age of New Media*. Boston, MA: MIT Press.

Index